# THE
# OCTOPUS

*By*

## Elizabeth Dilling

**Sons of Liberty
Box 214
Metairie, LA 70004**

**PRINTED IN THE U.S.A.**
**FIRST PRINTED OCTOBER, 1940**
**REPRINTED 1985**
**REPRINTED 1986**

# The Octopus

## B'nai B'rith

The most colossally-financed, "O.G.P.U.", coercive spy and propaganda machine in the United States is the pro-Red, anti-Christian B'nai B'rith Anti-Defamation League (with an appropriation of a half million dollars for 1938 alone—"B'nai B'rith Magazine", 6/38). Through its Gentile accomplices, it reaches even into the private mailing list of the individual. Its propaganda and ramifications extend from coast to coast. Your information concerning national and world affairs is colored by it. "B'NAI B'RITH serves American Jewry", is its slogan.

Its aim, in which it largely succeeds, is **national control,** through coercion or inducements, of speakers, books, articles, sermons, radio preachers, renting of halls for public meetings—in brief, of American freedom of speech, press and assembly. It stops at nothing in its efforts to publicly discredit any individual who dares oppose or expose any subsersive activity that is Jewish, or who mentions anything unflattering to Jewry. It is **breeding,** instead of lessening, anti-Semitism.

As a smokescreen, in 1938, it announced that it is against "Communism", as well as "Fascism", whereas its official organ, "B'nai B'rith Magazine", now called "The National Jewish Monthly", without exception, praises and never criticizes Marxists (Communists and Socialists), Jewish and Gentile, of every label.

The uninformed public is unaware that Communism and Socialism are names for the identical system of Karl Marx, which is also furthered under many other group and party labels.

### Nation-Wide Tentacles

In conjunction with other radicals, B'nai B'rith sponsors the National Conference of Jews and Christians, with James

3

M. Yard, a militant Communist-supporter, heading the Chicago branch. It, to quote its aide, Stanley High, "has set up its machinery in 310 cities. It reaches 1,000 campuses. Two hundred daily papers subscribe to its feature service. Its radio recordings appear regularly on 65 local stations. During 1939, under its auspices, Protestant, Catholic and Jewish speakers appeared together at 10,000 meetings in 2,000 communities in all the 48 States." (Saturday Evening Post, 6/1/40/.)

During 1939, B'nai B'rith's Anti-Defamation League distributed, according to "American Mercury", 7/40, 1,771,309 pamphlets, or, as reported in the "American Hebrew", 2/16/40, "over a million pamphlets of significance for **Jewish security and welfare** were distributed to **non-Jewish** readers."

### Suppressing Christianity

It reports being successful in various cities in eliminating, as repugnant to Jewry, Christmas and Easter celebrations from American public schools, and also references by Christians, in books, Passion Plays, etc., to the Scriptural version of the Crucifixion and to other Biblical passages, denounced as "anti-Semitic". Authors, publishers, ministers and radio speakers are coerced into deleting these.

For example, to quote a B'nai B'rith report in "B'nai B'rith Magazine", 3/38, p. 239:

"He" (the Secretary) "reported that the League had handled **750 cases of anti-Semitism** during 1937, in the following categories: books, 51; education, 28; employment, 41; investigations, 200; magazines and pamphlets, 74; movies and stage, 56; **PASSION PLAY, 23**; propagandists, 115; radio, 33; resort, hotels, real estate, 44; miscellaneous, 85."

### Using and Threatening Ministers

As a Chicago minister, who was guilty of reading the Bible account of the Crucifixion over the radio, personally related, a Jewish committee waited on him and warned him that if he did it again, "We will put you off the radio like we did a Grand Rapids minister."

Christian ministers who distribute the pamphlet "Refugee Facts", or other propaganda "bunkum" sponsored by B'nai B'rith, are unmolested, if not aided financially.

Christian Gentiles are preferred and for the most part utilized, as fronts for the work of spreading B'nai B'rith propaganda which is compounded of deceptive half-truths, melodramatic, emotional appeals to Christian charity, outright lies, any kind of statement likely to be swallowed by the uninformed Gentile public.

### When Facts Are Irrefutable, Smear!

"B'nai B'rith Magazine", 7/40, recommends a book, "Mr. Smith Meet Mr. Cohen", under the heading "Eight Ways to Fight" (opponents as "anti-Semitics"). The book is by Communist James Waterman Wise, son of Rabbi Stephen S. Wise, and Lee J. Levinger, an author of B'nai B'rith propaganda. How Levinger's son, Samuel, was honored, by Rabbi Wise and son James, for dying fighting for the Spanish Reds, was told by "B'nai B'rith Magazine" (3/38, p. 234).

Among these "Eight Ways to Fight", recommended by Levinger and Wise and "B'nai B'rith Magazine", Method #3 shows how, instead of **answering the charges** made by an "anti-Semitic" opponent, the **person making the charges** should be attacked and shown up as a "Nazi rat". A cartoon illustrating this method portrays a hand focusing the rays of a pocket flashlight on a **rat** labeled with a Nazi **swastika.**

Method #8 advises Jews to take their stand with the Leftists **despite** criticisms.

### Is This a Jewish Nation?

In Method #5, on "Discipline", satisfaction is expressed at the recent **restriction of radio time** "for controversial discussions prejudicial" to Jewry. A picture illustrating this method shows an uplifted hand holding a candle-snuffer about to snuff out a candle labeled "Coughlinism".

Method #6 shows the need for **alteration** of children's text books in the schools and **Sunday Schools.** Of Bishop Gilmour's "Biblical History", it asks, "Who knows how

### B'NAI B'RITH

*Our Motto: Benevolence, Brotherly Love and Harmony*

## AMARILLO LODGE NUMBER 802

### AMARILLO, TEXAS

Aug 15th, 1940

Mr. Guy W Keeling,
1600 Van Buren St.,
City.

Dear Sir:

Enclosed you will find a pamphlet " Jews in America,"
sent you with the compliments of B'nai Berith.

We will appreciate your reading the contents, and accept
it with the spirit in which we are sending it to you.

Yours very truly,

ABE FEFERMAN (PRESIDENT)

---

## Jews in America

By The Editors of Fortune

● Do the Jews control industry in America?

● How big a part do they play in banking?

In the automobile industry? In retailing?

In the theatre and the movies?

The results of this research, appeared originally in Fortune magazine. Later published in book form by Random House. The edition of Digest & Review have procured the rights to reprint this book, and a slightly condensed version appears on the following pages.

Mr. Keeling Attributes His Ousting As Radio Commentator to B'nai B'rith Power

6

many innocent minds this has corrupted?" The paragraph quoted from it, as a horrible example, merely sums up Bible teaching about the Jewish dispersion, believed by Christians.

The beautiful, **soundly Scriptural,** Austrian Passion Play is denounced in "B'nai B'rith Magazine", 7/37, as "one of the most vicious anti-Semitic diatribes I have ever witnessed . . . comparable only to the world famous and greatly-to-be-deplored Passion Play of Oberammergau."

But are Christians to be attacked because the **Bible,** God's Just and Holy Word, from cover to cover, Old and New Testaments, is highly unflattering to Jewry as a race? Is Christian teaching to be forbidden?

Because of this, must Christians in America submit to **Jewish censorship and deletion of the Bible** and its teachings? **Is this a Jewish nation?**

## Jews Make U. S. Chamber Lie

For an example of Jewish power in high places, compare deleted with undeleted copies, otherwise identical, of the very same edition of a pamphlet issued by the "U. S. Chamber of Commerce, Washington, D. C.", dated "November, 1934", and numbered "1685", entitled, "Combating Subversive Activities in the United States".

The evidence is plain. It is unnecessary to relate stories told of how the Jews forced the U. S. Chamber of Commerce to call in and destroy every available copy of this edition soon after it came off the press, and to delete, in re-issuing it, all mention of Jews in Communist activities. The U. S. Chamber pamphlet had quoted from pages 17 and 20 of Congressional Report #2290 (a Report of the investigation of Communist propaganda made by a Congressional committee headed by Congressman Fish, presented to Congress 1/17/31).

| Congressional Report No. 2290 stated (p. 17): | U.S. Chamber of Commerce pamphlet No. 1685 **originally** stated (p. 10): |
|---|---|
| **"Composition of communist membership of foreign origin** in the United States, estimated | "The Congressional committee, on the basis of the **foreign language press,** estimated that |

7

from **foreign-language press** and evidence submitted before the committee, on membership strength and not on percentage, is **as follows: Jews**, Russians (Slavs), Lithuanians, Hungarians, Finns, Czechoslovaks, Ukrainians, Yugoslavs, Poles, Germans, Scandinavians, Italians, Mexicans, Greeks, Rumanians, Armenians, Portugese, Spanish, South Americans, English, Irish, Scotch, French, Estonians, Lettish, **Chinese, Japanese.**"

the **composition of the communist membership of foreign origin** in the United States ranked in the **following** order: **Jews**, Russians (Slavs), Lithuanians, Hungarians, Finns, Czechoslovaks, Ukrainians, Yugoslavs, Poles, Germans, Scandinavians, Italians, Mexicans, Greeks, Rumanians, Armenians, Portuguese, Spanish, South Americans, E n g l i s h, Irish, Scotch, French, Estonians, Lettish, Chinese, Japanese."

U.S. Chamber of Commerce pamphlet No. 1685 **deleted** stated (p. 10):

"The Congressional committee, on the basis of the **foreign langauge press**, estimated that the **composition of communist membership of foreign origin** in the United States ranked in the **following order: *** Russians, Lithuanians, Hungarians, Finns, Czechoslovaks, Ukrainians, Yugoslavs, Poles, Germans, Scandinavians, Italians, Mexicans, Greeks, Rumanians, Armenians, Portuguese, Spanish, South Americans, E n g l i s h, Irish, Scotch, French, Estonians, Lettish, Chinese, Japanese."

(Note: * "Jews" deleted here, making Russians as **first** in order, a misquotation and misrepresentation.)

Congressional Report No. 2290 stated (p. 17):

"The **Daily Worker, published in New York,** is the **national official organ** in the **English** language of **the Communist Party** of the United States. It has an alleged daily **circulation of 35,000** . . ."

"The **largest daily communist** newspaper is the **Morning Freiheit,** published in **Yiddish** in New York City. It has a paid circulation through the United

U.S. Chamber of Commerce pamphlet No. 1685 **originally** stated (p. 11):

"The **national official organ** of the Communist Party, in **English,** is the 'Daily Worker,' published in New York with a stated **circulation of 35,000,** this **exceeded** only by the 64,000 circulation of the **Jewish communist** daily, 'Morning Freiheit.' "

U.S. Chamber of Commerce pamphlet No. 1685 **deleted** stated (p. 11):

8

States mails of only 5,617, but a total sworn circulation of 64,067, largely in New York City and vicinity." (Page 20.)

"The **national official organ of** the Communist Party, in **English, is** the **'Daily Worker,'** published in New York with a stated circulation of **35,000."** . . . . . . . .
. . . . . . . . . . . . . . . . . . . . . . . . . . . . . .
. . . . . . . . . . . . . . . . . . . . . . . . . . . . . .
(Note: Last three lines deleted, thus omitting the largest Communist Party publication.)

The list of Communist auxiliary organizations on pages 16 and 17 of Congressional Report #2290 include **"Jewish Freiheits".** These are mentioned in original copies of the U. S. Chamber of Commerce pamphlet #1685, but deleted in copies of later ones.

In addition, the same Congressional Report #2290, page 28, states: "In the vicinity of New York City the communist camps include a very high percentage of **Jewish** boys and girls, estimated to be as high as **90 per cent."**

### "Rev." Brooks a B'nai B'rith Mouthpiece

An interesting example of how deceptive B'nai B'rith propaganda is put out by its Gentile mouthpieces, with the prestige of sound uninformed ministers dragged in to help put it across, is shown by a characteristic leaflet of "Rev." Keith L. Brooks' American Prophetic League, released for distribution among Fundamentalist Christians.

On one side of Brooks' leaflet is printed a "Manifesto to the Jews by American Fundamentalists". This is composed of innocuous, sleep-producing expressions of "goodwill" to Jews and denunciation of "anti-Semitism in **whatever** form it may take", with sixty-seven impressive names of America's leading Fundamentalist ministers listed as signers.

### Tying Lies to Prominent Names

The other side of this leaflet is B'nai B'rith propaganda, reeking to Heaven with falsity, headed "ANSWER ANTI-JEWISH PROPAGANDA WITH STATISTICS." It should have been headed "Answer Truths With Lies in Order to Fool Christians".

9

Note Brooks' B'nai B'rith sources by comparing the statements below. References to B'nai B'rith articles, unless otherwise specified, are to their series compiled in book form entitled, "Facts About Fictions Concerning the Jew", by "Anti-Defamation League, B'nai B'rith, 130 North Wells Street, Chicago, price $1.00."

**Brooks' "Manifesto" leaflet says:**

"The **Communist Manifesto** of 1848 was devised by **Karl Marx, a Jew**

"who had been **baptised into the Christian faith**, and who to his end denounced the Jewish race. His co-signer **was Frederick Engels, a German.**"

"Nicolai **Lenin,** Russia's Red leader, **was NOT a Jew** and denounced the Jews for opposing him."

"**Russia** is controlled by **13** leaders, only **one a Jew.**

"Of the **19 commissars, 4 are Jews.**

"**Communism** in the U.S. is led by **Browder, Hathaway, Ford, Minor, Haywood, Bedacht** and Mother **Bloor,** none of them Jews."

**B'nai B'rith says:**

"**Karl Marx** as the author of the **Communist Manifesto (1848)** must be regarded as the founder of Communism. **Karl Marx** was born **a Jew.**" (B'nai B'rith article XXII, p. 9.)

"He was **baptized into the Christian faith** at the age of six . . . he was an outspoken antagonist of Judaism. His co-laborer in his philosophic work **was Frederick Engels, a German.**" B'nai B'rith article V, p. 10.)

"**Lenin was not a Jew.**" (B'nai B'rith article XXII, p. 18.)
"On March 15, 1918, Lenin's government issued a manifesto attacking the Jewish workers for their anti-Bolshevist attitude." (B'nai B'rith article V, p. 12.)

"The supreme directing body in Russia is the Polit-bureau. It consists of 9 members and 4 candidates." (**13** are listed showing **one a Jew.**) (Same article, next page, 13.)

"Of the **19 commissars** 14 are Great Russians and Ukrainians. One is an Armenian and **4 are Jews.**" (Same article, same page, 13.)

"The leaders of Communism in America are Earl **Browder,** William Z. Foster, Clarence **Hathaway,** James **Ford,** Robert **Minor,** William Patterson, Harry **Haywood,** Ella Reeve **Bloor** and Max **Bedacht.** Not a single one of them is a Jew." (B'nai B'rith article V, p. 9.) (Same state-

**Brooks' "Manifesto" leaflet says:**

"In New York City, the world's largest Jewish city, only about a thousand Jews belong to the Communist Party. In a thickly settled Jewish district Earl Browder himself running for Congress could not muster enough votes to make a showing."
**"Jews do NOT control U.S. banking."**

"Of **420 directors** of the **19 member** concerns of the **New York Clearing House—30 Jews.**"

"In the largest banks of New York there are **no Jews** at all, in spite of the fact that many of their customers are Jews."

"Investment houses of **Kuhn Loeb & Co.**, **Speyer & Co.**, **Seligman & Co.**, **Thallman & Co.**, and **Lehman Bros.**—the largest Jewish concerns—**do not compare in power with Gentile firms** like **J. P. Morgan & Co.**, **National City Co.**, **Dillon-Read**, **Chase-Harris-Forbes Co.**, **Guarantee Co.**, **Bankamerica**. The Morgan Co. does nearly **20%** of all the **foreign loan** business. **Kuhn, Loeb & Co.**, the **highest Jewish concern, only 2.88%**, and this company is part Gentile in control."

**B'nai B'rith says:**

ment in B'nai B'rith article XXII, p. 1)
"In New York with a Jewish population of over 2 million there are approximately one thousand Communists . . . In New York trenchant Jewish opposition to Communism was manifested at municipal elections last November." (Same article, same page, next paragraph.)

**"They do not run banking."** (Page 6 of B'nai B'rith pamphlet distributed free, "Anti-Semitism in the U.S.?", by Russell W. Davenport, managing editor of "Fortune" magazine.)

"Of the **420 listed directors** of the **19 members** of the **New York Clearing House** in 1933 only **30 are Jews.**" (Same source, same page, 6.)

"There are practically **no Jew**ish employees of any kind in the largest commercial banks—and this **in spite of the fact that many of their customers are Jew**ish houses. (Same source, same page, 6.)

"of which **Kuhn Loeb & Co.**, **Speyer & Co.**, **J. & W. Seligman & Co.**, Ladenburg, **Thalman & Co.** and **Lehman Bros.** are the best known though they **do not compare in power with** the great houses owned by non-Jews. . . . If these houses are ranked upon the amounts of foreign loans outstanding on March 1, 1935, **J. P. Morgan** with **19.87** percent, **National City Bank** with 11.71, **Dillon-Read** with 11.44, **Chase, Harris, Forbes** with 8.45, **Guaranty Co.** with 6.68 percent, **Bancamerica-Blair** with 6.18 percent . . . all rank above the **highest Jewish** house, which is **Kuhn Loeb & Co. with 2.88 per**cent. . . . Furthermore, these so-called Jewish houses are by no

11

| Brooks' "Manifesto" leaflet says: | B'nai B'rith says: |
|---|---|
| | means e x c l u s i v e l y Jewish." (Same source, same page, 6.) |
| "Of the 1375 member concerns of the New York Stock Exchange, 252 are Jews. This is 18%." | "On the New York stock exchange, 252 of the 1375 members, or 18 percent, are Jews." (Same source, next page, 7.) |
| "In Movies Jews control 3 of 8 principal companies. Of 85 names engaged in production, 53 are Jews." | "Three of the 8 principal companies are owned and controlled by Jews. Of 85 names engaged in production . . . 53 are Jews." (B'nai B'rith pamphlet, distributed free, "Jews in America by the Editors of Fortune", p. 9.) |
| "The number of Jews in Federal positions is lower than their percentage in the population. There are few Jews in high administrative and policy-making posts." | "the percentage of Jews in federal service is sharply lower than the percentage of Jews in total population. In high administrative and policy-making posts the Jewish fraction is much smaller than would be justified on a pure population basis." (Same source, p. 6.) |
| "Jews have a subordinate place in the field of heavy industry." | "Jews . . . have an even more inconspicuous place in heavy industry." (Same source, page, 6.) |
| "(Scrap iron business 90% Jews.) | "Scrap iron and steel is owned 90 per cent by Jews." (Same source, same page, 6.) |
| "No influence in auto industry, coal mining, rubber, oil, chemicals, shipping, transportation, railroad, ship building, airplane building. | The same source (same page) continues minimizing Jewish industrial influence in the same order as Brooks: "automobiles", "coal industry", "rubber", "petroleum", "chemical industry", "shipping and transportation", "railroading", "shipbuilders", "aviation". |
| "Found only in light industries, largely the distributing end. | "To find Jewish participation in industry it is necessary to turn to the light industries. And even there it is necessary to turn from the manufacturing to the distributing end." (Same page, following on to p. 7.) |
| "Underwear and dress-cutting and men's clothing, high percentage Jews. | "In the underwear and dress-cutting trades using rayon 80 to 90 percent are Jews . . . 85 per- |

| Brooks' "Manifesto" leaflet says: | B'nai B'rith says: |
|---|---|
| | cent of men's clothing . . . " (Same page, 7.) |
| "Department Stores of N.Y. City largely Jewish, but in Chicago the largest concerns are non-Jewish. | "Department stores are largely Jewish-owned in New York . . . But in Chicago the two leading stores are Marshall Field and Carson, Pirie, Scott & Co., one of Yankee origin and the other Scotch." (Same page, 7.) |
| "Chain stores only 5% Jewish. | "The department-store chains like May, Allied, Interstate, and Gimbel are Jewish but the Five and Ten, etc., chains like Woolworth and Kress are 95 per cent not." (5% Jewish.) (Next page, 8.) |
| "Mail order business is non-Jewish. (Sears & Roebuck now owned by Robert Wood.) | "Montgomery Ward in the mail-order field is non-Jewish while Sears, Roebuck has a Jewish history (Julius Rosenwald) but active management of Sears, Roebuck now is in the hands of General Robert Wood. (Same page, same paragraph.) |
| "Drug store chains 10%." | "Drug store chains are about 90 per cent non-Jewish." (10% Jewish.) (Same page, same paragraph.) |
| "New York Times, largest newspaper, Jewish owned, but considered one of the most reliable papers." (Proceeds to claim Jewish newspaper control almost non-existent.) | "Save for the prestige of the New York Times, which must rank on any basis of real distinction as the leading American newspaper, the interest of Jews is small." (Same source, page 11.) |
| "This should be sufficient to show that Jews DO NOT dominate the American scene." | "Jews do not dominate the American scene." (Same p., 11.) |
| "U.S. has 4,500,000 Jews. Were they more evenly distributed about the country, their presence would scarcely be noticed." | "Were the four and a half millions of American Jews scattered more or less evenly over the whole industrial acreage . . . their presence as Jews would hardly be noticed." (Same source, page 11.) |

## Rev. Smith, Another B'nai B'rith Mouthpiece

Rev. Rembert Gilman Smith, retired Methodist minister,

13

is another acting as a mouthpiece for B'nai B'rith. His most recent pamphlet assailing Father Coughlin is entitled "The Achievements of the Rev. Chas. E. Coughlin". References to B'nai B'rith articles are to the series bound in book form entitled, "Facts About Fictions Concerning the Jew, Anti-Defamation League of B'nai B'rith". Note Smith's sources.

**Rembert G. Smith says** (in his above pamphlet):

"Karl Marx was a Jew but he was baptized in the Christian faith at the age of six." (P. 11.)

"Friedrich Engels, who signed 'The Communist Manifesto' . . . with Marx, was a German." (Same paragraph.)

"Lenin was a Russian nobleman; Stalin is not a Jew." (Same paragraph.)

"The Jews in Russia . . . suffered under the czars, but they did not favor Bolshevism. (Same paragraph.)

"Most of the Jews in Russia were of the Menshevik Party, which was opposed to the Bolshevik Party. (Same paragraph.)

"The Kerensky government . . . had the support of most of the Jews in Russia.

"In 1918, Lenin, actually criticized the Jewish workers for their opposition."

"the Jews suffered greatly, and thousands of them would have starved had it not been for re-

**B'nai B'rith says** (in its volume of articles):

"Karl Marx, although born a Jew was baptized at the age of six." (B'nai B'rith article XXII, p. 9.)

"Frederick Engels, an 'Aryan,' was the co-author of the 'Communist Manifesto'." (Same article, same page.)

"Lenin was not a Jew. He comes of a family of Russian nobility. Kalinin and Stalin are definitely non-Jews." (Article XXII, p. 18.)

"The truth is that the Jews opposed Bolshevism. The Russian Jews suffered terrific persecution under the Czarist government." (Article V, pp. 11-12.)

"The great part of the Russian Jewish population belonged to the Menshevik Party, which was a democratic party, and opposed to the Bolshevik Party." (Same paragraph, page 12.)

"The Jews, with a few exceptions, were supporters of the Kerensky Provisional Government. (Same paragraph.)

"On March 15, 1918, Lenin's government issued a manifesto attacking the Jewish workers for their anti-Bolshevist attitude." (Same paragraph.)

"The distress among the Russian Jews was so great that these would have died of starvation

14

| Rembert G. Smith says: | B'nai B'rith says: |
|---|---|
| lief which was sent from the United States. | had it not been for the American Jewish relief." (Same source, next page, 13.) |
| "Today, the **body** in control over the government of Russia is composed of **thirteen** men, of whom only **one** is a **Jew**; | "The supreme directing **body** in Russia is the 'Polit-bureau.' It consists of nine members and four candidates." (**13** are listed, **one** as a **Jew**.) (Same source, page 13.) (Also used by Keith Brooks. |
| "there are **nineteen commissars**, of whom only **four are Jews**. | "Of the **19 Commissars**, 14 are Great Russians and Ukrainians. One is an Armenian and **four are Jews**. (Following paragraph, same page.) |
| "The communist regime in Russia has been very severe on the Jews. **Synagogues** have been turned **into workmen's clubs**." (Same paragraph, p. 11.) | "The Russian Bolshevik government has dealt blow after blow upon Jewry. **Synagogues** were converted **into workmen's clubs**." (Following paragraph, same page. |
| "an advocate of communism . . . ceases to be **a Jew**, when he becomes **a communist**." (Following paragraph, same page.) | "**A Communist** who was **a Jew** is now an apostate." (Same source, next page, 14.) |
| "There are prominent **Protestants** and Roman **Catholics**, who have become **communists**." | "there are **Communists** who were born **Protestants** and **Catholics**." (Same paragraph.) |
| "**The leaders of the communist party** in this country **are**: Browder, Foster, Hathaway, James Ford, Minor, Heywood, Mother Bloor and Bedacht. Of these **not one** is a **Jew**." (Same source, page 12.) | "In the United States, **the leaders of the Communist Party** are Earl **Browder**, William Z. **Foster**, Clarence **Hathaway**, James **Ford**, Robert **Minor**, William Patterson, Harry **Haywood**, **Mother** Ella Reeve **Bloor**, Max **Bedacht**, **Not one** of those mentioned **is Jewish**." (B'nai B'rith article XXII, p. 1.) |
| "**In Philadelphia, there are** about **seventy-five** Jews who are members of the **communist** party. (Same paragraph.) | "in Philadelphia, with a Jewish population of two hundred fifty thousand, **there are about seventy-five communist** members." (Same source, same page, following paragraph.) |
| "**In New York**, where there are **over two million** Jews, **there are** only **one thousand** members of | "in **New York** with a Jewish population of **over two million**, **there are** approximately **one** |

15

| Rembert G. Smith says: | B'nai B'rith says: |
|---|---|
| the communist party. (Same paragraph.) | thousand communists." (Same paragraph.) |
| "In Chicago, where there are four hundred thousand Jews, there are about one hundred and fifty Jew Communists. (Same paragraph.) | "in Chicago, with a Jewish population of four hundred thousand, there are about one hundred fifty communists." (Same paragraph.) |
| "In Pittsburgh, where there are forty-five thousand Jews, there are only thirty members of the communist party. (Same paragraph.) | "in Pittsburgh, with a Jewish population of forty-seven thousand there may be thirty communist members." (Same paragraph.) |
| "Last November, an anti-communist ticket was nominated in New York City. Most of the nominees for the important offices were Jews. (Same paragraph.) | "In New York . . . last November . . . an Anti-Communist ticket came into being. Endorsement for most all major offices went to Jews. (Same paragraph.) |
| "Among prominent writers in the United states against communism are: Walter Lippman, David Lawrence, Frederick Wile, Simeon Strunsky, Arthur Krock, E. D. Coblentz, Paul Block, Isaac Marcosson, and Gilbert Seldes, who are all Jews." (Same page.) | "Distinguished American Jews who help to formulate public opinion . . . are all violently opposed to Communism. These include such brilliant writers as Walter Lippman", "David Lawrence", "Frederick William Wile", "Simeon Strunsky", "Arthur Krock", "E. D. Coblentz", "Paul Block", "Isaac Marcosson", "Gilbert Seldes", "George Seldes", Emil Lengyel, and many others." (Same page.) |

# ANSWERING B'NAI B'RITH FALLACIES

## MARX

B'nai B'rith propaganda simply asserts but makes no attempt to give proofs or authorities for its "facts". To adequately show the fallacy of its above statements would require several books; but the following are illustrations of the falsity of the whole.

In an attempt to lay to "Christian" training any blame for Karl Marx' atheistic, Red revolutionary activities, B'nai

B'rith (and its mouthpieces, Keith Brooks and Rembert G. Smith, as previously quoted) says:

"KARL MARX, ALTHOUGH BORN A JEW, WAS BAPTIZED AT THE AGE OF SIX AND WAS BROUGHT UP IN A COMPLETELY CHRISTIAN ENVIRONMENT, HAVING NOTHING TO DO WITH JEWS OR JUDAISM." (B'nai B'rith article XXII, p 9.)

### Marx Baptized for "Business Reasons"

Karl Marx (1818-1883), whose real surname was Mordecai, was a descendant of a long line of rabbis. His father, Heinrich, took up the practice of the law and was a convinced disciple of that bitter enemy of Christianity, Voltaire. In 1824, when Marx was six, the family, suddenly, were all baptized as Christians. Liebknecht, Jewish revolutionary, intimate of Karl Marx, wrote in his "Memoirs" that this acceptance of Christianity by Marx' parents was compulsory, being due to a Prussian Government edict compelling all Jews holding official positions or practicing learned professions like the law, to give these up unless they chose to renounce Judaism. ("The Cause of World Unrest", Grant Richards, Ltd., London.)

### Jewish Unbelief and Materialism

Jesus Christ bitterly denounced the unbelieving Jew (John 8:37-44, Matt. 3:9-10, Luke 16:31, 13:34). Every book of the Old Testament warned Jewry as a race that if its unbelief and materialism continued, it would be dispersed (as at present) and punished (Ezek. 39:23-24, Deut. 28:64-67, 11:26-28, Zech. 13:9, etc.).

### Marx' Denunciation of Jewry

B'nai B'rith says Marx "WAS AN OUTSPOKEN ANTAGONIST OF JUDAISM" (B'nai B'rith article V, p. 10).

B'nai B'rith's mouthpiece, Keith Brooks, as previously quoted, echoes: "MARX TO HIS END DENOUNCED THE JEWISH RACE".

Marx, being a militant Atheist and materialist, denounced all forms of religious faith including Judaism, but that he

17

was a Jew and surrounded himself with Jews is undisputed.

A better understanding is gained by the following, from an article entitled "Jew Baiting on the Left", in the May, 1940, issue of the Jewish, Marxian-Socialist, Zionist magazine, "Jewish Frontier". It says that Bakunin, who was Marx' closest associate in founding the "First International" (a world association of Communist-Socialist parties), in 1871 wrote of Marx as follows:

" 'He is a Jew and is **surrounded** by a crowd of little, more or less intelligent, scheming, agile, speculating Jews, just as Jews are everywhere, commercial and banking agents, writers, politicians, correspondents for newspapers of all shades, in short, literary brokers, just as they are financial brokers, with **one foot in the bank and the other in the Socialist movement,** and with their behind sitting upon the German press; they have taken hold of all newspapers, and you can imagine what a nauseating literature is **the** outcome of it.'

## Jewish Capitalism and Marxism

"And he continues: 'Now this entire Jewish world, which constitutes an exploiting sect, a people of leeches, a voracious parasite, closely and intimately connected with one another, **regardless not only of frontiers but of political differences** as well—this Jewish world is today largely at the disposal of **Marx or Rothschild.** I am sure that, on the one hand, the **Rothschilds appreciate the merits of Marx,** and that, on the other hand, **Marx feels an instinctive inclination and great respect for the Rothschilds.** This may seem strange. What could there be in common between communism and high finance? Oh! The communism of Marx wants a **strong State centralization,** and where this exists there must inevitably exist a **central state bank,** and where this exists, **there the parasitic Jewish nation,** which speculates upon the labor of the people, will always find means for its existence.'

"A year later, in 1872, . . . Bakunin wrote, 'In reality this would be for the proletariat a barrack regime, under which

18

the workingmen and working women, converted into a uniform mass, would rise, fall asleep, work and live at the beat of the drum; the privilege of ruling would be in the hands of the skilled and the learned, **with a wide scope left for profitable crooked deals carried on by the Jews,** who would be attracted by the enormous extension of the **international speculations of the national banks.'** "

This brings to mind how Otto Kahn, partner in Kuhn, Loeb & Co., (in writing, 4/7/30) admitted financing such Communist authors as Mike Gold of the Communist Party's "Daily Worker", etc., and how the "Jewish Communal Register" of 1917-18, published by the "Kehillah (Jewish Community) of New York", 356 Second Ave., N. Y. (p. 1019), praised Jacob Schiff, head of Kuhn Loeb & Co., for financing the Russian Red revolution.

### Marx on "The Jewish Question"

This same "Jewish Frontier" article, concerning one of Marx' essays, "The Jewish Question", says it, to quote: "could have become a classic of 'scientific' anti-Semitism . . . **'Money',** he says, **'is the zealous God of Israel outside of whom no other God is permitted to exist.'** " (The Bible speaks similarly.)

Concerning another of Marx' articles, **"Money Is the Jewish God",** it says: "Marx' idea that the concepts of 'Jew' and 'capitalist' are interchangeable is epitomized in these two sentences" (of Marx'), " 'The emancipation of the Jews is in its last analysis the emancipation of mankind from Jewry' and 'The social emancipation of the Jews is the emancipation of society from Jewry.' "

In reply to this, the Marxian-Socialist "Jewish Frontier" mildly retorts: "Painful as it is, in the case of a **man of his stature,** one sometimes cannot help likening his attitude to that post of 'detachment' with which a certain type of Jew occasionally tries to persuade his Gentile audience that he is better than the bulk of his people."

### B'nai B'rith and Jewry Honor Marx

The burning in Germany of the books of **Karl Marx,**

"father of Communism", and other Reds was **denounced** by B'nai B'rith magazine (6/33) as "Nazi terrorism". Concerning anti-German, Jewish protest demonstrations, it criticizes one representing 600 Jewish organizations, saying: **"B'nai B'rith favors protest meetings called by NON-JEWS of prominence."**

And that is the way they work their propaganda off on dumb Gentiles!

The Jewish Encyclopedia (Vol 8) describes Marx' arrests, exiles and Red revolutionary activities in only the most favorable, deferential way, and says: "The **great** work of Marx's life with which his fame is most enduringly identified is 'Das Kapital.'"

"The Encyclopedia of Jewish Knowledge" (Jacob de Haas, editor, 1938) with equal deference describes Marx and his "great" works.

Karl Marx, militant atheistic opponent of all faith, is universally honored by Jewry and by B'nai B'rith's official magazine. For example, in feature articles, one answering "Yes", the other "No", to the question **"Is Judaism Doomed in Soviet Russia?"** (3/33 issue), both praised Marxist Soviet Russia. To quote the "No" man (Norman Bentwich, a contributing editor of B'nai 'B'rith magazine):

"It is certain that the **principal prophet** of the proletarian movement was the German Jew, **Karl Marx, whose picture hangs in every public institution** and whose book 'Kapital' is the gospel of the Communist creed; that another German Jew, Ferdinand Lasalle, whose heroic statue adorns the Nevski Prospect of Leningrad, was one of the inspirers of the early revolutionary parties; that Jews have, from the beginning to the present day, played a part in the creation and the maintenance of the Revolution; and that for no community has the Revolution brought about a greater change of status than for the Jews." (They have dominated Russia since the Red revolution.)

"The essential feature about their community is that the Jews, and particularly the younger generation, feel at home and part and parcel of the new order. They are proud of their share in the councils of the Revolution of Trotsky who organized the Red Army (though among non-Jews he is in disgrace and his name is not mentioned) and of the Jews holding high positions in the Foreign Office and other ministries, in the Army and the Navy, in the economic councils and academies. . . .

"When we landed in Leningrad, our interpreters and guides from the State Tourist Organization were usually Jews and Jewesses. . . . **They are conscious Jews in spite of their Communism. . . .**

"There had to be **destruction** before there could be new life, as well in the Jewish body as in the body politic of Russia. The spiritual motive of the Revolution goes back to the principles of Socialism in the teachings of the Hebrew prophets even though the Communist denies the rock from which he is dug." (This is a favorite blasphemy of radical Jewry, as blind now as then to the spiritual teachings of the Hebrew prophets they killed.) The Hebrew prophets, instead, promised every man his own vine and fig tree (Micah 4:4).

### Marx—Satan's World-Wide Agent

Marx' ponderous wordy writings "explaining" all life, history and humanity as mere results of clashing matter, Satanically excluding and denying any existence of a Divine Spirit, faith in One being denounced as harmful superstition and ignorance requiring extermination as the necessary prelude to progress, are the text books of all Socialist-Communist followers, and are given the fancy names of "dialectical", "historical" and "scientific" "materialism".

These Hellish teachings of Atheism have motivated the countless church burnings, the murdering and torturing of Christian clergy, the persecution of millions of Christians, wherever Marxism has gained power, as in Russia, Hungary, Mexico, Spain. They are taught in every Socialist and Communist school in the U.S.A.

Yet "Jewish Contributions to Civilization", issued by the "Jewish Publication Society of America" (1920), eulogizes Karl Marx and blasphemously likens his Hell-inspired, anti-

God, venomous theories to "the exalted indignation of an Isaiah" (pp. 45-6).

## ENGELS

MARX' "CO-LABORER IN HIS PHILOSOPHIC WORK WAS FREDERICK ENGELS, A GERMAN", says B'nai B'rith and its mouthpieces.

Engels' birth was German by location but, as to his race, authorities differ. Edwin D. Schoonmaker, for example, says: "the spiritual fathers of the New Russia" were "Marx and Engels, authors of the Communist Manifesto, **both Jews** and foreign Jews at that" ("Democracy and World Dominion", Richard R. Smith, N. Y., p. 210). Prof. Shadwell says Engels was a Jew ("The Socialist Movement", Philip Allan & Co., London, Vol I, p. 50). The London Spectator, in 1920, said of Marx and Engels "both German Jews". Etc, etc.

## LENIN

B'nai B'rith (and its mouthpieces) says: "LENIN WAS NOT A JEW. HE COMES OF A FAMILY OF RUSSIAN NOBILITY" (B'nai B'rith article XXII, p. 8).

It is agreed that Lenin (Oulianoff) was the son of a Russian nobleman (non-Jewish) **but** not agreed whether by birth or **adoption**. Photos of Lenin's Satanic, Asiatic, un-Russian looking countenance offer a mystery. D. Petrovsky, Russian historian (in "Russia Under the Jews", p. 86) relates the story told by Simbirsk natives that Lenin, as a child, was left behind, there, by a company of prisoners passing through, and later his Jewish convict father, Ilko Sroul Goldman, wrote inquiring his whereabouts. Lenin had then already been picked up and adopted by Oulianoff.

Victor Marsden, for many years London Morning Post correspondent in Russia, and during the revolution, wrote: "Lenin is a half-blooded Jew", and "Oulianoff by adoption, a Calmyc Jew, by birth, married to a Jewess, and his children speak Yiddish." Another authority refers to Lenin as a "Russo-Tartar, or a Kalmuck Jew". Etc.

# JEWS IN RUSSIA

B'nai B'rith (and its mouthpieces) says: "THE GREAT PART OF THE RUSSIAN JEWISH POPULATION BELONGED TO THE MENSHEVIK PARTY, WHICH WAS A DEMOCRATIC PARTY AND OPPOSED TO THE BOLSHEVIK PARTY" (B'nai B'rith article V, p. 12).

What twaddle calculated to deceive sucker Gentiles! But what an **admission** to those who know the Mensheviks and Bolsheviks, meaning minority and majority, were branches of the same Red Marxian party in Russia! B'nai B'rith thus **admits** the "defamation" of experts for years: that most of Jewry in Russia (and elsewhere) is tied up in Marxism.

Concerning the cause of the Russian Revolution, "Revolutionary Radicalism", Vol. I, pp. 209-10, "The Report of the Joint Legislative Committee of the State of New York Investigating Seditious Activities", 1920, commonly called the Lusk Report, states, to quote:

"The **Marxian doctrines gained increasing foothold** especially through the efforts of **Plechanov and his followers including Lenin."** It goes on to tell how, in 1903, their joint Marxist party, called the Social Democratic Party, split over tactics. The Bolshevik (meaning majority) faction, led by Lenin, "insisted on **immediate** revolt against the imperial government, while the minority faction" (Menshevik) "argued that Russia was not **ready** for a revolution". (They were right for the 1905 revolution failed.)

They split, Plechanov heading the Menshevik (minority) faction, and his follower Lenin the Bolshevik (majority). To quote: "Each section retained the name it was given in 1903 though the Mensheviki soon became the majority instead of the minority of the Social Democratic Party." They were quarreling rivals but, to quote, "Nevertheless on various occasions the **Mensheviki cooperated with the Bolsheviki."**

## Lenin's Feuds With Other Jewish Reds

B'nai B'rith, to whitewash Russian Jewry of charges they

were Reds, says: "ON MARCH 15, 1918, LENIN'S GOVERNMENT ISSUED A MANIFESTO ATTACKING THE JEWISH WORKERS FOR THEIR ANTI-BOLSHEVIST ATTITUDE" (B'nai B'rith article V, p. 12).

Whether or not such a manifesto was ever issued, this is more **bunkum**. The Bolshevik faction of Reds who emerged on top of the other Red factions (all Jewish dominated) seized power in a "military coup d'etat", Nov. 7, 1917, and being a minority, had to use the utmost ruthlessness to **stay** on top. In the assembly elected November 25, 1917, "Of the 730 members of the assembly only 165 were Bolsheviki". So Lenin promptly decreed it dissolved. (N. Y. State Lusk Report, p. 226.)

Like the brigands who won out in the French revolution and then slaughtered each other off, "The Bolsheviki acknowledged that their worst enemies, those against whom they used the severest form of 'Red Terror' including wholesale executions, were not members of the bourgeoisie, but members of the **other two Socialist parties**, the Mensheviki and Social Revolutionaries, against whom they raised the absurd accusation of being 'counter revolutionists'" (N. Y. State Lusk Report, pp. 226-7).

### Marxist Ferocity

This course, which runs true to Marxist theories of force, has been followed by every Red regime, whether Russian "Bolshevik", German "Spartacist", the bloody French "Commune" (1871), or Spanish "Loyalist" (1936-9). In Barcelona, long an Anarchist stronghold, during the recent Red civil war, Socialists and Communists fought against the Anarchists for control, slaughtering each other for three days in the streets, the Socialist-Communist faction emerging on top. This was while the Socialists-Communists-Anarchists were all allies in fighting the war against the Christian Franco forces. It was not that the Anarchists lacked butchering spirit; they were simply beaten at it.

Lenin's Bolshevik feuds with rival Mensheviks and other Marxists meant rivalry, nothing more. The bitterest family quarrels are between rivals for political leadership of the same movement. The "pots and pans" fly continually between the numerous, alternately splitting-and-re-uniting, quarreling-and-cooperating, Socialist-Communist Marxist parties in the U.S.A.

## Marxist Feuds in U.S.

Stalin's former Communist Party leaders, Jay Lovestone (Jew), Leon Trotsky (Jew), Albert Weisbord (Jew), have each formed rival Marxist parties in the U. S. which air each others' faults in their separate papers. Each hopes, by exterminating opposition, to become the "Lenin" kingpin of the Red Revolution in the U.S.A.

Norman Thomas is the Gentile window dressing for the (largely Jewish) Socialist Party, formerly headed by Morris Hillquit (Jew) and Victor Berger (Jew). Thomas jointly, as fellow director with Sidney Hillman and Communist Wm. Z. Foster, etc., since 1922, has voted huge communist-Garland-Fund sums to the principal Communist Party, and other Red revolutionary, organizations.

Between the above mentioned Marxist parties and the Socialist Labor Party (founded by Daniel de Leon, Jew, who "first formulated the idea of a Soviet Government" followed by Russia, Lenin said); the (Jewish) Social Democratic Federation, headed by Louis Waldman (Jew); the immense Socialist "Jewish Forward" with its following of several hundred thousand Yiddish-reading Jews who read its Socialist paper, the largest Yiddish paper in the world (printed in New York and Chicago with editions for principal cities); the Communist Party's International Workers' Order (largely Jewish) with 198,000 members and 200 schools; Stalin's Communist Party with 100,000 due payers, plus several million members of its subsidiaries and "Workers' Schools" in all principal U. S. cities; the Socialist Jewish "Workmen's Circle" with its more than 75,000 members and 159 Marxist schools where children are taught Yiddish; the Communist Party's "Jewish People's Committee" claiming 400,000 members; the Socialist Rand School, N. Y.; etc.

25

—the mass Red Marxist movement advances continually in the U.S.A., as it did in Russia, amidst feinting and boxing of participants and shaking hands between rounds. **Its backbone is Jewry.**

## Marxists Have Same Creed

Whether a man be a Presbyterian, Baptist, Methodist, Episcopalian or Catholic, he is still a Christian adhering to the same Bible, same faith and same Saviour for salvation.

Whether a man be a follower of the Socialist Party, or the Socialist Workers' Party (of Trotsky), the Independent Labor League (of Lovestone), Communist League of Struggle (of Weisbord), Communist Party (of Stalin), he is a **Marxist** adhering to the same Marxian creed of anti-God materialism and revolutionary "class struggle", for "salvation" through the Marxian collectivist state.

As Emile Vandervelde, long a world leader of the Socialist International, said, **"The ideal of us all, our ultimate aim is Communism"** ("Collectivism and Industrial Revolution", 1907, p. 174, by him).

Said Red Bernard Shaw: **"Communism is the same as Socialism, but better English"** ("Spectator", 10/24/25).

## Jews and Kerensky

The same B'nai B'rith article, quoted by its stooges, "defames" instead of whitewashes Jewry with the assertion that in Russia: "THE JEWS WITH FEW EXCEPTIONS WERE SUPPORTERS OF THE **KERENSKY** PROVISIONAL GOVERNMENT" (Article V, p. 12).

You may read in the New York State Lusk Report, Vol. I, how, in inciting the Russian Red revolution, "The Social Democrats" (Bolsheviks-Mensheviks) "distributed hundreds of thousands of leaflets among Russian soldiers" urging "that the soldiers should disobey their officers" and lay down their arms (p. 215), and that this revolution met with "swift success . . . attributed in large measure by Lenin to a **fortuitous cooperation** between **contending groups and factions"** and so the Czar abdicated (p. 217).

26

## Kerensky's Soviet Overthrows Lvoff

"At the same time alongside of the provisional government headed first by Prince Lvoff, the **Socialist and Anarchist elements** of Petrograd's population established a **Soviet** of Soldiers', Workmen's and Sailors' Deputies. . . . Its president was at first Tcheidze and **its vice-president Kerensky**". Tcheidze was a Menshevik leader (p. 218). Both were Marxist Reds, Kerensky being a leader of the socialist Social Revolutionary Party.

"In May, 1917, the **Soviet**" (Kerensky's) "forced the resignation of the first cabinet . . . **Kerensky** who **succeeded** Prince Lvoff, the first premier of the provisional government, proved to be a weak and vacillating character" (p. 218).

## Lenin Overthrows Kerensky

"The liberal decrees of the provisional government had **destroyed** the discipline of the army and the **disintegration** of the once powerful Russian military machine became almost complete" (p. 219). Then Bolshevik Lenin, proving to be the strongest of the Reds, took over in November, to carry on the wrecking work of his Red predecessor, Kerensky.

## "Most of the Jews Were Social Democrats" (Germany)

B'nai B'rith, to whitewash German Jews of Hitler's charges that they were Reds, says: "MOST OF THE JEWS WERE SOCIAL DEMOCRATS" (Article V, p. 11). This means that B'nai B'rith **admits** most of the German Jews were **Marxist Reds**.

About Marxism in Germany: "The principles of the Karl Marx Communist Manifesto were adopted as early as 1869 as the basis of the first **Social Democratic Party**". In 1875, followers of Lasalle, Marx' fellow Jewish Revolutionist, made some changes in the program against Marx' "vigorous opposition", but in 1891, the Social Democratic Party "Congress revised its program and **adopted a thorough and comprehensive Marxian position . . . which remained the basis of the Party from that time forward. . . .** The party had over

27

3,000,000 votes in 1903" (N. Y. State Lusk Report, pp 87-8).
It was led, in Marx' lifetime, by Marx' students Wilhelm Liebknecht and August Bebels. Its Left-Wing was led, before the world war, by Karl Liebknecht (Jew) who with Rosa Luxemburg (Jew) led the bloody "Spartacist" revolution, which for two weeks threatened Germany's Sovietization, until they were killed, Jan. 15, 1919.

## Parvus, Social Democrat, Soviet Agent

It is well known how Helphand Parvus (Israel Lazarevitch), a member of the German Social Democratic Party, persuaded the Kaiser's Government to conduct Lenin and crew, then temporarily exiled in Switzerland, back into Russia in a sealed train like a vial of germs (April 17, 1917), as agitators for Red Revolution that would "lay Russia low" and thus stop Russia from fighting Germany.

In the comment of anti-Nazi Westbrook Pegler on Lenin's above expedition, he repeats what every informed person knows, that Jews were foremost in Russian Communism, saying: **"Although a large proportion of the original Communists were Jews,** the fact remains that nothing which they did could have been done without the first assistance of the German government which was given recklessly but deliberately for the sake of a temporary military advantage."** (Pegler's 7/23/40 column.)

## Kuhn Loeb & Company

The work of the before mentioned Helphand Parvus (alias Israel Lazarevitch) in setting up in various countries the bank accounts that financed the Russian revolution, and bought arms and brought Trotsky (Bronstein) from New York, etc., is revealed strikingly in The Sisson Report (by Edgar Sisson, President Wilson's "Special Representative in Russia, of the Committee on Public Information", 1917-18, during the Bolshevik Revolution).

The Sisson Report* presents a series of corroborating

---

* Note: Quotations on this from the Sisson Report appear in a booklet which can be secured, free, from Father Coughlin, Royal Oak, Michigan, entitled "An Answer to Father Coughlin's Critics".

documents showing how Kuhn Loeb & Co., international bankers of New York (Jacob Schiff, then head, L. L. Strauss and Felix Warburg, partners), assisted by Max Warburg, the partner's brother in Germany and the above Parvus, Soviet agent, arranged the financing of the Russian revolution and how they maneuvered to keep the Czarist Russian government from getting money, to cripple it.

## Who Is the Liar?

Kuhn Loeb & Co., wreaking vengeful fury on Father Coughlin as an "anti-Semitic" liar for revealing this over the radio, stated, "The firm of Kuhn Loeb & Co. has never had any financial relations or other relations, with any government in Russia, whether Czarist, Kerensky or Communist" (New York Times 11/29/38 early edition; also American Hebrew 12/2/38, p. 4), making similar denials for the late Jacob Schiff, head of Kuhn Loeb & Co.

But the "Communal Register" of the "New York Kehilla" (listing, p. 72, Schiff and Felix Warburg of Kuhn Loeb & Co., also Louis Marshall, as members of its own Kehillah executive committee) **praises Schiff for doing just that!** The name of Louis Marshall, Jewish leader who forced Henry Ford's apology, is shown in the Sisson Documents as also meddling in the Russian revolution.

In the Encylopedia of Jewish Knowledge, 1938, edited by Jacob DeHaas, one of Jewry's 120 chosen leaders, is this concerning Jacob Schiff: "As a Jew he struck a distinct note in giving $500,000 for the Galveston Experiment in distributed immigration, in his fervent support of liberal immigration, and in his unrelenting opposition to Russia whilst its government persecuted the Jews, and his **investing a million rubles in the bonds of the Kerensky government as soon as that revolution was successful.**" Jacob Schiff's letter is then quoted from "Jacob Schiff His Life and Letters", Vol. 2, by Cyrus Adler (another of Jewry's 120 chosen leaders), as follows:

" 'I realize fully what is at stake for the firm of Kuhn Loeb & Co. in the decision we are going to make. But come what may . . . I cannot sacrifice my profoundest convictions for the sake of whatever business advantage . . . I am willing that Kuhn Loeb & Co. should join in the loan and the leadership of the transaction provided that we are assured in writing by the commission, on behalf of the British and French governments, that not one cent of the proceeds of the loan be given to Russia.' "

Concerning the Galveston Experiment it is stated elsewhere in the Encyclopedia that Schiff's Galveston "bureau was in operation between and including the years 1907-14, during which upwards of 10,000 Jewish immigrants from Russia, Poland, and Rumania, etc., were distributed by the Galveston office . . . the **machinery of B'nai B'rith** was used for distribution . . . each family or group of families making **a nucleus for other settlers.**"

### Kuhn, Loeb Power Then

The Jewish Communal Register 1917-18 (of the New York "Kehillah" or Jewish "Community") in its biographical sketch of Jacob Schiff, a rhapsody of praise, tells (p. 1018) how he came from Germany in 1865, returned to Germany, to quote: "where he **made connections with the chief banking houses.** Upon returning to the United States he entered the banking firm of Kuhn Loeb & Company, New York, of which he later became the head. His firm became the financial reconstructors of the Union Pacific Railroad, and since then is strongly interested in **American railroads.** Mr. Schiff's principle of 'community of interests' among the chief railway combinations led to the formation of the Northern Securities Company thus **suppressing ruinous competition.** The firm of Kuhn, Loeb & Co. **floated the large Japanese War Loans of 1904-5, thus making possible the Japanese victory over Russia.** Mr. Schiff is director of numerous financial companies, among them the Central Trust Company, Western Union Telegraph Company, the Wells Fargo Express Company. He has been several times vice-president of the New York Chamber of Commerce.

"Mr. Schiff is widely known for his many philanthropic

30

activities and for his interest in education. Of his numerous philanthropies only a few can be mentioned here. He founded the Chair in **Social Economics** at **Columbia University**; he presented the fund and the building for **Semitic** studies at Harvard . . . Mr. Schiff has always used his wealth and his influence in the best interests of his people. **He financed the enemies of autocratic Russia and used his financial influence to keep Russia from the money market of the United States.** When last year, Mr. Schiff celebrated his seventieth birthday, all the factions of Jewry in the United States and elsewhere united in paying tribute to him."

## Kuhn, Loeb and American Banking

It is another story how, with international connections and brother Max Warburg heading a bank in Hamburg, Germany, brothers Paul M. and Felix Warburg came to America, married the sister-in-law and daughter, respectively (1894, 1895), of Jacob Schiff and became partners in Kuhn Loeb & Co. Then, how America's banking and money system (1914) came under the control of the Federal Reserve System (a private, not a government system, as is generally supposed) through Paul M. Warburg's efforts.

Concerning Warburg and the U. S. Federal Reserve Bank, and similarly set up foreign banks manipulated by an international group, to quote: "Mr. Warburg did not tell the American people that the privately owned Central Banks of England, France and Germany were the result of long years of conniving on the part of international money controllers." ("Money Creators", by Gertrude M. Coogan, Sound Money Press, Chicago.)

## Kuhn Loeb & Company Power Now

Now, Kuhn Loeb & Co. rank first in control of all American railroads (41.1% of all U. S. rails) and second in general financial control in the U.S.A., with a control of 10 billion, 853 millions of dollars of assets in rails, banks and utilities, according to the June, 1939, report on "The Structure of the American Economy", by the "National Resources Committee", composed of Government officials: Harold Ickes, chairman, Henry Wallace, Frances Perkins, Harry Hopkins, etc., members (U. S. Government Printing Office, $1.00).

Kuhn Loeb & Company's subterranean methods of covering up its control and its huge interests in industries are revealed on pages 162, 306-7, 311-12, 315, of the same report.

What a contrast with the little 2.88% rating given Kuhn Loeb & Co. by B'nai B'rith and its stooges!

### More B'nai B'rith Revelations

The rest of the same B'nai B'rith article (V) and appendix to it, pertaining to Jewish membership in Russian parties, although intended as whitewash for suckers, is instead, a revealing admission of Jewish Marxism. Besides citing Jewry's participation in the Bolshevik, Menshevik, and other Red Marxist parties of Russia, it adds this: "As for that part of the Jewry which was united politically as **Jewish** it grouped itself in the only mass-like Jewish party, the **Bund**. Part of Jewry sympathized with the **Zionists**. The Bund as well as the **Zionists** have been persecuted by Bolshevism from the first days of the October upheaval of 1917 to the present day . . . The Bolsheviks persecute all parties so that very many Jews, members of these parties, have been shot or linger in prisons . . ." (Article V, p. 30.)

### The Bund, Marxist

Certainly, "Dog eat dog" is the law of Marxism, and shooting off rivals is a great Marxian sport. But the Russian Bund, nevertheless, was a Jewish **Marxian Socialist Party**. The New York Jewish Communal Register 1917-18, p. 1455, says:

"CENTRAL VERBAND OF THE BUND ORGANIZATIONS OF AMERICA, 202 E. Broadway. PURPOSE: Financial aid to the **Jewish Socialist Bund in Russia,** Poland and Lithuania. Branches in all cities in the United States and Canada. . . . Their members were found in the vanguard of the Jewish trade unions and swelled the ranks of the **Workmen's Circle.** . . . The Bund played an important part in

32

educational work of the Jewish masses of the United States. Since the Russian Revolution in 1917, the Central Verband of the Bund has been active in collecting funds to assist the Russian Bund in its work against counter revolution forces and against the agitation by the Black Hundred for massacres of Jews."

This plainly tells that the Russian Jewish **Bund fought against,** and their brothers in America raised money to help them **prevent,** the counter-revolutionary **overthrow of the Bolshevik revolution in Russia,** also that Gentiles who **opposed** Bolshevik tyranny and held the Jews responsible for it wanted to massacre them.

### Soviet Government "Principally Jewish"

After 132 days of the murdering, torturing, Soviet terror regime of Jewish Bela Kun (Cohen) and his Jewish cohorts in Hungary, who even baked nuns alive in an oven (1919), when anti-Red Gentile forces regained power, they killed Jews on sight.

The Lusk Report, quoted above, indexing the **"Hungarian and Soviet Governments principally Jewish",** says of Bela Kun's Hungarian Soviet: "Of **thirty-two** principal Commissars, **twenty-five** were **Jews,** which was **about the same proportion as in Russia."**

The before-quoted "Jewish Frontier" article "Jew Baiting on the Left", cites the following by the prominent Marxist, George Sorel, in his chapter "Plea for Lenin", added to his "Reflexions on Violence":

" 'It seems that the **Jews** who joined the revolutionary movement are chiefly responsible for the terrorist measures for which the **Bolsheviks** are being blamed. This hypothesis seems to me all the more plausible as the intervention of the Jews in the Hungarian Soviet Republic was not fortunate.' "

### The Russian Jewish Bund in U.S.A.

How the Bund in the U.S.A. formed the Jewish Socialist Federation of America is told in the Jewish Communal Register, 1917-18, pp. 1256-61; also how the Bund was foremost in forming the National Workmen's Committee of radical Jews whose first convention in New York City, Sept. 4-6, 1915, represented "a total membership of **half a million** Jewish workmen . . . representatives of all **radical** wings" (p. 1448 of same).

Further, concerning this alien Socialist Jewish **Bund,** transplanted to the U.S.A. by Jewish immigrants, it says: **"A net of Bund branches was spread throughout the United States** and Canada. For a number of years these branches, whose primary object was to collect funds for the Bund in Russia, were the most active and influential bodies in the **Jewish radical world.** Their members formed the vanguard of the Workmen's Circle and swelled the ranks of the Jewish **trade unions.** The activities of the branches were coordinated and supervised by a Central-Verband which was elected at the annual conventions" (p. 1257). "The Agitation Bureau was accordingly organized for the purpose of conducting Socialist propaganda in Yiddish . . . the Bureau was supplanted by the Jewish Socialist Federation" (p. 1258). "Over a hundred branches in 26 states are at present affiliated with the Federation" (p. 1259 of same "Jewish Communal Register", 1917-18).

### Dubinsky and Hillman, Russian Reds

Likewise, the same B'nai B'rith article V (p. 9) "whitewashes" as not "Communists" the revolutionary Socialist Jewish labor leaders in the U.S.A., David Dubinsky and Sidney Hillman. Both served in Russian prisons for Red revolutionary activities and both have never ceased to undermine Americanism with their Red Marxist activities since they left Russian prisons and came to these shores; Dubinsky as a Socialist Party leader, recently raising thousands of dollars for Red Spain, as part of the Socialist and Communist Parties' campaign; Hillman being eulogized by Lenin for raising great funds for Soviet Russia, etc., and now a leader in the Socialist-Communist American Labor Party of New York and President Roosevelt's right hand man, etc.; both sponsoring (1939) the Communist Party's

34

hero, Tom Mooney, whose letter to "Comrade Stalin" pledging his aid to Red revolution if freed from prison appeared in the Communist Party's "Labor Defender" magazine (11/32).

## Zionism, Marxist

Zionism is not only Jewish nationalism but is Marxian-Socialist in leadership, theory, and in practice in Palestine, being notable there for absence of religion and being carried on in Marxian manner with collective funds, lands, cooperatives and farming communities, run like in Soviet Russia, with over 85% of Jewish Palestinian workers organized in the Histradruth, the Jewish labor organization (p. 40 "Guide to New Palestine", issued by Zionist Information Bureau for Tourists in Palestine", 1937). The Histradruth is affiliated with the **Socialist,** Second International, and aided in the U.S.A. by the Socialist "League for Labor Palestine" which issues the "Jewish Frontier" magazine (275 7th Ave., N. Y.).

## TYPICAL ZIONIST LEADERSHIP

### Solomon Goldman

For example, take Rabbi Solomon Goldman, Russian-born Red and 1940 President of the Zionist Organization of America (Z.O.A.). He tells (in Who's Who in American Jewry, 1938-9) that he had been vice-president of the Z.O.A. since 1933; is member of the American Jewish Congress (headed by red Rabbi Stephen Wise); since 1929 executive committeeman (Chicago branch) of the Socialist Party's League for Industrial Democracy (which combined its student and unemployed branches with the Communist Party's in 1935); member, since 1927, of **B'nai B'rith's** Hillel Foundation which organizes Jewish groups and propaganda on American college campuses; etc.

Goldman was on the sponsoring committee to honor communistic Albert Einstein (Jewish Frontier, 6/39); board member (1940 and previously) of that notorious legal-spearhead of the Red movement, the American Civil Liberties

35

Union, which defends Red treason wherever it lifts its head, and every phase of Marxism, obscenity, violence, atheism, etc.

## Attitude Toward Christ

One who has heard Goldman speak, or read his writings, quickly discerns that hatred of Christ and Christianity burns in him like a carefully banked fire, only a tongue darting out from time to time to betray the heat within.

Goldman, for three hours, in his book review (2/20/40) at his synagogue, denounced his radical friend Sholem Asch for "straddling" and turning out a book, "The Nazarene", neither Christian nor Jewish. He blamed Asch for not coming out plainly and denouncing Jesus; for building up Mary Magdalene's voluptuous scented physical appeal and then lacking courage to finish with the conclusion that there was an affair between them. He praised Nowack's "Life of Jesus" which he explained shows Jesus as a bastard dreamer and Judas Iscariot a hero who, after he saw that Jesus could not free Israel or Himself from the Roman yoke, said, "I see, Rabbi, you are a fake", and then did his duty to Israel by betraying Jesus.

## Judaizing Christians

However, Goldman's own B'nai B'rith is distributing to members at a reduced price, Sholem Asch's book, "The Nazarene", with praise of it as a novel and this note, to quote them: "A secondary purpose of the story is to **destroy all theological** and political reasons for friction between Jews and Christians" (B'nai B'rith Anti-Defamation Review, 12/39, p. 3).

The only cause for friction, the "unbridgeable chasm", as Goldman put it, between Jewry and Christianity, is that Jewry will **never** accept Christ as Divine. Acceptance of Christ's Divinity **is** Christianity. Without it, Jesus becomes just another "Rabbi" self-deceived, or perhaps a racketeer, but as a successful prominent Jew, acceptable to Jewry as such. One Rabbi expressed it, "as a Jew, I am proud of Jesus"; but as the Divine Son of God, Jewry rejects Him today as they did when He was on earth. "After these things Jesus walked in Galilee: for He would not walk in Jewry, because the Jews sought to kill him." John 7:1.

Anything creating in Christians disbelief in Christ's **Divinity,** therefore, helps Judaize Christians and prepare them for materialistic Marxism. Modernist "Christians" who, like Jews, disbelieve the Bible, are subversive Jewry's warmest allies in Marxism, and also in fighting any truth-telling about Jewry as criminal "anti-Semitism". There are also Fundamentalist "Christians" who can be bought for this purpose, even as Judas was.

### Another Zionist, Communist Brainen

Another example is Russian-born Reuben Brainen, both a Communist and a Zionist, who is hailed in an eulogistic article in B'nai B'rith magazine, entitled "Brainen At 75" (Aug.-Sept., 1937 issue), explaining that Brainen, "a pioneer Zionist whose interest in and activity for the Jewish homeland antedates the first World Zionist Congress, is one of the builders of Hebrew literature, and the courageous exponent of Jewish colonization of Soviet Russia."

The Communist Party's "Daily Worker" (11/23/38-12/2/39) tells of Brainen: sitting on the platform at New York Communist Party rallies; as national committeeman of Icor, the Communist Party organization to aid the Jewish colonization of Biro Bidjan in Soviet Russia; as honorary president of the Party's "Jewish People's Committee" (of 400,000 members) ; etc.

Brainen helped Theo. Herzl organize the first World Zionist Congress (1897) ; has been honorary vice-president of the Zionist Organization of America; vice-president of American Jewish Congress; has attended all Zionist and World Congresses to date; contributor to the Jewish daily "The Day" (Who's Who in American Jewry, 1938-9).

### Stephen S. Wise

Hungarian-born Rabbi Wise, founder of the first Federation of American Zionists (1897) and president of the Zionist Organization of America from 1936 on, and leader in all things Jewish, has sponsored the principal Red activities in the U.S.A. A long partial list of his Red affiliations appears in "The Red Network" by Mrs. Elizabeth Dilling. His son, James Waterman Wise, is a Communist Party writer, vice-president of "Icor" (Communist), etc. His daughter, Justine Wise Tulin Polier, wife of a radical, Isadore Polier, is herself connected with the communist Friends of the Soviet Union, etc. She was appointed Judge in New York by the Jewish-Italian radical Mayor LaGuardia, 1935.

## More on Marxist Zionism

Describing the start of the Socialist Zionist movement ("Poale Zion"), the Jewish Communal Register, 1917-18 says the Jewish masses "were **Socialistic through and through** . . . **Zionism thus received a Marxist basis** and appealed strongly to the masses" (p. 1376). It says: "Poale Zionism is the center of the East Side, from which come forth almost all Jewish American movements, or without which no movement can prosper" (p. 1381). "Thanks to the American Poale-Zion, the Federation of Labor . . . adopted resolutions favoring the creation of a Jewish home in Palestine. . . . The movement for national **radical schools** has been created by the initiative of the Poale-Zion, and is growing from day to day" (p. 1380).

## Zionism Versus Bolshevism

It is the militant **exclusive** nationalism of Zionism, not its Socialism, which irks the Bolshevik who is working for international Socialism controlled from headquarters in Moscow, U.S.S.R. (Union of Soviet Socialist Republics), instead of Palestine.

To quote Horace M Kallen, chosen by world Jewry as one of the 120 leading Jews: "Between the protagonists of the Zionist idea and programme and the abstract and doctrinaire humanitarianism of the Jewish internationalists of the **Bolshevik or other Socialist sects** there was fought out concomitantly with the tragedies of the Ukraine, Hungary, and Poland, **a battle for the leadership of the Jewish com-**

munity and the control of the Jewish institutions". (P. 245, "Zionism and World Politics".)

## Jews and Revolutions

Kallen says of Jewry: "Members of the race are particularly conspicuous in the Polish and Hungarian rebellions, in the republican uprising in Germany of '48. Even more conspicuous were they in the new internationalism. . . . This internationalism is a conclusion from the philosophy of Socialism. Its strongest authoritative voice was that of the Jew, Karl Marx; its most heroic practical defender the Jew, Ferdinand Lasalle; its unseen root the economic doctrine of the Jew, David Ricardo." (P. 53 of same.)

Horace M. Kallen, Jew, who wrote this, then and for years, has been connected with the pro-Communist, Freudian-filth-purveying, New School for Social Research, New York. The spirit and political scope of Zionism are set forth very clearly in his book "Zionism and World Politics" (1921). He describes Zionism as "a position in which the postulates of Socialism are fused with axioms of nationality" and, like the "Jewish Communal Register", says "the lower East Side of New York is full of exclusively **Yiddish**-speaking 'cosmopolitans'; they really compose a **Socialist Ghetto**", adding "the self-conscious Jewish workmen are not merely **Socialists,** they are also **Nationalists**" (p. 89).

Kallen shows how the Socialist labor movement and Socialist Zionist movement dominate Jewry and how Zionist representation "in the international Socialist organization has consequently become the acknowledged representative of the Jewish proletarian and it has secured from this organization and others the endorsement of the Jewish claim to Palestine" (p. 91).

### Zionism Is World-Wide Socialist Jewish Nationalism

Kallen writes of the first world Zionist Congress at Basle, 1897, under Theo. Herzl as "an irrefutable demonstration of **Jewish national solidarity**" regardless of "diversity" of "life and thought", rich or poor (p. 74).

He tells (p. 97) how the Rothschild millions were poured

into Zionism (Read again Bakunin's statement about Jewry having one foot in the Socialist movement and the other in the bank—Marx and Rothschild).

He relates how in 1914, with the advent of the war, Zionism became a world political force, everywhere, with Judge Louis D. Brandeis leading it, aided by Felix Frankfurter (protege of Brandeis and brains of the Red movement in America for over 20 years, as well as designing power, with Brandeis, of the New Deal), Eugene Meyer and Nathan Straus, financiers (p. 136).

## Brandeis' Words

Enlarging on Brandeis' views, he says: "Zionism, thus, is in Brandeis' view, the salvation of the Jew who elects to build his life elsewhere than in Zion, no less than of the Jew who chooses the destiny of a Judean." He cites the necessity Brandeis urged of organizing every Jew **as a Jew** inside any country as a separate **nationality** and Brandeis' admonition to Jewry: **"Organize, organize, organize, until every Jew in America must stand up and be counted—counted with us—or prove himself wittingly or unwittingly of the few who are against their own people"** (p. 139).

And this same Jewish **nationalist,** Brandeis, has been followed by his protege Frankfurter to hold sway in our Supreme Court which **is** the American Constitution through the Supreme Court's interpretations of it, according to Frankfurter.

It would seem that Americans should separate the leaders of such avowedly **separate** national groups from control of **America.** Fear of just such a logical conclusion has made some Jews squeamish about open advocacy of Zionism.

## Zionism and World War

Kallen also tells in "Zionism and World Politics" how the present world Zionist leader, Chaim Weizmann, chemist, in 1914, through his service to the British government in contributing "toward the creation of T.N.T.", along with "Sir Herbert Samuel and the Rothschilds", gained the ear of "Englishmen of influence" to secure Palestine for Zionist Jews (p. 165), and how Zionism's "greatest asset was the known fact that the **President of the United States had come to believe in the Zionist program** and had promised his best efforts in helping to carry it out. **It counted** heavily in Mr. Balfour's consultations with **Justice Brandeis** during the former's mission to the United States" (p. 166).

Brandeis had the ear of President Wilson, and as it was necessary to bring the U.S.A. into the war that England might win to secure Palestine for the Jews, the result of the negotiations of Balfour and Brandeis with President Wilson was that the U.S.A. entered the world war April, 1917, urged on by a press filled with Belgian atrocity stories, babies' hands cut off, etc. Palestine was won for the Jews.

### Balfour Declaration Followed

Kallen says (p. 169): "On November 2, 1917, after nine months of conference, negotiations, and consultation", the Balfour Declaration was made public. This was a letter from Arthur J. Balfour, British Secretary of State, to Lord Rothschild of the Zionist Organization, assuring Palestine to Zionist Jews, if England won. President Wilson's enthusiastic public letter acclaiming the Zionist program is also quoted (pp. 174-5).

### Claims Zionism Brought U. S. Into World War

Samuel Landman, a World Zionist Organization officer from 1912 on, in his pamphlet published in London, 1937, entitled "Great Britain, the Jews, and Palestine", says: "The fact that **it was Jewish help that brought the U.S.A. into the war on the side of the Allies** has rankled ever since in German—especially Nazi—minds, and has contributed in no small measure to the prominence which anti-Semitism occupies in the Nazi program."

He tells how in 1916 the Zionist organization gave up hopes of a deal with Germany to get Palestine for Jewry and turned to the Allied governments instead. To quote **Landman:**

41

"An interesting account of the negotiations has already appeared in the Jewish press, and need not be repeated here in detail, except to recall that immediately after the **'gentleman's agreement'** between Sir Mark Sykes, authorized by the **War Cabinet,** and the **Zionists,** cable facilities through the War Office, the Foreign Office, and British Embassies, Legations, etc., were given the latter to communicate the glad tidings to their friends and organizations in America and elsewhere, and **the change in public and official opinion, as reflected in the American press, in favor of joining the Allies in the War,** was as gratifying as it was surprisingly rapid. . . . In Germany, the value of the bargain to the Allies, apparently, was duly and carefully noted."

### British Government Admits It!

The British Royal Commission (Peel Commission), in its report issued in July, 1937, frankly admits that: "The Balfour Declaration was issued in 1917 in order to enlist the Jewish support for the Allies. . . . We came to the conclusion from information we received from every part of the world that it was vital we should have the sympathies of the Jewish community."

But this was not thus officially revealed until 19 years later!


## WILL JEWRY REPEAT IN 1940?

Ever since 1933, when Hitler started dislodging Jews from power in Germany, the American public has continually been fed by the press with "atrocity" stories vamped on the old cutting-off-Belgian-babies' hands lines.

### Shaving—"The Sadistic Operation"

Sometimes these stories are so far fetched as to be ridiculous. For example, there is shown in the Jewish Sentinel, 7/18/40, a picture of one Jew shaving the face of another Jew, with a beard apparently intact, two uniformed men watching them at a little distance. Below it, another pic-

42

ture shows some five bearded Jews standing, as though about to pull it, in front of a small wagon, empty except for one Jew seated in it. Seven soldiers stand around the wagon with photograph-conscious looks. The caption under these two pictures is lurid enough to jerk tears from stone:

"Fiendish Persecution in Poland—These two pictures, brought recently from Poland by an American girl, reveal the unspeakably brutal methods employed by Nazis against Jews in that prostrate land. Above, an orthodox Jew having his beard shaved off by another Jew at the order of Nazi officers standing by as the sadistic operation is carried out. Below, Jews forced to pull a large horse carriage on one of the streets in Warsaw."

Perhaps in America, also, wagon-pulling and daily shaving **should** be classified as "fiendish persecution" and "sadistic operations".

### "Fifth Columnism" or Truth?

When Col. Lindbergh truthfully points out that the American press these past years has erroneously made the American people believe that under Hitler the German people, actually the most powerful in Europe, have been starving and their air force was so weak they had to fly their planes back and forth in order to have them counted more than once, he is dubbed a "Nazi agent" and a "Fifth Columnist", despite the fact, impossible longer to conceal, that German might has demonstrated its ability to defeat one nation after another with ease.

### Bellowing for War

Jewish journals from coast to coast are, and have been, trumpeting for war, and a dictatorship war regime, against Hitler at any cost.

Typical, is this masthead and heading on the editorial page on the 5/23/40 issue of "The Sentinel", self-avowedly devoted to **Jewish** interests:

43

## THE IMPERATIVENESS OF AIDING THE ALLIES

"The national defense program" of President Roosevelt **"must** be carried out in every detail", it says, **"as set forth by Walter Lippmann** in crystal clear fashion and **stirringly voiced in Wm. Allen White's** appeal to leading citizens throughout the land".

White has been Jewry's faithful radical mouthpiece for years. Lippmann, formerly an avowed Marxist "Red Light", now ostensibly a "conservative", is now, as he was in the World War, one of the Jewish-Frankfurter-Baruch war crowd. Lippmann and Frankfurter then were both Assistants to Secretary of War Baker (self-avowed Socialist). Lippmann was also an assistant to Edward Mandel House for the Peace Conference which drew the blueprint of Europe's new hates. House wrote the plan for Socialist revolution in the U.S.A. in his novel "Philip Dru Administrator". The Socialist hero became dictator of the United States.

### Claude Pepper

It is no accident that Claude Pepper, that incessant war monger who called Col. Lindbergh "the chief of the fifth column in this country" (Chgo. Daily News, 8/6/40), should be speaker for B'nai B'rith. Of him B'nai B'rith wrote as follows:

"CHICAGO:—A last-minute rain failed to dampen the enthusiasm of 25,000 men and women who filled Grant Park for a mammoth Flag Day celebration, **sponsored by the Chicago B'nai B'rith Council.** Featuring the event were the address of **Claude Pepper** of Florida . . ." (B'nai B'rith Magazine, July-August, 1940, p. 350.)

### Another Parrot for B'nai B'rith

Nor is this A.P. dispatch proudly reproduced in the paper of Dr. J. Frank Norris, 8/2/40, an accident:

"PASTOR TO BURN NAZI FLAG IN SUNDAY PRO-
TEST. . . . Rev. Mr. Norris believes the United States
should send England 10,000 bombing planes at once, 1,000
armed motorboats to help repel the invaders, ships to evac-
uate children from the country, and supply food, clothing
and munitions, including guns and tanks. He added there
are **3,000,000 'Hitlerites'** in the United States, each of which,
he said, **should be placed in a concentration camp or deported.**"

Like that of other mouthpieces of B'nai B'rith, the propaganda of Rev. J. Frank Norris, "Fundamentalist" minister,
concerns Jewry having no particular connection with Marxism, and the Jews not having killed Christ(!), etc. Some of
his statements appear in B'nai B'rith article V (pp. 23-4)
in company with similar statements by notorious Reds and
Modernist "Christians" (John Haynes Holmes, Harry
Emerson Fosdick, S. Parkes Cadman, atheist Harry Elmer
Barnes, etc.).

### Norris Reverses Himself

Those unacquainted with B'nai B'rith power and technique were confused by the quick change in Norris' mes-
sages shortly after he returned from Germany, the summer
of 1937, eulogizing its conditions and praising to the skies
the freedom of preaching Christianity there. He was
promptly dubbed a "Nazi agent" by the Red press and
"reached" by B'nai B'rith. How they afterward financed
literature, meetings, and nation-wide broadcasts for him in
return for his eulogy of Jewry, misleading B'nai B'rith
propaganda, and vilification of Germany, has been revealed
by himself and others, like Ormsby McHarg (one time
Asst. Secy. of Labor and Commerce), who heads the Citizens' National Committee, 41 E. 42nd St., New York City.

In June, 1939, when Jewry's war became imminent, Norris ceased his habitual lambasting of the Federal Council of
Churches and the New Deal as Red, reversed his peace policy, and pitched in to back Roosevelt's war program, broadcasting a warlike lift-the-embargo appeal over a nation-wide
hookup in the fall of 1939. He praised New Dealers in his

paper and featured as speaker in both of his churches, Elliott Roosevelt, whose unsavory divorce and beer convention activities were well known. It was Elliott's brother, James, who in person bore to the May, 1938, B'nai B'rith Convention, President Roosevelt's letter of eulogy and felicitations (Reproduced in full in 6/38 issue of B'nai B'rith Magazine, p. 341). A mere message was not enough! President Roosevelt has received more than one Jewish medal for his services to Jewry.

B'nai B'rith article V, in which Norris' statements appear, is the message of Sigmund Livingston B'nai B'rith Anti-Defamation League Secy., to this same Convention.

B'nai B'rith financially supports the Federal Council of Churches and runs jointly with it the nation-wide "Religious News" broadcasts. Norris even featured in his paper, 6/21/40, as a "fine fraternal message", greetings from radical Edgar De Witt Jones, an ex-President of the Federal Council of Churches whom he had so long lambasted.

### B'nai B'rith Has Over 500 "Valuable" Speakers!

B'nai B'rith boldly announced in its Anti-Defamation League "A.D.L. Review" of 10/39, p. 4: "MORE THAN 500 SPEAKERS THROUGHOUT THE COUNTRY WHO COOPERATE WITH THE SPEAKERS' BUREAU RECEIVE REGULAR MAILINGS OF ANTI-DEFAMATION LEAGUE EDUCATIONAL MATERIAL . . . WHICH HAS PROVED VALUABLE IN THE PREPARATION OF **SERMONS, ADDRESSES** AND **RADIO** BROADCASTS."

"Valuable" to whom? Certainly not valuable to those who want **truth** or who place **America's** welfare ahead of the welfare of those Jews at home and abroad who insist on a **separate international nationhood** for themselves within all nations. "B'nai B'rith serves **Jewry**", is the B'nai B'rith slogan.

### Pushing for War

The same Jewish forces, pushing in 1917 for United States entry into war, are now pushing with terrific power for the conscription and mobilization of Americans to fight Germany to restore Jewry to power in Europe. They aim, through B'nai B'rith's huge network, spread for spying and repression, backed by Presidential dictatorial emergency powers, to crush and punish as "fifth-columnism", anti-Semitism", or "Nazism", any opposition or criticism of this war program.

## Punishing "Anti-Semitic" Opponents
### Emanuel Celler

Emanuel Celler, member of B'nai B'rith, American Jewish Congress, American Jewish Committee, etc., and sponsor of bills for aliens and Reds, backer of Communist Tom Mooney, speaker for the communist American League for Peace and Democracy (Daily Worker, 5/6/38), etc., introduced the measure to permit wire tapping to catch people opposing the present war program. To quote:

"In the face of charges that Congress is being stampeded into passage of dictatorship legislation in the name of national emergency, the House today by a voice vote adopted a joint resolution giving the Federal Bureau of Investigation authority to tap wires to prevent interference with national defense preparations by conspiracy . . . or in **any other manner.** Only a handful of congressmen were on the floor when the measure was **jammed through** following a **favorable report by the judiciary Committee.** . . . Previously Rep. **Emanuel Celler, chairman** of the **Judiciary Committee** had explained that the resolution has the approval of Atty. Gen. Robert H. Jackson" (Chicago Tribune, 8/7/40).

## Marxist Socialist Party Immune!

Jackson's letter assuring the red Socialist Party it will need fear no investigations or hampering is reproduced on the front page, 7/27/40, of the "Socialist Call". As in England, the Earl Browders and the Daily Worker will go on, while the so-called "anti-Semitics" will sit in jail.

## Adolph Sabath

Adolph Sabath, Jewish Congressman with a notorious

Red-aiding record, has introduced another measure asking twenty-one years' imprisonment and fines up to $5,000 for "fifth column activities" including "inciting religious or racial prejudice" (Chgo. Times, 8/6/40). Telling such truths as are in this article would undoubtedly rate the limit of punishment with the Red Jewish Sidney Hillmans, Sabaths, Cellers, and their aides at the National helm.

## $250,000 To Push Conscription

The reluctant revelations of T. R. Wyles, Chief Civilian Aide of the Secy. of War, concerning collection and disbursing of a $250,000 fund to push the present conscription bill, is reported in the Chicago Tribune, 8/7/40. "It was this group that Sen. Rush D. Holt (D., W.Va.) yesterday described as 'Wall Street lawyers, international bankers and directors of munitions enterprises' and the real backers of the selective draft proposals" (Same source).

## They Want Red Dictatorship

The American Ass'n. for Economic Freedom, Washington, D. C., headed by Jewry's faithful servitor, Wm. Allen White, in its pamphlet, "Program for America" (printed in the red New Republic, 7/5/39), calls for **Socialization of America,** with no goods permitted to be **manufactured, shipped** or delivered unless **licensed** by the State with blanket licenses **controlling all businesses in every industry.** A complete Dictatorship State, a "directed economy", is called for.

Francis Pickens Miller, professional organizer, "a member of the interventionist group in charge of agitation and propaganda for the Roosevelt administration's project to release fifty or more destroyers to Great Britain, admitted today he requested the allotment of radio time for a speech by Admiral Wm. H. Standley next Saturday night on 'American Aid to Great Britain'" (Chgo. Tribune, 8/9/40).

Miller is Secretary of the Washington, D. C. Committee of the above red American Ass'n. for Economic Freedom, headed by outstanding Red lights, all with records in the Dilling "Red Network" and "Roosevelt Red Record and

48

Its Background": Wm. Allen White, chmn.; Wm. Jett Lauck, vice-chmn.; Zionist Rabbi Stephen S. Wise; Frank P. Graham; Wesley C. Mitchell; Eduard C. Lindeman; Paul H. Douglas; John A. Ryan; James Myers; Guy Emery Shipler; Bishop McConnell; Wm. E. Sweet; Henry Pratt Fairchild; also Wm. Simkin of the American Friends Service Committee, very closely aligned with B'nai B'rith in serving Jewish interests; Meyer Jacobstein, Jewish banker who was director of war emergency courses during the World War, mediator in clothing industry, new president of First National Bank & Trust Co., Rochester, publisher, Rochester Evening Journal and Sunday American since 1933; Isadore Teitelbaum of red Rabbi Wise's (Zionist) American Jewish Congress, delegate and a commissioner of the **World Jewish Congress.**

## Will We Be Jailed or Killed?

WILL OTHERS JUST MISS DEATH BY BEING DRIVEN OFF THE ROAD, AS HENRY FORD WAS, BEFORE BEING MADE TO RECANT CRITICAL TRUTHS ABOUT SUBVERSIVE JEWRY? OR ELSE?

## Jews in Government Posts

B'nai B'rith says: "THE PERCENTAGE OF JEWS IN FEDERAL SERVICE IS SHARPLY LOWER THAN THE PERCENTAGE OF JEWS IN THE TOTAL POPULATION. IN HIGH ADMINISTRATIVE AND POLICY-MAKING POSTS THE JEWISH FRACTION IS MUCH SMALLER THAN WOULD BE JUSTIFIED ON A PURE POPULATION BASIS" (B'nai B'rith pamphlet, "Jews in America By the Editors of Fortune", p. 6).

Said the Brooklyn Jewish Examiner, 10/20/33: "The Roosevelt Administration has selected more Jews to fill influential positions than any other previous administration in American history. One of the key Roosevelt advisors is Bernard M. Baruch. In the absence of the President from Washington, Mr. Baruch is regarded as 'Unofficial President.'"

## The Power of Frankfurter

For over twenty years, Felix Frankfurter, protege of Judge Brandeis (Red-aider and militant Jewish Zionist Nationalist), has accomplished infinitely more to aid Red destruction of America than any ordinary Communist or Socialist Party member. He was an organizer and has provided brain power and propaganda for the American Civil Liberties Union, legal spearhead for the Reds, which notoriously bails out, propagandizes and legally fights for I.W.W.'s, Anarchists, Socialists, Communists, Red Revolutionary conspirators who are undermining American institutions, wherever they are found from coast to coast.

## A New Deal Master

A sizzling seventeen-page summary of Frankfurter's subversive activities with documentary proofs was presented to the United States Senate in protest against his U. S. Supreme Court appointment by Mrs. Elizabeth Dilling in January, 1939. But Frankfurter, as was known then, despite this or anything else, was slated to go into power, being not a servant, but one of the **masters,** of the New Deal.

It was the untruthful, vicious ballyhoo campaign against the Dept. of Justice, then suppressing Reds, which was carried on by Frankfurter's group (See National Popular Government League in "The Red Network" by Dilling) which in 1924 succeeded in doing away with all Dept. of Justice funds for suppression of Reds, thus freeing and enabling the Red movement to grow to its present mammoth proportions.

## A Menace

In connection with the Red campaign of violence and rioting for Sacco and Vanzetti, the Red murderers who died yelling, "Long Live Anarchy!", Mass. State executive Frank A. Goodwin said: "The leader of the movement to set these two murderers free is Felix Frankfurter". "I then believed and still believe that Frankfurter and men of his type are **a menace to the country and to American institutions."** Pres. Theodore Roosevelt wrote a scorching letter to Frankfurter on the same lines denouncing Frankfurter for his subversive battle in behalf of Moscow's pet, Anarchist-Communist Dynamiter Tom Mooney.

Patriots who knew Frankfurter's subversive activities raised such an uproar when Frankfurter was nominated to the Massachusetts Supreme Court by Gov. Ely, on recommendation of Jewish Judges Brandeis and Cardozo and their close associate Oliver Wendell Holmes, that rather than be publicly rejected, Frankfurter declined the nomination, June, 1932.

## Frankfurter, Stimson and Knox

Of course, the Republican interventionists, Henry L. Stimson and Col. Frank Knox, have been loaning their names to radical and Jewish organizations or they would not be where they are, Knox, for example, having long been on the board of the Chicago branch (headed by Communist-supporter James M. Yard) of B'nai B'rith's National Conference of Jews and Christians, etc., etc.

## Stimson and Frankfurter

A clearer idea of the political set-up now threatening to plunge America into war can be gained from an article in "The American Hebrew", 1/20/39, p. 7, entitled "Felix Frankfurter". To quote: "Born in 1882 in Austria, the son of a long line of Rabbis, Justice Frankfurter arrived in this country in 1894 . . . Prof. Frankfurter's first experience in the field of administrative law, which he was later to teach at Harvard, came as Assistant United States Attorney in New York under **Henry L. Stimson**" . . . He "was confidential assistant to Newton D. Baker when he was **secretary of war during the Wilson Administration**" (which dragged us into war for Jewry).

## Power Behind the Throne

"Justice Frankfurter has been publicized so much in certain circles as **'the power behind the throne' in the Roosevelt Administration that many persons do not realize that his role in this Administration has differed little from what**

51

it was in the Administrations of Hoover, Coolidge, Harding, Wilson, Taft and Roosevelt the first. To all of these he supplied the bright young men who were willing to win their legal spurs at minimum cost . . ."

## Willkie

"Another evidence of the prevalent belief today in the fairness of Justice Frankfurter came recently in a statement from that well-known utilities man, **Wendell Willkie, who was willing to accept Frankfurter** as one of the three arbitrators who could adjust the Tennessee Valley Authority controversy with the private utilities."

This was printed, remember, in the Jan. 20, 1939, issue of "The American Hebrew", before Willkie was thought of by the public as a Presidential candidate and started acting as a spokesman for Jewry, backing intervention and calling for making "anti-Semitism" criminal (Chgo. Herald-Examiner, 7/6/40).

## Brandeis-Frankfurter, New Deal Master Mind

Simon and Schuster (Jewish publishers) issued "The New Dealers" in 1934. Referring, in connection with Frankfurter (p. 317 on), to "that other great Jew Bernard M. Baruch . . . perpetual advisor to all Presidents of all parties, at all times, upon all subjects", it, continuing, asserts: "Felix more than any other one person is the **legal mastermind of the New Deal,** altho he is in large part only the **transmitter of the apostolic succession of Louis D. Brandeis.** . . . His intimacy with Roosevelt dates back to the Wilson Administration when Frankfurter's work on the War Labor Policies Board brought him in frequent contact with the Navy . . . they have continued their association ever since. . . . And Felix urged in letters to his friends and in conversation Roosevelt's nomination for the Presidency, being one of the few liberal intellectuals who saw that Roosevelt was **their man. . . .**

"When Wallace and Tugwell planned their new farm administration they asked Frankfurter to recommend a Solicitor for the Department of Agriculture. He suggested **Jerome N. Frank,** a liberal Jewish lawyer of Chicago.

"When the first draft of the Securities Bill prepared by Huston Thompson was practically wrecked, Moley sent for Frankfurter to rewrite it. Felix brought down **Professor Landis,** a younger protege named **Ben Cohen,** and borrowed still another of his proteges, **Thomas G. Corcoran.** . . When the Tennessee Valley Authority was organized and needed a smart lawyer, Frankfurter produced **David Lilienthal,** whom he had been farming out in Wisconsin in training for just such a job. Lilienthal knew public utilities and the laws governing them from right to left. For Secretary Ickes, Frankfurter produced **Nathan R. Margold;** for Miss Perkins . . . **Charles E. Wyzanski, Jr;** and Secretary Hull found waiting for him in the State Department another Frankfurter economic protege in the shape of **Herbert Feis.**

"Thus there are Frankfurter men established in key posts thruout the Administration. Most of them are young and brilliant heirs to the tradition of **Holmes, Brandeis and Cardozo,** transmitted through the Harvard Law School under Professor **Felix Frankfurter.** . . .

"Most of the Frankfurter products brought their own rolls and mustard along to Washington, until there are now between seventy-five to a **hundred** men in the Administration who studied under Frankfurter. . . . Some Departments and emergency organizations won't accept any lawyer who is not on the Frankfurter white list. The fact that so many liberal lawyers are **Jews** has succeeded in giving an accidentally **Semitic** cast . . . to the legal front of the New Deal. . . .

"So Frankfurter's part in the New Deal was not confined to the provision of its legal personnel. He was an active though detached member of the Brain Trust . . . and he advised the Administration on its main strategy with regard to the Supreme Court. He urged against allowing any of the **revolutionary** legislation to come before the Court until Congress had reaffirmed its intent by re-enacting the emergency measures. This strategy would also allow the **Grim Reaper** to do his stuff on some of the **conservative dodos** on the bench. So Frankfurter advised the Administration to 'go slow' and that was his parting word to almost every

53

one of his lieutenants in each of the experimental wings of the **Roosevelt Revolution."**

The "Grim Reaper", death, enabled them to capture the Supreme Court, instead of packing by enlarging it, and Frankfurter was put on it.

## COURT MARTIAL FOR TRUTHTELLERS
### Frankfurter Against Lindbergh, Col. Smith

To quote: "Another man who has been close to Lindbergh is Col. Truman Smith of U. S. Army Intelligence and the army's chief specialist on Germany. . . .

"For instance, when Germany moved into Poland last year, Col. Smith was able to tell the War Department the points which the Germany army would take, and almost the exact hour it would take them. At first, the War Department would not believe his information, eventually had to admit its soundness. . . .

"Opinion in the War Department is unanimous that Col. Smith is an extremely able officer, but reports of his collaboration with Lindbergh, brought to Roosevelt by **Justice Felix Frankfurter, caused the President to demand his court martial.** Gen. Marshall, however, persuaded Roosevelt that this would cause bad public reaction, and instead sent Col. Smith south to the maneuvers." (Pearson and Allen column, 8/12/40.)

## WHO IS PUSHING US?
### The Stimson, Knox, Kuhn-Loeb Tie-up

To quote: "**Sir William Wiseman,** chief of British intelligence and 'undercover' man during the first World War, is a **partner of Kuhn, Loeb Company,** New York banking house with labyrinthian connections in London, France, and other international finance quarters.

"Sir William returned to the United States several months ago.

"**Henry L. Stimson is counsel to Kuhn, Loeb Company...**

"Henry Stimson is now Secretary of War in the Cabinet of President Roosevelt, who heads the war party of the Nation.

54

"Recently a considerable block of stock was opened to public sale by the **Chicago Daily News**. Among the largest buyers was **Kuhn, Loeb Company.**

"**Colonel Frank Knox,** Chicago Daily News Publisher, is now Secretary of the Navy in the same Cabinet." (Quoted from Boake Carter in Social Justice, 7/15/40, p. 6.)

Furthermore, Frank Knox' Chicago Daily News has recently formed a hookup with the New York Post owned by George Backer, an executive of the Communist-Socialist American Labor Party, and head of the American section of the Jewish ORT World Federation. He is son-in-law of the Kuhn Loeb & Co. partner, Mortimer Schiff (Chgo. Tribune, 6/23/39), offspring of Jacob Schiff, who financed the Russian revolution.

### "International Financiers" Remove Woodring

After Harry H. Woodring was removed, 6/20/40, as Secy. of War by Pres. Roosevelt, to put **Henry L. Stimson,** "Republican interventionist", in his place, Woodring, in a letter to Sen. Vandenberg, to quote, "condemned the Roosevelt administration's conscription program as a step toward totalitarianism that cannot be justified on the basis of miliary necessity. . . . Opponents of conscription said the letter proved their contention that the **army was opposed to compulsory military service** and did not recommend it **until forced to do so two days after Stimson** took his oath of office. . . . Woodring himself was quoted by friends as saying, three weeks before his removal that 'a small **clique of international financiers'** wanted to force him out of office because he opposed their demands for 'the United States to declare war and get into the European mess with everything we have, including our man power.'" (Chgo. Tribune, 8/3/40.)

### Acheson, Frankfurter's "Hot Dog Boy"

Another of the war-mongering Committee to Defend America by Aiding the Allies is Dean Acheson, former secretary (1919-21) to the radical Zionist-Jewish-Nationalist Justice Brandeis. Acheson was one of the Brandeis-Frankfurter "100 Hot Dog Boys" appointees as Under Secy. of the Treasury, 1933.

Acheson, with his law partner George Rublee (former Harvard law instructor and still connected, and on the Wilson-Baruch war industries board, 1917), and Chas. C. Burlingham (also connected with Frankfurter's Harvard law department), and Thos. D. Thatcher, have issued a 3,000 word brief finding supposed loopholes in the American law **against** releasing U. S. war vessels to other countries, which, they declare, make it legal to now **release fifty American destroyers to England!** (Chicago Tribune, 8/12/40.)

## Pershing's Jewish Connections

General Pershing, who appealed for war intervention for England, opposing Col. Lindbergh (8/4/40), has family ties with the international banker, Jules Bache, who is head of J. S. Bache & Co. and President of British Domes Mines, Ltd. To quote the Jewish Sentinel (8/1/40, p. 11):

"Congratulations to banker Jules Bache on his approach to the status of great grandpa. His granddaughter Muriel, who is the daughter-in-law of Gen. John Pershing, is preparing a nursery for early 1941."

## Stimson, Adler and Conscription

The Paul Mallon column, 8/8/40, stating that the original conscription bill was drawn by the Military Training Camps Ass'n. of New York, says: "Prominent in the group were **Henry Stimson,** later appointed Secretary of War, and a man whom Stimson has now installed as his assistant secretary, Judge Robert M. Patterson. Such men as President James B. Conant of Harvard" (Frankfurter's center of influence); "Julius Ochs Adler . . ." (Jew, since appointed Chief Civilian Aide to Secy. of War Stimson), etc.

## Who Pays?

Whose money is paying to whip up U. S. war intervention through the fabulously expensive nation-wide advertisements of the "Committee to Defend America by Aiding the Allies", whose "front" is the faithful stooge for Reds and Jewry, Wm. Allen White? This Committee was called together originally by Frederick R. Coudert (Willkie backer), legal advisor during the World War (1915-20) to the British Embassy, working with Jewry to propagandize us into the World War holocaust to reap ingratitude, bloodshed and crushing debts, still unpaid.

Senator Holt (Congressional Record, 7/11/40) said that financially supporting this Committee were, to quote, "Not only international financiers, may I say, but individual members of corporations that are profiting as a result of this war. . . . You hear plenty of war talk on the air", he said, and pointed out that such men (Jews) as **I. D. Levy**, chairman of the board of directors, WCAU, and director of Columbia Broadcasting System, and **Jerome H. Lauchhelm**, bank director, and director of Columbia Broadcasting System, were financial backers of this Committee; also **Irving Berlin** (Baline), Russian-born Jew, now "blessing" America in his song as world Jewry's new country; **Douglas Fairbanks, Jr.**, Jewish movie actor; **Paul Muni** (Weisenfreund), Polish-born Jewish actor; also **Sam Goldwyn** (Goldfish), Polish-born Jewish motion picture producer.

Radio war propaganda and **hate films** are **foremost** in stirring up war fever, as he said.

### Kuhn Loeb & Co. Again

Also cited as financial backers of this interventionist Committee are: **Mrs. Daniel Guggenheim,** widow of the late Jewish international copper king, connected with the Guaranty Trust Co., the National Bank of Commerce, the American Surety Co., etc.

Also the wife of **John Schiff,** partner of Kuhn, Loeb & Co., grandson of Jacob Schiff, who financed the Russian Revolution.

**Frederick Warburg,** another Kuhn, Loeb & Co. partner, grandson of Jacob Schiff, his mother being Frieda Schiff, his father Felix M. Warburg, lamented when he died as a "Prince of Israel".

Joseph Thomas, partner of the Jewish banking house of **Lehman Brothers,** of which Gov. Herbert Lehman, active in radical and Palestinian affairs, became partner in 1908.

Also Henry Luce, publisher of "Fortune" (and its B'nai B'rith propaganda); to quote Sen. Holt: "It is stated he started his magazine program after he had secured a loan from Lamont, of Morgan & Co. and others. Luce says we should go further into the war. He helped to pay for the 'Stop Hitler' advertisement. Perhaps that will explain why Life Magazine tries to show the country that we are in danger of invasion. Week before last Life Magazine had the Germans over here already." Luce studied at Oxford, England, and J. P. Morgan, international banker, keeps homes in New York and at "12 Grosvenor Sq., London, W., and Wall Hall, Watford, Eng." (Who's Who in America, 1940-41.)

## HOOVER'S WARNING ABOUT THE "JEW DEAL"

It is not without cause that the popular nickname of the New Deal has been the **"JEW DEAL"**.

Rabbi George Fox (money raiser for Soviet Russia's Biro Bidjan), in his page in the Jewish Sentinel, 7/11/40, complained that Willkie had not yet placed a Republican Jew to the front on his campaign advisory board, but suggested that perhaps his reason for not doing so was to **protect** Jews from such criticisms as have worried ex-President Hoover. To quote:

"We know that Willkie is not anti-Jewish. It is perhaps not known that at least two of his campaigners were of Jewish extraction. We know from personal sources that some of his most valuable advisors are Jews. His own business relations, as well as those of members of his family, with Jews, is of the closest. . . .

"Some months ago, the only living ex-President of our country told the writer that he was greatly pained and alarmed by the spread of anti-Semitism in this land. He attributed it to various reasons, and then said that **he felt that the presence of so many Jews in the government in Washington was also a cause for the growth of anti-Semitism.** Mr. Hoover did not justify this reason; he simply

58

stated what he thought is a fact. He also believed that efforts ought to be made to prevent more Jewish young men from going there. . . .

"The writer's answer to the ex-President was that the Jews . . . if they had the ability to contribute to the work of maintaining our government and helping to solve its problems, it was their duty to do so; and that to encourage anti-Semites by depriving the Jew of the opportunity to serve his country, was wrong, sinful and un-American. We still believe this." Willkie obeyed and "announced the appointment of Walter I. Sundlun of Providence, R. I., to his personal staff. Sundlun is president of the Congregation of Temple Beth-El in Providence, and an officer in several other Jewish organizations in his state". (Chgo. Tribune, 8/31/40.)

## Some Governing Jews

B'nai B'rith Magazine (11/32) boasted editorially:

"In the state of New York, a Jew, Herbert Lehman, is Democratic candidate for governor. In the same State, a Jew, George Z. Medalie, is Republican candidate for United States Senator. In the State of Illinois, a Jew, Judge Henry Horner, is Democratic candidate for governor. In the State of Ohio, a Jew, Gilbert Bettman, is Republican candidate for United States Senator."

Red-aider **Gov. Herbert Lehman,** whom Pres. Roosevelt called his "good right arm", was executive committeeman of the New York Kehilla (p. 72, Communal Register, 1917-18) along with those mentioned in conjunction with the Russian revolution, Louis Marshall, "Prince of Israel" Felix M. Warburg, Judah L Magnes (of the communist Garland Fund, now in Palestine, then head of this same Kehillah).

## Jew Heads Illinois National Guard

**Governor Henry Horner** (Levy) of Illinois (member of Adolph Kraus Lodge, B'nai B'rith) has (1940) replaced Gentile Roy Keehn with a Russian-born Jew, **Samuel Lawton** (Solomon Slewiski) as **head of the Ill. National Guard,** jumping him over the head of his Gentile senior Thos. S.

Hammond; also replaced Gentile Weymouth Kirkland with the notorious Jewish politician **Jake Arvey** as **Judge Advocate General of the Ill. National Guard.** ("Lightnin' ", 6/40, pp. 2 and 3.)

Jewish **Sam L. Nudelman,** a "bankrupt" appointed State Director of Finance by Horner (Lightnin', 2/40), has been Ill. State boss for Horner since the latter's illness.

### Red Jew Hillman

**Sidney Hillman,** Russian-born Jewish **Red,** is one of Roosevelt's supreme National Defense Council in charge of labor relations and the training of **millions of America's youth,** and on Hillman's board are Red Emil Rieve and others like him.

**Julius Ochs Adler** of the New York Times, who has been going around the country yelling for more arms, millions of boys to arms, has been made Civilian Aide to Secretary of War Stimson, 8/4/40.

Jewish Admiral **Joseph Taussig** has been war mongering against Japan.

The Jews, J. David Stern, Bernard Baruch, Frederick Wm. Wile, Gabriel Heatter, Eugene Lyons, Jules Semon Bache (international banker with family ties with Gen. Pershing), Barnet Nover, Abraham Cahan, Zionist Nahum Goldmann, Rabbi Louis Newman, are all sounding the Jewish call to arms.

### Jew Secretary, U. S. Treasury

**Henry Morgenthau, Jr.,** is Secy. of the U. S. Treasury, **in control of all American gold and of the secret stabilization fund of two billion dollars,** long buying gold and silver from the Red governments of Mexico and Russia, **stabilizing them.**

### Jew La Guardia

Roosevelt's Red Jewish aide **Fiorello La Guardia** is Mayor of New York with his Jewish Red appointees in power on the bench, board of education, etc. Justine Wise Polier, Rabbi Wise's daughter, was appointed **Judge by him,** Joseph Schlossberg, Red Russian Jew, has been on the New York City Board of Higher Education since 1935, etc.

## New York School System

James Marshall, son of Louis Marshall (elsewhere mentioned in connection with the New York Kehillah, Henry Ford and the Russian Revolution), as president of the N.Y. board of education, has been, they boast, **"controlling a school system of 38,000 teachers and 1,110,000 pupils.** Son of the late Louis Marshall, Jewish leader, he is a militant fighter for **progressive** causes" (B'nai B'rith Magazine, 6/38, p. 349). Marshall, in his article in this issue, says that **Jewish "assimilation is no good".**

## Some Other New Deal Jews

A few others of the host of Jews who are influential in the New Deal Administration include: Wm. C. Bullitt, Jacob Baker, Alexander Holtzoff, Justice Sam Rosenman, David Lilienthal, Wm. Morris Leiserson, E. A. Goldenweiser, J. David Stern, David Dubinsky, Lee Pressman, Chas. Michelson, Abe Fortas, Lawrence Steinhardt, Harry F. Guggenheim, Emanuel Celler, Sol Bloom, Herbert Feis, Albert Einstein, James P. Warburg, Adolph Sabath, Isadore Lubin, Nathan Margold, Leo Wolman, Louis Kirstein, Lincoln Filene (for whom John Roosevelt works), Samuel Dickstein, Chas. Wyzanski, Jr., Max Zaritsky (Presidential elector, 1936), Chas. Taussig, Jacob Straus, Nathan Strauss, Jerome Frank, Louis H. Bean, Abraham M. Fox, Benedict Wolf, David J. Saposs, L. H. Seltzer, Edward Berman, Jacob Perlman, Morris L. Jacobson, A. H. Meyers, Jack Levin, Harold Loeb, Wm. Seagle, Herman A. Gray, Alexander Sachs, Frank Bloom, Nathan Witt, Ismar Baruch, Maurice Mandell, Mordecai Ezekiel, Ben Cohen, Felix Cohen, Morris Watson, Arthur M. Blaine, Arthur J. Altmeyer, Samuel Becker, Jacob Billikopf, Henry Ellenbogen, Leon Sacks, Rabbi Ferdinand Isserman, Emil Rieve; and Red Jewish writers for New Deal Red propaganda: Nadir Moishe, Henry Alsberg, Meyer Levin, Elmer Rice (Reizen-

61

stein), Clifford Odets, Mike Gold, Albert Maltz, Alfred Kreymborg, John Howard Lawson, Geo. Sklar, etc.

## Communist Propaganda Films

Heirs of the Jewish Communist Ernst Toller, late suicide and Hollywood script writer, are suing James Roosevelt, charging he adapted Toller's play, "Pastor Hall", without payment. Mrs. Roosevelt has been pictured in the press made up for her part in the prologue to this "hate propaganda" film. Communist Toller, the author, was leader of the bloody murdering Red revolution in Germany, 1918, was "chairman central committee Bavarian Soviet, 1919; and member of Red Guard; in prison 1919-24" (The American Labor Who's Who, 1925).

# PEPPER'S DICTATORSHIP PROPHECY HORRIFIES

The words of Claude Pepper, warmongering mouthpiece for B'nai B'rith Jewry, horrified (Chicago Tribune, 8/14/40) informed ones who fear complete dictatorship powers, sought by Jewry, may be pushed through Congress before Gentile patriots awaken to find themselves muzzled by Celler and Sabath laws, already passed or introduced, punishing "anti-Semitism" and all opposition. To quote:

"The senator, who several weeks ago introduced in congress a seven point program for establishing a dictatorship in this country, also stated that other New Dealers subscribe to his theories. . . .

" 'Senator Pepper said that the President should have, in his opinion, the authority to take over all private industry and all private business and private endeavor, or any part of it, that has any connection with national defense.' Asked whether this, in fact, would not include 'almost everything, all business and industry,' the New Dealer replied, according to Lewis, that it would . . . 'And he said with particular emphasis that he sees no reason why Mr. Henry Ford should be allowed to produce what Henry Ford wants to produce.' . . .

"Asked by Lewis whether these amazing theories of government were his alone or whether there are other New

Dealers who share them, Senator Pepper, whose oath as senator binds him to uphold the constitution, was said to have replied that 'a great many others subscribe to the same views.' And, according to Lewis, he promised in conclusion: **'THE WHOLE THING IS GOING TO COME.'**"

## Conscripting Money and Liberty

Senate Bills 4213 and 4214 and amendments to Senate Bill 4164, taken in connection with the Burke-Wadsworth Conscription Bill, would make the President absolute **Dictator.** S. 4164, in part, provides:

"Whenever war or the imminence of war creates an emergency which in the judgment of the President is sufficiently serious to necessitate an increase in the Military Establishment by the drafting of manpower, the President is authorized and directed to cause to be taken a census of the net wealth and income of every citizen of the United States, . . ." and ". . . shall cause to be computed each person's ability to lend to the Government. . . ."

## DIES DARE NOT REVEAL JEWISH MARXISM

The only reason that **Jewish powers** behind Congress permitted the creation or continuance of the Dies Committee was the hope of its unearthing "Nazi" "anti-Semitic" enemies of Marxist Jewry.

The reason why no Congressional Committee, Fish, Dickstein, Dies, or any other, has ever attempted to investigate or denounce Red Revolutionary **Socialist** organizations is because the overwhelming mass of Jewish people are aligned with such. **Mass Jewry is too powerful a force to touch.**

The Dies Committee was continued (1940), on the assurance that it **"would not hold public meetings during the political campaign"**, to unearth "Naziism" or "anti-Semitism", and to get after only one splinter of the Marxist movement, Stalin's Communist Party, which is guilty of adhering to the Nazi-Soviet pact, generally hated by Jewry; but **not** to investigate the overwhelming mass of Red Revolutionary

Marxism which is, in the U.S.A., grouped largely into Jewish Socialist organizations.

### B'nai B'rith Hails Half Million Jewish Reds

Complimenting it on its stand for **Jewish racial solidarity,** B'nai B'rith Magazine (4/34, p. 235) hailed the Red New York City conference of leading Socialist Jewish organizations, which formed the **Jewish Labor Committee** now representing more than 500,000 Jews, saying:

"With the leading **Jewish Socialist** organizations, large trade unions and other labor bodies represented by over one thousand delegates, this recent conference equalled in size and resembled in character the one that was held at the outbreak of the war. It was estimated that the delegates acted and spoke for more than **a half a million** organized Jewish toilers, and spoke for them in behalf of specific **Jewish** interests, but from a distinctly labor point of view. . . .

"To show the world that we have great armies of labor is a very good thing, but to have the same world note that these hosts are largely of a **radical** frame of mind, is something about which we have in the past been somewhat **squeamish.**"

### The Jewish Labor Committee

The elected officers were as representative a group of Red alien-born Jews as one could find, carrying on in America the Red activities which exiled them. They were: B. C. Vladeck (deceased), chmn.; J. Baskin, Secy. (Gen. Secy., Workmen's Circle (Socialist Jewish) since 1914); David Dubinsky, treas. (Pres. Int'l. Ladies' Garment Workers' Un.); vice presidents: Jos. Schlossberg (Secy.-Treas., Amalgamated Clothing Workers' Un.); Max Zaritsky (Pres., Intl. United Hatters, Cap & Millinery Workers' Un.); all leading Socialists and former Red revolutionists in Russia; Morris Feinstone (Polish-born Secy., United Hebrew Trades); Alex. Kahan, I. Weinberg, Saul Rifkin.

For example: Dubinsky, repeatedly arrested in Russia, served eighteen months in one Russian prison, was then exiled to Siberia, escaped after five months and came to

64

U. S. (American Labor Who's Who, 1925.)

Israel Weinberg, "acquitted on one count of charge of murder in San Francisco preparedness day parade bomb explosion, 7/22/16, eight other indictments still pending." (Same source.)

Adolph Held, Socialist, Polish-born Jew (Pres., Jewish Socialist Daily Forward Assn., Pres., Amalgamated Bank, N.Y.C., etc.), took Vladeck's place, Dubinsky is still treas., Baskin, Secy., Charles Zimmerman (Lovestone Communist), an exec. committeeman, etc. ALL SPONSOR COMMUNIST PARTY, AS WELL AS SOCIALIST, ACTIVITIES.

The 1940 national executive committee of the Socialist "Jewish Labor Committee" is comprised of representatives of the following Socialist Jewish organizations; Int'l. Ladies' Garment Workers' Un., Amalgamated Clothing Workers' Un. of Am.; United Hatters, Cap & Millinery Workers' Int'l Un.; Workmen's Circle; Forward Association (which issues the Jewish "Daily Forward" paper in Yiddish); Jewish Socialist Verband; Jewish Workers' Party (Left Poale Zion); New York Joint Board, Cloakmakers' Un.; New York Joint Board, Dressmakers' Un.; New York Joint Board, Amalgamated Un.; United Hebrew Trades; Greater N. Y. Bakers' Joint Council; Jewish Section, Socialist Party; Committee for Jewish Masses in Poland.

### Communists Gather Half Million Jews

"Jewish Life" (magazine published by the "N.Y. State Jewish Buro, Communist Party", 50 E. 13th St., N. Y. City, 1/38 issue), reporting the convention of the Communist Party's **"Jewish People's Committee"**, said:

"Close to 1,000 delegates representing HALF-A-MILLION American Jews participated in the National Conference and the anti-Polish Pogrom march on Washington under the auspices of the Jewish People's Committee. . . . A spokesman for Jewish reaction, Dr. S. Margoshes, tried to pooh-pooh the whole conference by saying: 'About a thousand delegates, representing mostly Left and Communist-controlled Jewish organizations, assembled in Washington over the week-end.'" But the article goes on to say, "Half a million Jews constitute a significant cross section of American Jewry."

Wm. Weiner (Welwel Warszower), Financial Secy. of the Communist Party, convicted of passport fraud, has been replaced (1940) as national head of the Jewish People's Committee "For United Action Against Fascism and Anti-Semitism" (1133 Broadway, Room 1427, N. Y. City), by Rabbi Moses Miller; Harry Mintz, Reuben Saltzman, Bernard J. Harkavy, M. Gertner, Dr. A. L. Bunin, Ben Meyers, M. Olkin, Max Perlow, Irving Potash, Prof. H. Slochower and Tobias Wendy, being other national officers of it (1940).

### U. S. Jewry in Three Red Groups

"Jewish Life" (4/38 issue) states: "Three federated Jewish bodies encompass between them the **majority of Jews**; the **American Jewish Congress,** controlled by the **Zionists** and representing the majority of Zionists; the **Jewish Labor Committee** and the **Jewish People's Committee,** both of which have had national conventions in the past months, at which their respective positions were very clearly stated."

In other words, the **majority of Jews** are encompassed by three Marxist national networks, two being Socialist and one Communist.

### B'nai B'rith Hails Reds

And B'nai B'rith Magazine (5/38, p. 329) successively on the same page gloated over conventions in N. Y. City of this communist "Jewish People's Committee" with "1,000 delegates", and the red "Jewish Labor Committee" convention "attended by 1,200 delegates, said to represent more than 500,000 organized Jewish workers", and rejoicingly chronicled that "The achievements of the Jewish people in the Soviet Union have been made possible by the assistance of the Soviet government".

The Socialist "Jewish Frontier" (8/40, p. 23) refers to

the Communist Party as the **"Stalinist brigade which is also the Jewish brigade"**, and asserts the prominence of Jewry in the Communist Party of U.S.A., which is so well known to any informed person. To quote:

"Four students of New York City College have been arrested on grounds of interfering with a student military parade on their campus. All four are Jews. The Communist press carries daily reports of 'pacifist' activities in other colleges. Whenever participants in such demonstrations are mentioned by name, the names are generally Jewish. The Stalinist controlled American Youth Congress has placed pickets. . . . The names of the pickets announced in the press are also Jewish. . . ."

## U. S. COMMUNIST PARTY LEADERSHIP

B'nai B'rith says: "THE LEADERS OF COMMUNISM IN AMERICA ARE EARL BROWDER, WILLIAM Z. FOSTER, CLARENCE HATHAWAY, JAMES FORD, ROBERT MINOR, WILLIAM PATTERSON, HARRY HAYWOOD, ELLA REEVE BLOOR AND MAX BEDACHT. NOT A SINGLE ONE OF THEM IS A JEW" (B'nai B'rith article V, p. 9).

Thus do B'nai B'rith and its stooges claim that the leaders of the Communist Party are, besides Max Bedacht, the Gentiles Browder, Foster, Minor, Hathaway, Bloor, and the Negroes, Haywood, Patterson and Ford, and these are featured by the Communist Party, as Norman Thomas is by the heavily Jewish Socialist Party. However, if Bedacht, genl. secy. of the Communist Party's International Workers' Order (I.W.O.), is not a Jew, that is a discovery!

The I.W.O. was formed (1930) by the withdrawal of the left wing of the **Jewish** Socialist Workmen's Circle, which conducts 159 schools for children in which they are taught Marxism and to read and speak Yiddish. The I.W.O. has 198,000 members, 1,900 chapters, and conducts some 200 Red schools, its largest section being Jewish (Daily Worker, 11/18/38). Heading the Communist Party's I.W.O., besides Bedacht, are the **JEWS** William Weiner (pres.), Rubin Saltzman (natl. secy.), Emanuel Levin (natl. educational dir.), Sam Pevzner (natl. youth secy.).

## Congressional Report on Jewish Organizers

Congressional Report #2290 (by the Fish Committee), about the Communist Party, says: "The district organizers are responsible for Communist activities throughout their districts, such as forming nuclei among factory workers, conducting political campaigns, arranging mass demonstrations, circulating Communist literature, and in raising funds. **A large percentage of all the known Communist district organizers are of Jewish origin**" (p. 14).

## Rushmore Reveals Communist "Brain" Jewish

When Howard Rushmore, American-born Gentile, recently quit the Communist Party and quit working on the staff of the "Daily Worker", official organ of Stalin's Communist Party, he said it had (to quote Chgo. Herald-American, 12/27/39): "an editorial board made up of a well-to-do Negro and five Russians. . . . Head of this Stalin brain trust is **Sam Don**", managing editor. "None of the 'Daily Worker' staff knows his **real name.** . . . Next to him in power is **Harry Gannes,** foreign editor, now under federal indictment charged with passport forging. . . . Other members of the editorial board are **Milton Howard** (assumed name) 'historian'; **Alan Max,** labor editor, and Sender Garlin, former Moscow correspondent. All are Russian born or of Russian descent. **The real brain of the American Red organization are Alex Bittleman, Jack Stachel, F. Brown and Sam Don,** none of them citizens."

None of these Jews, the "real brain", of the Communist Party in America, are mentioned as such by B'nai B'rith.

Carl Brodsky (Jew) is given as the responsible representative of the "Daily Worker" during recent libel suits filed against it, and the Jews Alex. Trachtenberg, Carol Weiss King, Isaac Shorr, Irving Fraikin, as its (1929) incorporators (New York Times, 2/3/39). Jewish Nat Wein is its advertising head (Westbrook Pegler, 2/14/39).

Israel Amter and Chas. Krumbein, Jews, are top Party leaders, and a list a yard long could be added here.

### Russia's New "Latvia", "Estonia", "Lithuania"

In August, 1940, because of suits and fear of suppression as an alien organ, for legal purposes, the "Daily Worker" was placed in the name of three little old radical, American-born ladies, up in the eighties in age. One Red quipster says they ought to be called "Latvia", "Estonia", and "Lithuania", after the States recently taken over by Russia.

### B'nai B'rith-Fortune Research Says

Even the B'nai B'rith-Fortune "Research", aiming to whitewash Jewry, thought it necessary to explain originally (p. 141, "Fortune", 2/36):

"The reason for the general impression of Jewish and Communist identity is simple . . . the Jewish members of the Communist Party are very commonly the intellectual and hence the articulate members of that party. The second-generation Jewish intellectual with his **background of Talmudic dialectic is mentally predisposed to Marxism to a degree which he himself rarely appreciates. And Marxism with its internationalism and anti-nationalism** is eminently fitted to the emotional needs of a people **without a fatherland.** The attachment of men of other blood to the earth on which they were born is sometimes incomprehensible to the traditionally earthless Jew. But most important, Jewish intellectuals are attracted to radicalism because the Jewish intellectual very understandably feels that the 'system' is against him. . . . In consequence **he is frequently a radical.** And since he is able and idealistic and courageous and articulate he becomes **the voice of radicalism.** He provides, under his own name or under **non-Jewish names chosen for tactical reasons,** a very great deal of the magazine writing, the propaganda, the general literature, of the movement in New York."

### RUSSIA NOW*

B'nai B'rith says: "THE SUPREME DIRECTING BODY IN RUSSIA IS THE 'POLIT-BUREAU'. IT

* See documented lists of Russian Commissars in "The Rulers of Russia", distributed free by Father Coughlin, Royal Oak, Michigan.

CONSISTS OF 9 MEMBERS AND 4 CANDIDATES".
13 ARE listed, only one, Kaganovitch, as a Jew. (P. 13,
article V, which was Secy. Livingston's B'nai B'rith Convention message, 1938.)

## Wise, Who Is "Wise", Says "Bunk"

Communist James Waterman Wise, whose recent book
"Mr. Smith Meet Mr. Cohen", showing "eight ways to fight
anti-Semitism", is written in collaboration with Lee J. Levinger, head of B'nai B'rith's Research Bureau, himself denounced such twaddle as the above as a false "panic stricken" way of fighting anti-Semitism, in his article in the Communist Party's "New Masses", entitled, **"Are Jews Communists?"** (10/29/35). He said:

"Jews are not Communists, is the burden of a panic-stricken statement issued jointly by Dr. Cyrus Adler, president of the American Jewish Committee, Alfred M. Cohen, president of the B'nai B'rith, and B. C. Vladeck, chairman of the Jewish Labor Committee. . . . Let us analyze their statement . . . it falls into two parts. The first attempts to show that the Jews of Germany and of other countries were not and are not Communists; the second, that Communism and the Soviet Union are themselves foes of Jews and Judaism. As to the facts and figures—investigations will **disprove** the proud boast **that Jews have played no part in Communist parties** of various countries . . . but refutation of a single paragraph will indicate the falsity of its entire structure.

"Of Soviet Russia, it says: 'Among the thirty-six commissars who constitute the Soviet government, only two are Jews. . . .' . . . Is it possible that the heads of the American Jewish Committee, the B'nai B'rith and Jewish Labor Committee have never heard of Litvinov, of Yaroslavsky, of Kaganovitch, of Radek, of Bela Kun? . . .

"Let Messrs. Adler and Cohen and Vladeck consult the files of their own organizations. Let them refer to the work of the Ort and the Agrojoint and the Joint Distribution Committee. Let them make public the facts as to hundreds of thousands of Jews living in Agricultural colonies

70

in the Crimea and the Ukraine, and the even larger numbers who are sharing in the industrial development of Soviet Russia. Then let them dare speak of 'declassed Jews' and 'hindrances to the development of the Revolution.'"

Wise razzes them at length pointing out the prominence of Jews in Communism and in Russia. Wise (as well as they) knows that ORT, Agrojoint and the Joint Distribution Committee, leading Jewish organizations financed by B'nai B'rith and American Jewry generally, have poured fabulous sums into Soviet Russia.

For example, "Who's Who in American Jewry, 1938-9", lists the Russian-born "American" Jew, Joseph A. Rosen, as head of the Joint Distribution Committee "reconstruction work" in **Soviet Russia,** and as director of Agrojoint, directing "settlement of some 250,000 Jews on farms in the Ukraine and Crimea" in **Soviet Russia** and supervising "industrial readjustments of thousands of Jews" in **Soviet Russia,** while also acting as "consulting agriculturalist of Union of All Russian Cooperative Agricultural Societies" of the **Soviet Government.**

Picture, if you can, B'nai B'rith and other American Jews pouring the tremendous sums they have poured into the above Jewish projects in Russia, if they themselves were actually hostile to Russia's Communist Govt. system, which is enforced on everyone living under it, or if Russia's Communist Govt. were hostile to Jewry!

### Rabbi Wise's Magazine Praises Russia

"Opinion" Magazine, edited by the red Zionist leader, Rabbi Stephen S. Wise, his Communist son, the above James Waterman Wise, being on and off its editorial board, stated (12/33): "With the rise of the Soviet regime . . . never has the world witnessed such a spectacular change of front on the part of a great state toward Jews. . . . The State which previously did not employ any Jews at all, now employs in White Russia **61% JEWISH OFFICIALS. . . .**" (The percentage of Jewish population in Russia is **LESS THAN 2%.**) ". . . A Jew is commander-in-chief of the Ukrainian Army; a Jew is President of the State Bank;

Jews occupy almost all important ambassadorial positions of the Soviet Union; the universities, professions, judiciary and administration, have now a greater percentage of Jews **THAN ANY OTHER NATIONALITY.** Anti-Semitism has been declared a state offense, and is **PUNISHED AS COUNTER-REVOLUTION."**

### American Jewry Claims Red Commissars

Jewish Commissars Maxim Litvinov and Lazar Kaganovitch of Red Russia are both proudly listed in "Who's Who in American Jewry, 1938-9", with an imposing array of high posts held by them in the Soviet Govt. Kaganovitch's daughter is the wife of the "Supreme Boss", Stalin. Litvinov's real name is given as Finklestein-Wallach. He has used many aliases in his longtime criminal activities in connection with Bolshevist plots—arms running, disposing of rubles in Paris stolen from the bank at Tiflis by Stalin, etc.

Molotov recently replaced Litvinov as Commissar of Foreign Affairs, presumably because a Gentile was necessary to deal more smoothly on foreign affairs with "anti-Semitic" Germany.

B'nai B'rith magazine (11/39, p. 82) pictures, with enjoyment, Von Ribbentrop, representing Germany, having to visit the Molotov home to be entertained by Molotov's wife, a Jewess, as his hostess, and says: "The Jew, like the representatives of all groups in Russia, has, in a number of instances achieved a prominent position in governmental affairs. Some have done it through sheer ability; others through marriage. Mrs. Molotov, wife of the Commissar of Foreign Affairs, is one of the Jews who has achieved a prominent position through marriage."

### Lists Foreign Jews

The international racial character of Jewry, its holding itself to be an unassimilated, dispersed, nation-within-all-nations, is illustrated by the fact that "Who's Who in American Jewry, 1938-9", without any separate or foreign section as justification, lists along with Jewish residents of the United States on the same pages, under the identical heading, "Who's Who in American Jewry", not only Kaganovitch and Litvinov of Soviet Russia, but Leon Trotsky, exiled Soviet Commisar living in Mexico; Diego Rivera, the huge, gross painter, Trotsky's close associate, of Mexico; Leon Blum, anti-Christian filth writer and Red Front leader of France; Hore-Belisha, a pernicious power in England as Secy. of War; and even practicing Catholic priests in foreign countries!

## DESTROYING CHRISTIANITY

Communist apostate Jewry, of course, sneers at all spiritual faith, but with Jewish Reds in power in Russia, Jewish racial ties have operated so that the Marxian revolution against religion, "the opium of the people", as Marx called it, has meant violence almost entirely against **Christianity.**

The American Hebrew editor wrote (American Hebrew, 11/18/32, p. 12): "According to such information as the writer could secure while in Russia a few weeks ago, **not one Jewish synagogue** has been torn down, as have hundreds—perhaps **thousands** of the Greek Catholic Churches. . . . In Moscow and other large cities one can see Christian churches in the process of **destruction** . . . the Government needs the location for a large building."

### Jewish Russian Power, According to Jews

Of Russia, the Jewish Chronicle, 1/6/33, said: "Over one-third of the Jews have become officials".

Said the "Call of Youth", youth organ of the Workmen's Circle, Jewish Socialist fraternal insurance society (3/36): **"A great percentage** of young **Jews in the Soviet are officials,** and are thus arousing the envy of other groups of the Russian population who still remember the 'rightless' status of Jews in the former regime. Besides, the predominant part of Russian Jewry is crowded in cities, which fact might possibly help to breed the **anti-Semitic** virus that is liable to become dangerous in the future." (Because Jews have such power.)

The Jewish Sentinel, 8/8/40, p. 25, announces "MANY JEWS LEAVE RUMANIA FOR **SOVIET** OCCUPIED

BESSARABIA", but reports (p. 4) that campaigns have been inaugurated by the Soviets in their newly captured Lithuania and Latvia against Zionism. "Zionist editors of Jewish newspapers have been ousted and replaced by Jewish Communists". Moscow **Bolshevist** Jewry habitually strives with Zionist **Palestine** Jewry for mastery.

### B'nai B'rith Magazine Praises Soviets As Usual

B'nai B'rith Magazine, 1/40, p. 132, as usual, praises Soviet Russia, telling of the many Polish Jews rushing into the Soviet section there and saying: "As for **Communist** Poland there is no famine, no persecution of Jews as such. . . . But the Soviets were apparently dumbfounded at the strength of the Zionist movement there. They are setting about to root it out lock, stock and barrel".

The 11/39 issue (p. 66) of B'nai B'rith Magazine, again deploring that in Soviet-seized Poland "the Bund (Jewish Socialist Party)" was liquidated and Zionism banned by the Soviets (as Marxist rivals of Bolshevism), says that "All of this is most galling to Jews", but praises the Soviets and says that between a half million and a **million Jews** "have already fled from Nazi Poland to **Soviet** Poland. All, according to the A.P., have been received cordially and given work. The Red army has brought into Poland behind its tanks and cannons huge trains full of food". It admits, however, that "despite the efforts of the Red authorities to feed everybody, gruesome hunger exists".

### Will Jewry Continue in Power in Russia?

The 1939 Nazi-Soviet non-aggression pact made by Russia with "anti-Semitic" Germany has inspired considerable speculation and talk as to whether Jewry is, or will now remain, in power in Russia. Weak, murdering Stalin, after incessant butchering to remain on top, had more cause to fear his powerful close neighbor, Germany, than he did either to fear, or hope for help from, England and France, his more distant, ever-suppliant suitors for the same alliance.

Even now (Oct., 1940) England's government, strongly influenced by Jews and radicals, continues to woo Stalin

74

for the same Soviet alliance that Hitler walked off with in 1939, while French and English envoys cooled their heels outside of murderer Stalin's gates.

Stalin feared the spectre of his own overthrow. Hitler, as he heard Jewry's mounting cries **"Hitler must go!"**, resounding through the French and British press (echoed by America) portending war on Germany by world Jewry and its dupes, saw the need of keeping one of Germany's frontiers (Russia) "off of his neck" while he coped with the western "pack". He had more to offer and he won the pact.

Internal affairs in Russia are still densely shrouded in mystery. While there are those who believe that there is now a nationalist movement within Russia to displace Jewry from power, there is little to support this idea.

### RUSSIAN COMMISSARIAT 70% JEWISH

The only intimation of this, seen by the author, in the Jewish press is an item in the Jewish Sentinel (8/8/40, p. 30). It is headed "J.T.A." (Jewish Telegraph Agency) "Told of Jewish 'Elimination' in Russia".

"London, Aug. 5 (JTA)—A veteran diplomat with many years' experience in Moscow told the J.T.A. this week that a nationalist movement in Russia is marked by the 'painless elimination' of Jews. A few years ago, this observer said, the Narcomindel (Commissariat for Foreign Affairs) was **70 per cent Jewish and 30 per cent non-Jewish.** Today, the proportions are reversed and the number of Jews in this department is decreasing steadily. The same procedure reportedly is under way in all other government departments."

On the other hand, the Communist Party's Daily Worker (3/31/40, p. 3) tells of the numbers of Jews who have been elevated to high positions of power in the part of Poland seized by Soviet Russia, under the heading

### "MANY JEWS ELECTED TO HIGH SOVIET FROM FORMERLY POLISH AREA."

This article names among Jews elected as Deputies to the Supreme Soviet: Avram Mashevitsky, "humble Jewish teacher"; also Brokha Gutellevitch, "a Jewish seamstress";

also Meyer Shpringer, who "spent many years in Polish jails"; also Avram Ozirsky.

The Daily Worker (7/17/40, p. 2) tells that a Jew, Ginsburg, is "People's Commisar of Industrial Construction of the U.S.S.R.", that a Jew, Henkin, is Deputy to the Supreme Soviet of the U.S.S.R., "and others", and that there are now five and a half million Jews in Soviet Russia, one million more than in the U.S.A., since Bessarabia and Northern Bukovina recently were "liberated" (conquered by the Soviets).

It reports, to quote, **"The head of the Soviet air forces** is a former poor Jewish boy of Byelo-Russia, Jacob Smuchkevitch". Jewish actors and writers be-medaled by the Soviet Govt., it relates, include Markish, Kvitko, Pfefer, Halkin, Hofstein, Dobrushkin, and "Michoels and Guskin of the Moscow State Jewish Theatre".

It details that "In the Ukraine alone 439 different **Jewish** books have been published in the past year. . . . The Jewish poet Leib Kwitko is one of the most popular writers among the Soviet children", 6,422,000 copies of his works being circulated.

### Jews Still in Power Says "Patriot"

The London "Patriot" (4/18/40, p. 147) declares: "The idea that the Jew influence in the Soviets has given way to a Nationalistic policy is also utterly erroneous, for though the Kaganovitch family and other prominent Jews have been removed from their key positions, the Comintern, which is primarily controlled by the International Jewish influence, is still the supreme factor of the Soviet regime, and Jews are found at the head of every department or political cell."

The experiences related by men recently escaped from Soviet Russia (in the Service d'Informations Ukrainiennes of Paris, 4/7/40) are cited: "All the chief posts are occupied by Jews. The chief director of the Kalinine mine is a Jew. The chief of the militia is a Jew. The director of the school and most of the teachers are Jews."

To quote from the London "Patriot's" comment (4/18/

40) on Sovietization of the Baltic states: "Following the occupation of Estonia, Lithuania and Latvia by the Red Army the Evening Standard of 28 June gave a report from Moscow that 'the Sovietisation of national economic life is in full progress there.' That means the enslavement of the native populations for the benefit of the taskmasters who are placed over them. It is in keeping, too, with the 'Sovietization' **imposed on the Russian peoples** that **Jews are being put into positions of authority** in these Baltic States, and the Jewish Chronicle of 28 June stated that **a Jew, Dr. Leon Kogan,** has become Minister of Health in Lithuania."

## HISTORY OF JEWISH MARXISM IN AMERICA

Why are charges of "anti-Semitism" immediately hurled at any Gentile who opens his mouth against Marxism or its Reds? **"The guilty flee when no man pursueth",** says Scripture. Many an anti-Red Gentile, wholly dumb about Jewry's Marxist activities, has been led to investigate them merely because he was insistently called "anti-Semitic" for being **anti-Red.**

### Whence Comes Marxist Jewry?

Only one knowing the facts can understand why American Jewry now senses the need, through B'nai B'rith, of spending millions in propaganda, of gagging the press and radio, of throttling truth tellers, of buying decoy Christian Gentiles to dupe the public with bunk to prevent a Gentile Christian awakening to the truth that American Jewry, as a whole, is organized, grounded and soaked in imported Marxism, which is totally opposed to Christianity and American principles.

How did these organizations arise? The communist **International Workers' Order,** largely Jewish, with its 198,000 members and 200 schools teaching Yiddish and Marxism; the Jewish **Workmen's Circle** (Socialist) with its 75,000 adults and 159 schools teaching Yiddish and Marxism to 10,000 children, with Karl Marx' picture hanging on the classroom walls, as in their Chicago Center on N. California Ave., where each Sunday night the Anarchists meet; the

**Amalgamated Clothing Workers' Union,** largely Jewish, with 210,000 members (Chgo. Daily News, 5/13 38), headed by Russian-born red Sidney Hillman, now in charge of U.S. Govt. military training of millions of American Christian young people; the closely aligned **International Ladies' Garment Workers' Union,** whose platform and program is militantly Marxist, stating it is for "Internationalism", "against Fascism", "active in the American Labor Party" (Communist-Socialist), and stating "The struggle of the garment workers is a struggle not only against the garment bosses but against all the bosses and against the bosses' world. It is a struggle . . . for a **workers' world.** A special drive to aid the **Spanish Loyalists** was recently made. Nearly a quarter of a million dollars was raised by the proceeds of an extra day's pay for **refugee** funds." It issues journals in Yiddish and put on the red play "Pins and Needles". (Directory of Youth Org. by N.Y.A., 1940, p. 117.)

The International Ladies' Garment Workers' Union is primarily Jewish, with 250,000 members headed by the Russian revolutionist David Dubinsky (Roosevelt elector for New York in 1936). These unions, the Amalgamated Clothing Workers' Union and International Ladies' Garment Workers' Union, celebrate the revolutionary Red May Day as Labor Day yearly, and collect from their members for each alien Red cause as it comes along.

From whence come the 400,000 members of the Communist Party's **Jewish People's Committee?** The 500,000 members of the Socialist **Jewish Labor Committee?** The 40,000 members of the militant, radically-controlled **American Jewish Congress** (Zionist)? (Phila. Inquirer, 1/30/39.) Picture the United Hebrew Trades with "a quarter of a million men and women in the city of New York" (p. 1278, N.Y. Jewish Communal Register), who, as Marxist Reds, started sending their delegates to the first international Socialist Congress in 1889 (Workmen's Circle Magazine, May-June, 1940, p. 9).

From whence come the thousands of members of the

78

Marxist Jewish Zionist organizations—Poale Zion-Zeire Zion of America, Jewish National Workers' Alliance, League for Labor Palestine, Pioneer Women's Organization, Young Poale Zion Alliance, leagued together for exerting political pressure for **International Jewry,** plus the powerful Jewish federation of the "Stalinist" Communist Party and other Jewish-dominated Marxist parties?

## All Working For World Jewry

All are busy warmongering and boycotting German goods, thus cutting off German markets for American goods. Their exercise, through endless immigration committees, of pressure for **unlimited admission into the U.S.A.** of Jews and radicals, for "progressive" (Marxist) "Jew Deal" dictatorial governmental measures in America, and repression of all opposition, drives toward the "new Social order" of Marxism and power for **world** Jewry.

## European Jewish Origin Told by Workmen's Circle

The most graphic history of the whole Jewish Red movement now gripping our Government, White House, colleges, unions, business world—every artery of the Nation's life blood—is set forth in the "Jubilee" number (May-June, 1940) of the "Workmen's Circle Call" magazine, celebrating "Forty years of the Workmen's Circle", with articles by its leaders.

How Jewish Red plotters sewed the Red flag in Russia and armed for riotous demonstrations, were arrested by the Czarist police, fled by the **hundreds of thousands,** streaming to America, particularly after the unsuccessful Russian Red revolution of 1905, bringing their Marxism with them, how they long carried on in Yiddish, spreading networks of Marxist Socialist societies, schools and centers from coast to coast until now America is the largest Jewish center in the world and their Marxist dream of power is nearly accomplished here, is told in this Workmen's Circle magazine, much as it is told in the New York Jewish Communal Register of 1917-18.

### "Jew Deal" Socialism

"Outstanding Socialist Figures, 1900-1940" (p. 11), is the article, in this issue, by Benjamin Gebiner, Russian-born Workmen's Circle leader, who rejoices over the influence in America of the alien-born Jewish Socialist leaders, **Meyer London, Morris Hillquit, B. Charney Vladeck,** all Russian-born Jews, and Victor Berger, Austrian-born Jew, and urges completion of their Red program.

He says: "From the very platform of Congress **the Socialist movement** promulgated through its representatives, Meyer London and Victor Berger, a **program** of broad social reforms **that constitutes the best of the New Deal.**"

### The Jewish Vision

To quote another contributor: "The Workmen's Circle is forty years old. Its history is almost commensurate with the history of the **Jewish community** in America . . . it was in the eighties that **Jewish mass immigration** turned towards America . . . some of them had belonged to **the Bund,** the Jewish Socialist Party of Czarist Russia, and had even **been condemned to prison or Siberia for their revolutionary activity. And so they came to America with a vision. . . .**" (Israel Knox, editor, "Workmen's Circle Call" magazine, p. 4.)

### U.S.A. Largest Jewish Center

To again quote: "In the generation between 1880 and 1910, not less than **30% of all Jews** were on the road from one continent to another. . . . And today, the United States, with approximately five million Jews, has become, by far, the **largest Jewish center in the world** (indeed the largest at any time in Jewish history). . . . A good many of the Jewish pioneers ran away from military service. . . . **Socialist and Zionist movements with all their ramifications, spread like wildfire in eastern Europe.** Then the miracle came. These Jewish masses found a haven in the new land" (America). "They succeeded . . . in creating a Yiddish Socialist press, the beginnings of a trade union movement, and a radical movement . . . great Yiddish dailies with a circulation of about 350,000, weeklies, monthlies, all influencing and shaping opinions."

"With the second immigration, after the abortive revolution of 1905, thousands of progressive Jewish workers came to America. . . . A net of Yiddish schools was spread from the Atlantic to the Pacific. . . . One could easily go into panegyrics over the pioneering work done by teachers in our schools, or the literary values of books like 'Klassen Kamf'" (meaning Marxist "Class Struggle"). ("Forty Years of Jewish Folk Culture" by B. Graubard, dir. Chgo. Workmen's Circle "Mitl Shul", p. 6.)

To quote Joseph Baskin (Russian-born), gen. secy., Workmen's Circle: "After the 1905 revolutionary uprising in Russia . . . many of the revolutionary workers fled to America, and of these, the Jewish elements flocked to the Workmen's Circle". He tells of Workmen's Circle activities in forming the International Ladies' Garment Workers' and other unions, and how, "In 1917 the Workmen's Circle decided in favor of establishing Yiddish schools for its children". He says of their "Medical Department. This agency has all the characteristic elements of a system of socialized medicine" (Being pushed by the New Deal). ("Our Workmen's Circle", p. 22.)

Saul Goodman, a Workmen's Circle school teacher, in his article (p. 30), says: "the Workmen's Circle has 159 schools with about 10,000 children", and quotes from its official program: " 'Our school wants to unite the Jewish child of America with the millions of Jews who live . . . in Poland, Russia, Roumania, and other countries. . . . That is why the child should know the Yiddish language.' " Numerous pictures of these Young Circle League classrooms are included.

### The Russian Red Flag

Nathan Chanin, dir., Workmen's Circle Educational Dept., clearly pictures their **"educational"** ideas in his article to their young people (p. 35) in which he describes early struggles of their parents and himself in Russia. He says: "I recall the May Day demonstration . . . the people were secretly preparing for the eventful day. The girls in the ranks were sewing the **Red Flag,** the Flag of Freedom and of Socialism. The young men of our movement were **arming,** so that in the event of police attacks, at the start of the demonstration, our group would be ready to resist. . . . Then came May Day. . . . The Red Flag waved in the wind. There was an outpouring of songs of **Struggle and Revolution.** Police attacked us. We fought back. We fought tooth and nail—and dispersed.

"The leader of our Bund approached us and informed us that on the eve of the next day we were to be in readiness to distribute an **illegal** proclamation among the citizenry— a protest against the Czarist regime that had incited police against us and brutally assaulted us at the May Day demonstration." (That they had armed for, as Red revolutionists!)

"Firm belief permeated our ranks . . . belief in a **system** that would provide security and liberty for all. . . . I know you will ask: 'Do you still believe in this idea?' Yes, my friend, I believe in it today as I believed in it in my early youth. . . . We must bend our efforts to the **realization of this ideal.** And to this end we must be ready to sacrifice everything—**even our very lives."**

### Jewry Protects Russian Reds Through American Government

While these Russian revolutionary Jews were pouring into America, dedicated not only to the overthrow of the Czarist Govt., but of the American, or any but a Marxist, form of government, the American Govt. was forced to aid them in their designs. Jews exiled as Red revolutionists from Russia came to America in such large numbers, for the purpose of securing American citizenship to return under its protection to again agitate in Russia, that the Russian Govt. refused to honor American passports issued to **Jews.**

President Taft, at first, refused to break off the trade treaty which had existed since 1832 between the United States Govt. and Russia, as Jewry demanded that he do to punish Russia for this, but after Jewish millions had been poured into a nationwide pressure publicity campaign, he was glad to knuckle and do so.

## Breaks Russian Treaty

World-wide B'nai B'rith proudly claims its share in this undertaking. To quote its London publication: "The most widespread activity of the American B'nai B'rith has been the Anti-Defamation League, which has maintained a close watch on every form of discrimination against Jews or of attack on them in print, on the radio and on the screen . . . perhaps even more valuable has been the **political influence** which . . . B'nai B'rith has been able to exercise through the diplomatic channels of the **United States Government** in favour of Jews in Russia, Rumania, Germany and elsewhere . . . and as especially enjoying the confidence and support of the American Govt. in the protection of Jewish interests abroad. . . . B'nai B'rith . . . was instrumental in ultimately securing the abrogation by the United States of the commercial treaty with Russia owing to its refusal to vise the passports of American Jews visiting that country." B'nai B'rith influence, since 1933, on the U.S. Govt. against Nazi Germany in behalf of **Jewry, is also cited.** (From "B'nai B'rith—The First Lodge of England, By Paul Goodman, Past Pres., 1919. Published by the Lodge, London, 1936", p. 14.)

## Hamstringing U.S. Census and Protective Laws

The Jewish Communal Register of the New York Kehilla, 1917-18, tells how the inner Jewish government of Jews in America, the local Jewish Kehillahs (Communities), long organized in each American city (and all over the world), started electing representatives to the American Jewish Committee, organized Nov. 11, 1906, to fight for "rights of Jews in any part of the world" (p. 1415); how this combination of Jewry in 1909 prevented passage of a U.S. Census Bill to "ascertain the races of all inhabitants of the U. S.", so that Jewish immigrants could not be counted as such (p. 1416); and "opposed with success" naturalization laws "sought to deprive 'Asiatics' of the privilege of citizenship because it was believed that such laws would deprive **Jews** coming from Asia of the right to become citizens" (p. 1416) ; and prevented "extradition of Pouren and Rudovitz".

### Defends All Russian Reds

To quote (p. 1417) : "in 1909, the Russian Government sought the extradition of two political refugees, Pouren and Rudovitz, who had fled to this country. The Committee appreciated the bearing of their cases upon a **large number of Jews who had taken part in the Russian Revolution,** and who had sought, or who might seek, an asylum in this country; and in cooperation with others **succeeded in defeating the attempt of Russia."**

### Immigration

To quote (p. 1418) : "The danger that the enactment of repressive immigration legislation might deprive the **persecuted** Jews of Russia, of Roumania and of Galicia, of the opportunity of reconstructing their lives in this country, caused the Committee the greatest anxiety, and occupied much of its attention." REDS ALWAYS REPRESENT THEMSELVES AS **"PERSECUTED".**

(P. 1419) : "Three **restrictive** bills, containing a **literacy** test, were successively passed by Congress, but **all were vetoed;** one by President Taft, and two by President Wilson. In the three instances, the Committee presented arguments to the President of the United States urging his disapproval of the bills as passed. . . . Other **dangerous** amendments were defeated."

### The Russian Treaty Again

On Russia's refusal to honor American passports issued to Jews to circulate in Russia, the American Jewish Committee says (p. 1419-21) : "The Committee considered that it was one of its most important functions to bend every effort toward the solution of the passport question . . . and on May 18, 1908, dispatched a letter to President Roosevelt. This began the attempt. . . . Correspondence with the same end in view was also had with President Taft. . . . **All these endeavors proving ineffectual, the Committee decided to lay the facts before the people of the United States, and with the complete cooperation of almost every Jewish organization in the United States, a campaign of publicity was entered upon, which finally resulted** in the issuance by President Taft of a notice to the Russian Government of the intention of the Government of the United States to terminate the Treaty of 1832.

"This action was subsequently ratified by the Senate and the House of Representatives with but one dissenting vote in the latter House. . . . **The action** of President Taft and of the Congress of the United States **was subsequently approved by all the great political parties of the country, in the platforms adopted by them in 1912, and again in 1916.**"

## AND THEY BOSS ALL AMERICAN POLITICAL PARTIES TODAY!

According to p. 1426 of the same, officers of the American Jewish Committee at that time included: Louis Marshall, Pres.; Cyrus Adler, Vice-Pres.; Judah L. Magnes (head of the N.Y. Kehillah and on the communist Garland Fund); Cyrus L. Sulzberger, Herbert H. Lehman (now Gov. of N.Y.), Eugene Meyer, Jr., Felix M. Warburg and Jacob H. Schiff (of Kuhn Loeb & Co.), Jacob Wertheim (father of Maurice of the red "Nation"), etc., etc. Louis E. Kirstein, Irving Lehman, James Marshall (son of Louis), Samuel I. Rosenman (FDR advisor), are among the more recent executive committee members. They formed a joint council with the radical Zionist American Jewish Congress and B'nai B'rith (A.P., 6/17/38).

### To Again Quote the Workmen's Circle Jubilee Number
### How American Marxist Jews Subvert Europe

As exec. dir. of the Jewish Labor Committee, Isaiah Minkoff, of the Workmen's Circle, writes on "The Workmen's Circle and the Jewish Labor Committee", telling how the Committee was formed, in 1933 after Hitler took power, to fight for the "rights of the Jewish masses" in all countries, "to fight for the right of **free immigration** in all countries including Palestine", and "to intensify the **boycott** against Nazi-made goods and services." He says:

"We cannot at this moment give details of **our work** on behalf of the **underground** labor movement in totalitarian lands. . . . This very day individuals and groups in Germany, Austria, Czecho Slovakia and Nazi-Poland are carrying on **underground** work at the risk of their lives.

"The Workmen's Circle is more than merely one of the founders and affiliates of the Jewish Labor Committee. It is its very backbone. . . . The 40th Anniversary of the Workmen's Circle is therefore the holiday of all the unions, labor and progressive organizations affiliated with the Jewish Labor Committee **and the hundreds of thousands of their members.**" (P. 15, May-June, 1940, Workmen's Circle Magazine.)

HUNDREDS OF THOUSANDS OF MARXIST JEWS IN AMERICA WORKING, NOT ONLY HERE BUT IN CONJUNCTION WITH REDS ABROAD, TO SUBVERT EUROPEAN GOVERNMENTS IN BEHALF OF JEWRY AND MARXISM! YET THOSE ATTEMPTING TO EXPOSE OR OPPOSE THIS MOVEMENT ARE PORTRAYED AS "ANTI-SEMITIC", "FASCIST" OGRES.

The Workmen's Circle president, Reuben Guskin (p. 8), joins in rejoicing that, for the past forty years, **"during that golden epoch of socialist growth and sweep in our country,** the Workmen's Circle . . . always encouraged and sustained **socialist** trends, organizations, and the movement as a whole in America", and now "is associated with our fighting, vigorous aid organization, The Jewish Labor Committee", which **"serves the Jewish** and the non-Jewish **underground movement** in the Fascist countries. . . . And needless to say, the Workmen's Circle has always maintained its loyalty to the **Bund,** that organization of Jewish workers in **Russia and Poland."**

## New York School Board Member Hails Paris Red Commune and Congress

Reminiscences of "Half a Century of **Jewish** Labor" (p. 9) are by Joseph Schlossberg (Russian-born, member of the Board of Higher Education of the City of New York(!) and secy.-treas., Amalgamated Clothing Workers' Union, headed by Roosevelt's red Sidney Hillman).

He recalls how fifty years ago, in 1890, he participated in the **first Red May Day celebration,** proclaimed as such "by the first Congress of the Second International" (Socialist) "upon the initiative of American organized labor. The **Jewish** Workers of America were represented in that memorable Congress: the one year old **United Hebrew Trades** sent Louis Miller as its delegate."

He explains how the date was chosen for the Congress of this Red "Second International" to which Socialist parties of the world are still affiliated: "July 14, 1889, marked the anniversary date of the French Revolution, particularly the fall of the Bastile. The Socialists conceived the happy idea of reviving the shattered international labor movement by holding a Congress in Paris on the revolutionary anniversary date. . . . **The nightmare of reaction,** which had followed the **fall** of the **Paris Commune** and the Franco-German war, had lifted, and Europe began to breathe the air of freedom. **Europe of 1889 was generations ahead of Europe of 1940.**"

The Paris Commune was the Marxist Red regime which spilled the blood of some 70,000 people. **He, as a loyal Red,** describes "reaction" **against** this as the "nightmare".

### LaGuardia and Red Ballet

How these Red revolutionary Russian Jews are receiving support and appreciation for their efforts from high New Dealers is shown by the enthusiastic report of their "40th Anniversary Celebration", 5/5/40, in Madison Square Garden, New York, addressed by Jewish-Italian Mayor LaGuardia, member of Roosevelt's new Joint Defense Council with Canada. We are told that for entertainment a revolu-

87

tionary "ballet in three stirring acts told the story of 'Flame Red'" awakening **"the spirit of revolt** in the oppressed masses of Europe and twentieth century **America.** Twenty-four thousand inside, and over 15,000 outside, demonstrated to all opponents of **progress** and light that the Workmen's Circle has inscribed itself forever on the Golden Book of Mankind. No wonder **Mayor La Guardia said that he was proud to testify,** 'not only to this city but to the whole country, of the loyalty and devotion, and **of the great social usefulness** of the Arbeiter Ring'" (meaning "Workmen's Circle"). "To that our parents dedicated themselves forty years ago. To that we rededicate ourselves on this, their Fortieth Anniversary." (Pp. 34-6.)

### Red Youth Activities

Norman Dorfman, in "A National Organizer Speaks" (p. 39), reports new groups organized in "Memphis, Nashville, Chattanooga, Birmingham, to form a Southeastern District; faced a hostile press to sponsor L.I.D. lectures" (Socialist-Communist League for Industrial Democracy) "while bringing together under one roof for the first time a **mixed colored and white audience** . . . were the main backers of the Textile Workers in their general strike and the ILGWU in their organization campaign—and with **the** same courage backed Thomas for President in the reactionary South" (Socialist Party Thomas). "And what happened in Atlanta was duplicated in most of the towns throughout the country, in Ohio, Connecticut, Massachusetts, Texas, California, upstate New York, Indiana, Wisconsin and Canada." He says: "The groups which weathered the storms of our first ten years are definitely not of the 'polite' category, members were tested in the crucible of 'Social' fire."

## SOME JEWISH ORGANIZATIONS

Skip reading this, if you like, but how many Gentiles know anything about such **exclusively Jewish** organizations in the U.S.A., issuing periodicals in Yiddish or English, as B'nai B'rith with 82,860 members (10/1/39), 584 lodges in the U.S. and Canada, 35,000 members in its women's auxiliary, in addition to its Hillel Foundations in colleges and its Gentile network?

**Aleph Zadek Aleph of B'nai B'rith** (1003 K St., N.W., Washington, D. C.), with 8,619 boy members and 8,413 alumni members in 317 active chapters.

**American Jewish Congress** (radical Zionist), headed by red Stephen S. Wise with 40,000 members (Phila. Inquirer, 1/30/39), 4,000 in youth division, "To safeguard **rights of the Jew in all countries.** To further the development of the Jewish National home in Palestine". It lists its own snooping for "anti-Semitism" and "discrimination". "Investigates firms selling Nazi goods, **making known to the public** the names of those **firms** which persist in **disregarding** requests to cooperate in a **boycott.** Maintains two club houses as a temporary refuge for exiles from lands of oppression".

**The American Jewish Joint Distribution Committee** (100 E. 42nd St., N.Y.C.), raising funds "on behalf of **Jews of Europe**—active in more than 100 communities". Affiliations: B'nai B'rith, Hadassah, American Ort Federation, etc.

**Avukah (Student Zionist Federation)** (111 Fifth Ave., N.Y.C.), with 2,000 members in 60 U.S.A. colleges. "Offers Palestine fellowships of a year of work and study in a Palestine collective" (Soviet style). "Some of its members go to Palestine to live and work in the **collectives.** Raises funds for Zionist purposes".

**Brith Trumpeldor** (1400 Boston Road, Bronx, N.Y.C.). "To educate Jewish youth in the spirit of Zionism—to teach them to be useful citizens of **the future Jewish State**—first organized in Riga in 1925—today numbers many thousands of members in all parts of the world. World headquarters are in London, Eng., Vladimir Jabotinsky is World President". (Advocate of armed Jewish force.)

**Conference of National Jewish Youth Organizations**—devoted to problems of "Jewish interest" (1003 K St., N.W., Wash., D.C.). Affiliations: Aleph Zadik Aleph; Alpha Epsilon Pi, Avukah; Hashomer Hadati; Hashomer Hatzair; Hebrew Youth Cultural Federation; Hechalutz Organization of America; Jewish Youth Alliance; Junior Hadassah; Masada; National Federation of Temple Youth; Pioneer Women Youth Division; Sigma Omega Psi; B'nai B'rith Junior Leagues; B'nai B'rith Junior Women; Young Poale Zion; and National Council of Jewish Juniors.

**Habonim Zionist Pioneer Youth** (275 Seventh Ave., N.Y. C.), with 2,000 members devoted to Palestine and Jewish racial interests.

**Hashomer Hatzair** (305 Broadway, N.Y.C.), with 3,000 members for "Education towards **Zionism**". Affiliated with "World Movement of Hashomer Hatzair, World Zionist Org., United Palestine Appeal, Jewish National Fund, National Labor Committee for Palestine".

**Histradruth Hanoar Haivri** (111 Fifth Ave., N.Y.C.). "Favors the **communal** organizations of **Jewish life in America**. Affiliations: Histadruth Ivrith, National Organization for Hebrew Culture, National Youth Conference for Jewish Unity." Publishing in Hebrew a monthly, "Niv".

**Hechalutz Organization of America** (275 Fifth Ave., N. Y.C.). "Hechalutz is a **world-wide** youth movement composed of young Zionists". It calls for "loyal Jewish youth **well trained** for labor and **self-defense**. Maintains a training farm at Cream Ridge, N.J. Conducts study circles and programs on Hebrew language, history and topics related to Palestine. Purpose: To train Jewish youth for pioneer life in Palestine as members of the Histradrut." (Socialist Jewish Labor Federation in Palestine.)

**Jewish National Fund of America** (111 Fifth Ave., N.Y. C.), which buys lands in Palestine to be owned collectively by, and leased to, Jewish people (managed on Socialist lines); headed by red Rabbi Israel Goldstein. Affiliations: Avukah; Gordonia; Habonim; Hapoel Hamizrachi; Hashomer Hadati; Hashomer Hatzair; Hechalutz; Histradruth Hanoar Haivri; Junior Hadassah; Junior Mizrachi Women; Masada; Young Judea; Young Poale Zion Alliance; Young Israel; Young People's League of the United Synagogue of America; etc.

**Jewish State Zionists of America** (1472 Broadway, N.Y.

C.), with 1,000 members, part of the World Zionist Organization issuing a Yiddish monthly "Yudenstaat".

**ORT Federation of America** (212 Fifth Ave., N.Y.C.), headed by radical George Backer, owner of the New York Post, and executive of the Socialist-Communist American Labor Party of New York, son-in-law of Jacob Schiff of Kuhn Loeb & Co.; with 2,000 youth members in the U.S.A. "to support trade and vocational education among the **Jewish masses in Europe.** To assist . . . **cooperative** enterprises. . . . Today there are 407 Ort institutions in seven countries. Affiliations: Ort World Union; Joint Distribution Committee".

**Hadassah** (Women's Zionist Organization of America) (1860 Broadway, N.Y.C.), with a youth branch having "15,662 members in 250 units throughout the United States. Purpose: To support projects in **Palestine** and to carry on an **educational program in America.**" Youth branch affiliated with the communist American Youth Congress.

**League for Labor Palestine** (275 Fifth Ave., N.Y.C.); Socialist; with 3,500 members for "active support of the Histradrut Haovdim" (**Socialist** General Federation of Jewish Labor in Palestine embracing over 85% of Jewish workers there). "Conducts an annual summer seminar at the Hechalutz Farm in Cream Ridge, N. J."

**Masada Youth Zionist Organization of America** (111 Fifth Ave., N.Y.C.), with 1,500 members "dedicated . . . to establishments of an autonomous Jewish commonwealth in Palestine. The strengthening of **Jewish community life in America.** The defense of **Jewish** rights . . . promoting the study of Hebrew . . . propaganda and mass demonstrations combatting anti-Semitism. Affiliations: Zionist Org. of America, American Jewish Congress, Conference of National Jewish Youth Org."

**National Council of Jewish Juniors** (1819 Broadway, N. Y.C.), with 10,000 members in 118 sections. "Cooperates **in bringing children to this country each year** and maintaining them in private homes until they are self-supporting. Works with the National Council of Jewish Women

91

in its entire program of service to **foreign born**". Affiliated with communist American Youth Congress and Conference of National Jewish Youth Org.

**Order Sons of Zion** (220 Fifth Ave., N.Y.C.), with 5,000 members in 74 branches; devoted to Zionism. Affiliated with American Jewish Congress, World Zionist Org., Zionist Org. of America.

**Pioneer Women's Organization for Palestine** (275 Broadway, N.Y.C.).

**Shomer Hadati Organization of America** (1133 Broadway, N.Y.C.), with 3,000 boys and girls organized "under the banner of Torah and labor . . . to educate them to become devoted and loyal to the Torah of God, Israel, Eretz Israel (the land of Israel) **and Hebrew**". Affiliations: World Hdqts. of Shomer Hadati in Palestine, Hapoel Hamizrachi of America, Brit Olamit (World Movement of Hapoel Hamizrachi).

**United Jewish Appeal for Refugees and Overseas Needs** (261 Fifth Ave., N.Y.C.). Affiliations: United Palestine Appeal, American Jewish Joint Distribution Committee.

**Workmen's Circle and Its Young Circle League** (discussed elsewhere). Affiliations: Jewish Labor Committee; Workers' Defense League (of Socialist Party); International Ladies' Garment Workers' Union Sports League; Joint Boycott Council, HIAS.

**Young Israel** (200 W. 40th St., N.Y.C.), with 24,000 youth members; "for Jewish Orthodox youth . . . first convened **for the purpose of arousing** Jewish consciousness". Affiliations: "American Jewish Congress. Participates in the activities of the United Jewish Appeal; Jewish National Fund; Joint Distribution Committee", etc.

**Young Judea,** Junior branch of the Zionist Organization of America (111 Fifth Ave., N.Y.C.), with 20,000 members and 1,000 volunteer workers in 700 clubs. "To advance the cause of Zionism", inspire **"loyalty to the Jewish people"**. Affiliations: radical American Jewish Congress; communist American Youth Congress.

## "Conservative" Jewry!

**Young People's League of the United Synagogue of America** (3080 Broadway, N.Y.C.), listing itself as "A federation of **conservative** Jewish young people's organizations" with 40,000 members in 395 organizations and gives as its affiliations the **radical American Jewish Congress, communist** American Youth Congress, radical **B'nai B'rith** Hillel Foundation, **communist** World Youth Congress, besides the American Jewish Committee, Jewish National Fund, Young Judea, Hadassah, Joint Distribution Committee, Masada.

**Young Poale Zion Alliance** (275 Seventh Ave., N.Y.C.), "A Zionist Socialist organization of Jewish youth" with 1,500 members; youth branch of the "Poale Zion-Zeire Zion". "To rebuild Palestine as a Jewish national home on a cooperative **Socialist** basis. Affiliations: Poale Zion-Zeire Zion; Jewish National Workers' Alliance."

**Zionist Pioneer Youth** (Habonim).

(Quotations are from "Dictionary of Youth Organizations, 1940, issued by Federal Security Agency, National Youth Admin., 265 W. 14th St., N.Y.C.)

All linked together, excluding Gentiles, "conservative", "radical" Jewry, in a composite nationhood within America, operating through over 5,000 Jewish organizations.

## JEWISH HALL OF FAME

Nothing shows the Marxist mind of world Jewry clearer than the Jewish Hall of Fame from the 1938 World Almanac, cited in **favor** of Jewry by B'nai B'rith's echo, Rembert G. Smith. He tells in his "Fiery Furnace Flames Again" how this list of 120 "greatest living Jews" was chosen, "after a **poll of Jews all over the world**", from a list of "420 suggested names" of Jews who were alive Sept. 28, 1936, holding up "**living ideals** to Jewish youth".

During the summer of 1937, questionnaires and the suggested names were sent to organized Jewish Kehillahs (communities) of Egypt, Algeria, Holland, Belgium, Irak, Hungary, Denmark, Poland, Rumania, Palestine, South

Africa, Russia, Canada, Czechoslovakia, Morocco, Latvia, Italy, Bulgaria, Tripolitania, Tunis, Austria, Australia, England, Argentine, Irish Free State, Greece, Germany, France and the U.S.A. After conducting polls, these Jewish communities returned their "joint selections to The Ivrim, honor society of Jewish students in Chicago". **Thus the choice expresses the minds of world Jewry.**

Some of the world's leading Reds are included: Soviet Commissar Litvinov, German Soviet Revolutionist Ernst Toller, communistic sex-filth-purveyor Sigmund Freud, French Red-front-leader Leon Blum, Communist Albert Einstein, former communist-Garland-Fund director Rabbi Judah L. Magnes, English Marxist Harold J. Laski. **REDS OF EVERY HUE.**

ALFRED ADLER: deceased; former collaborator with filthy Freud; author of "Sexuality and Sexual Perversions"; contributor with Freud, Bertrand Russell, etc., to such radical magazines as "Modern Psychology" (1934), etc.; teacher at that sex and Marxist "garbage" center, New School for Social Research, New York, 1928-9, etc., along with another of the 120 world-chosen Jews, Horace M. Kallen.

CYRUS ADLER: deceased (4/7/40); founder and pres. of American Jewish Committee (for its browbeating legislation in favor of world Jewry and Russian Reds see p. 83); representative with Louis Marshall at Versailles Peace Conference in behalf of Jewry, 1919; formulator of League of Nations Commn.; mem., Jewish Agency for Palestine Joint Distribution Com. (working in Russia).

SHOLEM ASCH: Polish-born Yiddish Socialist novelist, now in U.S.; contrib. and corres. since 1903 to the Socialist Jewish Forward (Who's Who in Am. Jewry, 1938-9).

The sound "Sunday School Times", editorially (8/10/40, p. 630), says of his book "The Nazarene" (sold by B'nai B'rith): "I believe the book is a masterpiece of literature, a masterpiece of lust, a masterpiece of unscriptural falsehoods, and a masterpiece of blasphemy. . . . Like most modern writers, the author has taken full advantage of his opportunity to pander to the popular demand for lust and obscenity in his descriptions of men and women of nineteen centuries ago in the Roman Empire. .... The shining purity of the historical accounts of the same events and characters in the Bible are in sharp condemnitory contrast with the debased details over which Asch lingers and invites the reader to linger ... and contradicts certain basic facts given in the Gospels upon which this entire work is necessarily based ... putting into the mouths of the Bible characters, even of Christ himself, words that are not recorded in the Scriptures ... in a way that flatly contradicts the characters of the Bible history, and especially the character of our Lord himself."

DAVID BEN-GURION: leader of the Socialist "Histadruth" labor organization of Palestine and contributor to its "Jewish Frontier" in U.S.A.

BEN ZVI: another Socialist Zionist labor leader; contributor "Jewish Frontier", 3/36.

NORMAN BENTWICH: committeeman of the Red Marxist English Labor Party; B'nai B'rith; active Zionist; former British official in Palestine; contrib., Socialist "Jewish Frontier" (U.S.A.), praiser of Soviet Russia (see p. 20).

HENRI BERGSON: irreligious French philosopher, who added "intuition" to Marxist materialist evolutionary concept of nature.

MEYER BERLIN: pres., World Mizrachi Org., a Zionist organization devoted to Palestine, world Jewry, and the Talmud, founded about 1902 in Russia, having 200 societies in U.S.A. (Communal Register, 1917-18.) Hapoel Hamizrachi is its U.S. affiliate.

LEON BLUM: French Socialist leader; Zionist; sponsor Palestine "Histadrut" and its Red colonies; in "Leon Blum Salutes the Histadrut" (Jewish Frontier, 6/36), he says: "Every Socialist must admire the Jewish workers' organization in Eretz Israel"; author of fifthy book "Du Mariage" condoning incest, advocating promiscuity and seduction of young girls by middle aged men to initiate them in accommodating neighborhood boys; leader of the "Popular Front" of Socialist and Communist parties which undermined France.

FRANZ BOAS: one of the most active of Reds; was mem. of 1937 defense com. for exiled Soviet terrorist Leon Trotsky; mem., Soviet Govt.'s American-Russian Institute; backer of Spanish Reds and Moscow's Intl. Labor Defense, 1939; as the socialist "New Leader" (8/24/40) puts it, he "has been on literally **scores** of Committees with a Stalinite base".

LOUIS D. BRANDEIS: retired Supreme Court Justice; Zionist; "Father of the New Deal", whose "mantle" fell on his red protege Felix Frankfurter; largest individual financial supporter of the little communistic training school for Red agitators, "Commonwealth College", Mena, Ark., this and its free love, nude bathing, etc., being revealed by Ark. legislative investigation of Feb.-March, 1935; his advice to Jews is to "Organize" as a separate race. "Palestine, 1939", a book issued by the Palestine Pavilion of New York World's Fair, tells (p. 70) of the British Balfour Declaration promising Jews Palestine being influenced by Brandeis' close friendship with Pres. Wilson (who appointed Brandeis to the Supreme Court), and says, of Palestine Socialist-Communist cooperatives, which embrace practically every economic enterprise in Palestine from farming, bus lines, banks and the King David Hotel, to the development of the Dead Sea Potash: **"Alongside of this influence in Washington Mr. Brandeis** started a signal contribution to Palestine. He was father to the **cooperative** economic movement in this country, by fostering the first financial corporation for the economic development of the country along strictly cooperative lines." It tells how he keeps writing to a Palestine Socialist colony named for him.

ABRAHAM CAHAN: a leading Red propagandist in U.S.A.; "Born Russia, fled to U.S. to avoid arrest for revolutionary activity, 1882. Entered Socialist movement carrying on work among Jewish workmen 1882, founder of first Jewish Socialist society in Am., a founder 1897 editor since

1902 Jewish **Daily Forward,** N.Y.City" (Who's Who in Am. Jewry, 1938-9).

JUSTICE BENJ. CARDOZO: deceased; "like Justice Brandeis, had taken Frankfurter's proteges in his office as law clerks"; mem. of socialistic Survey Associates, and committeeman of B'nai B'rith's radically-controlled National Conference of Jews and Christians; helped radicalize Supreme Court.

ALFRED M. COHEN: hon. pres. of pro-Red, anti-Christian, Gentile-muzzling B'nai B'rith, and committeeman of its radically-controlled National Conference of Jews and Christians.

MORRIS RAPHAEL COHEN: Russian-born Socialist; prof., 1912-39, College City of N.Y.; exec. com. of the red American Civil Liberties Union "Committee on Academic Freedom", which fights for rights of teachers to teach Atheism, Communism, etc.; backer of Spanish church-burning Reds, etc.; a eulogistic article in B'nai B'rith Magazine (2/38 issue) tells of his resignation from teaching to devote his full time to "fighting anti-Semitism", and cites tributes paid him by red atheistic John Dewey, Felix Frankfurter, red free-love advocate Bertrand Russell, Judah L. Magnes (communist Garland Fund committeeman and Kehilla head), with this prophecy: "His new day cannot fail to be as brilliant as the old".

DR. JOS. B. DE LEE: obstetrician; mem. of B'nai B'rith; mem., Chicago Sinai Temple whose forum featuring leading Communist and Socialist lecturers regularly gathers audiences, in the Temple, of several thousands to hear Red propaganda.

ALBERT EINSTEIN: "Active in Zionist movement since 1921" (Jewish Who's Who, 1938-9); after exile as a Communist from Germany, came to U.S.A., Princeton U.; sponsor of Moscow's world-wide "Workers' International Relief" (Mass. House Report 2100, p. 122); one of intl. Communist Com. (Albert Einstein, Maxim Gorky, Heinrich Mann, Romain Rolland, Theo. Dreiser, Henri Barbusse,

97

Bernard Shaw, Mme. Sun Yat Sen) which organized, 1932, Moscow's world-wide Red revolutionary sabotage organization, called in the U.S.A. first "American League Against War and Fascism", later "American League for Peace and Democracy", and active in sponsoring various of its U.S.A. congresses (Daily Worker, 12/12/36, etc.).

To quote Einstein's fellow-committeeman, Bernard Shaw (12/13/32) : " 'Keep Einstein out of America? Why, they can't do that,' said Shaw. 'I am a Communist. And they haven't tried to keep me out. Einstein is an avowed Communist. I myself am not a practicing Communist . . . but Einstein signs extreme left manifestos and all that sort of thing.' "

Mem. atheist Freethinkers' Com. to honor Robt. Ingersoll; sponsor Communist Party's Intl. Labor Defense ball, N.Y. (communist "New Masses" 1/3/39) ; hailed Soviets in communist "Soviet Russia Today" (11/36, p. 18) ; sponsor Communist Party's Abraham Lincoln Brigade (Daily Worker, 2/2/40, 7/16/40, 4/19/39, etc.) ; supported Paul Beeck at communistic Commonwealth College (1/1/35 issue of its paper) ; eulogist of Soviet Biro Bidjan (Jewish Sentinel 6/18/36).

Communist Party's Daily Worker (3/16/39, p. 3) featured his picture and reported his congratulatory birthday telegram from the Soviet Academy, Russia, of which, it said, he has been corresponding member since 1922 and honorary member since 1927; co-author with the filthy Red sex writer, Sigmund Freud, of "Why War?".

Said he was "ashamed of democratic nations for failing to support Loyalist Spain" (Socialist-Communist regime), saying "I feel intimately united with the loyalist forces and their heroic struggle" (Daily Worker 2/5/37).

The Communist Party's National Committee magazine, "National Issues" (4/39, p. 7), said "The third Dies bill provides for the exclusion and expulsion of alien fascists and communists", and if passed, **"Albert Einstein would almost certainly have to 'go back where he came from' "**.

Press-agented as author of "relativity" theory, denounced

by scientists like Nicola Tesla, Chas. L. Poor, Thos. J. Lee, etc., as fake; his Jewish race loyalty evidently superceding Bolshevist loyalty, the communist Sunday Worker (5/28/ 39) reported him as saying "that the maintenance of Great Britain's present position was of utmost importance to Jewry". So he has switched from "pacifism" to urging warfare against Germany for Jewry.

JACOB EPSTEIN: of N.Y., then England; "sculptor" whose hideous distorted hunks, supposed to represent religious figures, are widely protested as blasphemous; designed tomb in Paris cemetery honoring pervert Oscar Wilde, and "bronze portraits" of numerous Reds.

LION FEUCHTWANGER: reported as facing death in a French concentration camp for Communist treason (Communist Party's Daily Worker, 6/19/40); B'nai B'rith magazine (1/33, p. 103), praising him, said he "sympathizes with Communism"; one of three Germans (with Thomas and Heinrich Mann) whose photographs were displayed in Soviet Union's World's Fair Pavilion (Daily Worker, 7/24/- 39); contributor to communist New Masses, in which he says, "By way of preface to the Russian editon of my collected works, I should like to say how deeply I am indebted to my Soviet readers. . . . I hope that the edition will thus do its modest part in **strengthening** and improving **the beautiful new world which my Soviet readers have helped to create.**"

RABBI LOUIS FINKELSTEIN: head of Jewish Theological Seminary of America; "cooperating educator" of New York "Reconciliation Trips" to Communist, Anarchist, I.W.W., Socialist, birth control, occult, etc., centers, directed by Clarence V. Howell, Communist Party supporter ("Reconciling" people to what?); member B'nai B'rith Hillel Foundation Commn., etc.

FELIX FRANKFURTER: the "weeny", scheming, little Brandeis protege who has long trained and placed Jewry's Marxist "Hot Dog boys" in key government spots. As a founder and active leader of the notorious American Civil Liberties Union, he has for over twenty years aided every phase of the Red revolutionary movement to destroy Christianity and the American Republic—the I.W.W.'s, Anarchists, Communists, atheism, obscenity—treason and violence in every form. His appointment to the Supreme Court was hailed by the entire Communist press.

To quote communist New Masses, 1/17/39: "No man is more needed on the bench than Prof. Frankfurter. . . . His court will pass upon the constitutionality of the Wages and Hours Act. It will also determine seven Labor Board cases including one involving the NLRB's right to order the reinstatement of sitdown strikers. . . . He will also hear the **Strecker case** which, **if unfavorably decided,** may be used as the basis for an attempt to deport Harry Bridges and may lead to an anti-Communist witch-hunt resembling that of the 1920's."

The Strecker case was decided the **Red** way. Back in **1933** the 12/28 issue of the Jewish Sentinel (p. 10) reported Frankfurter was being groomed to take Louis D. Brandeis' place on the Supreme Court, as he **did.** The Lovestone Communist "Workers Age" comment was: "Justice Frankfurter has been one of the **most active** and most emotional **undercover advocates of foreign intervention in the capitol.**" (6/29/40.) See also pp. 50-56.

SIGMUND FREUD: atheistic sex psycho-analyst; B'nai B'rith member; said "Religious ideas are illusions"; supporter communist World Congress Against War (Moscow News, 8/3/32); attributed most disorders to sex "inhibitions" or thwarted desire for intercourse, often with one's own father, mother, brother or sister; dreams about any conceivable object or subject he linked to sex organs; honored by Communist and Jewish press when he died, London, 1939; "Time" magazine (5/23/38) said: "His influence has been the greatest single factor in determining the course of **modern fiction**". Think of that, in connection with blasphemous, filthy, current sex fiction!

LOUIS GINSBERG: Russian-born prof. of Talmud, Jewish Theological Seminary, N.Y.; active in behalf of Red Spain (Daily Worker, 3/8/39); contributor to Communist pamphlet "Writers Take Sides" for Spanish Reds.

ALEX. GOLDENWEISER: Russian-born; anthropologist; former teacher at pro-Communist, sex-filth-peddling New School for Social Research, Socialist Party's Rand School, etc.; mem., 1937 defense committee for Communist Leon Trotsky; author of "Sex in Civilization", "Our Changing Morality" (!), etc.

NAHUM GOLDMAN: a leader of Zionist movement for socialistic Jewish nationalism.

RABBI SOLOMON GOLDMAN: Russian-born radical (see p. 35); on adv. com., B'nai B'rith Anti-Defamation Lg.; past pres., Zionist Org. of Am.; com. mem., communist American League for Peace and Democracy, 1938; sponsor communist Spanish Refugee Relief Campaign, 1939; exec. com., Socialist-Communist Lg. for Industrial Democracy, Red-aiding American Civil Liberties Union, etc. **His trinity consists of the Jewish God, the Jewish language, and the Jewish land**" (B'nai B'rith magazine, 5/32, p. 247, review of his book "A Rabbi Takes Stock").

HAYIM GREENBERG: editor of Socialist "Jewish Frontier" magazine (N.Y.) supporting Socialist "Histadruth" in Palestine.

JACOB DE HAAS: ed. of Encyl. of Jewish Knowledge, in which he eulogizes every Red Revolutionary Jew (Marx, Litvinov, Kaganovitch, etc.), upholding as a "pacifist" Ernst Toller (who signed the death warrant of Germans during his bloody Soviet regime), saying that after Toller's imprisonment "Moscow received him with open arms in 1928"; assoc. (England) of Zionist founder Theo. Herzl from 1896 on; Am. Jewish Congress delegate to Paris peace conf. 1919; "First to approach and win Louis D. Brandeis to Zionist cause; discussed Zionism with **Woodrow Wilson 1911**; part-author Balfour Declaration" (Who's Who in Am. Jewry, 1928).

FANNIE HURST: novelist, one of Mrs. FDR's Red friends; long time sponsor of many Socialist-Communist causes; recently active supporting Spanish Reds; contrib.

to communist Lg. Am. Writers' pamphlet for Spanish Reds; sponsor communist Medical Bureau to Aid Spanish Democracy and its Spanish Refugee Relief Campaign since 1937 (N.Y. Times, 5/10/37, Daily Worker, 4/11/39, etc.); mem., atheist Freethinkers Com. to honor atheist Ingersoll, 1933; sponsor red **Franz Boas'** "Am. Com. for Democracy and Intellectual Freedom" (Daily Worker, 4/5/40); sponsor communist Am. Youth Congress (Daily Worker, 2/21/-39); was an appealer for Anarchist murderers Sacco and Vanzetti, 1927; on Communist-aiding American Civil Liberties Union com. for Anarchist-Communist dynamiter Tom Mooney, also on its Nat. Coun. on Freedom from Censorship; was active in behalf of U.S. recognition of Soviet Govt.; etc., etc.

RABBI JOSEPH H. HERTZ: born Czechoslovakia; began as Rabbi in Syracuse, N.Y.; chief rabbi of British Empire since 1913; mem., bd. govs. of Hebrew U. in Palestine, headed by red Judah Magnes; his commendations of and foreword to the immoral, anti-Gentile Talmud are reproduced elsewhere (pp. 220-23).

VLADIMIR JABOTINSKY: deceased; Russian-born; organized Jewish troops to fight Arabs in Palestine; imprisoned for Palestine rioting 1920; broke with World Zionist Org. and formed "New World Zionist Org." (which he headed) through impatience to throw off British control of Palestine with armed Jewish forces (See its youth section, B'rith Trumpeldor).

JOSEPH JASTROW: Polish-born; "psychologist"; teacher 1927-33 at Marxian sex filth center, New School for Social Research; author of "The House That Freud Built", etc.; mem. of red American Civil Liberties Union defense committee for sex writer Mary Ware Dennett when convicted of obscenity; his eulogies of red American Civil Liberties Union national committeeman David Wallerstein read at its memorial meeting for him (Phila. Ledger, 12/21/32).

HORACE M. KALLEN: German-born; mem., Zionist Org. of Am.; teacher since 1919 at that Marxist and sex filth center, New School for Social Research, N.Y.; active

102

in Communist-Socialist groups: Soviet Russia's American Society for Cultural Relations with Russia; American Civil Liberties Union since 1921, its com. on Academic Freedom (for Reds) and one of its petitioners for filthy red Bertrand Russell (ACLU Bulletin 3/23/40), etc.; American Com. for Defense of Trotsky, 1937; mem. of communist Friends of Soviet Union welcoming com. for Soviet flyers; communist American League for Peace and Democracy com., 1936; sponsor communistic Consumers' Union; was arrested for blasphemous utterances (calling Christ an Anarchist) at memorial meeting for Anarchist murderers Sacco and Vanzetti, for whom Frankfurter agitated (AP, 8/27/28); like Frankfurter, was connected with the Nat. Defense Council of **Pres. Wilson** and mem. Commn. on Inquiry on Terms of Peace; mem., League of Nations Assn., Am. Palestine Development Coun.; his statements, to justify U.S. internationalist meddling, which he ascribed to George Washington, were declared forgeries (Chgo. Exam., 3/14/35).

BERYL KATZENELSON: "Palestine labor leader" and contributor to its Socialist "Jewish Frontier" in U.S.A.

REBECCA KOHUT: (N.Y.City) Hungarian-born; "communal" worker for Jewry; pres. since 1923 of World Congress of Jewish Women; on nat. sponsoring com., along with Socialist Norman Thomas and Reds of every hue, of radical World Peaceways directed by Estelle Sternberger of B'nai B'rith magazine staff; her eulogies of the Red Spanish Govt. appear in Daily Worker, 2/22/37, along with Fannie Hurst's, another of Jewry's 120 chosen leaders.

HAROLD J. LASKI: one of world's most active Reds; atheist; in his book, "Karl Marx", he proposes the plan of Red revolution which the New Deal has all but culminated. To quote: "The preparation for revolution is a qualitatively different problem from what it was in the days of the Paris barricades. . . . A State like England, which is wholly dependent on foreign trade, could not undergo a successful revolution except upon the assumption that her neighbours viewed its results with benevolence. . . . In a period of universal suffrage it ought to be possible to capture the seat of

103

power at the polls, and throw upon the capitalist the onus of revolting against a SOCIALIST democracy".

Felix Frankfurter, in his testimony at the Senate hearing, 1/39, on his appointment to Supreme Court, said he was a close friend of Laski and responsible for bringing him to the U.S. to teach at Harvard U. (1916-20); there Laski was charged with addressing and encouraging the Boston police strikers; concerning him, the "Harvard Lampoon" said (1/16/20): "It would be no mean blessing to have the next Soviet Ark that sailed transport this pseudo-instructor from the United States"; since his return to England, 1920, he has been connected with the London School of Economics, "intended to train the bureaucracy of the future Socialist state".

This communistic British Jew, in his latest book, "The American President: An Interpretation", nervily instructs Americans to give Pres. Roosevelt dictatorial powers; communist "New Masses" (9/3/40) referring to him as a Marxist who "acknowledges Lenin as one of the great political leaders and thinkers of all time", says of it: "He has written a campaign document for Roosevelt in which he **demands additional powers which FDR himself dares not yet openly request**"; sent greetings on first issue of Communist Party's Midwest Daily Record; sponsor of Soviet's Intl. Labor Defense Ball (Daily Worker, 12/29/38); etc., etc.

He is author of the euolgistic foreword to the **Communist Manifesto by Karl Marx** (Socialist Party of Am. edition); instructor red New School for Social Research, N.Y., 1937; author of "Why I am a Marxist" (Nation, 3/11/39), in which he ascribes his Marxism in part to "Jewish upbringing"; v.p. of the London counterpart (affiliated) of the red American Civil Liberties Union; contributor to Communist Party and Socialist periodicals in U.S.A.; in red New Republic (10/30/35, p. 339), he said: "**the defense of the Soviet Union is one of the highest duties a Socialist can fulfill**".

His message, as a fellow-atheist, to the World Union of Freethinkers' Atheist Congress (which includes Soviet Russia's Atheists), London, 9/9/38, is cited in its report (p. 93);

past pres. of the British atheist "Rationalist Press Assn. Ltd."; lecturer on "Religion as a Social Danger"; mem. exec. com. British Labor Party (Marxist).

HALPER LEIVICK: Russian-born; contrib. to Communist Party's Morning Freiheit 1922-9, since 1936 to The Day (edited by Am. Jewish Congress and Zionist exec. Samuel Margoshes); author of plays produced by Communist Party's Artef and other radical Yiddish players.

SALMON O. LEVINSON: Pres. and trustee of Lincoln Center, Chicago, a Communist meeting place and center of atheistic "humanism", issuing radical "Unity" magazine, edited by John Haynes Holmes (now and for years a leader of principal Communist and Socialist organizations), with Mrs. Levinson as chmn. of its publication com. and its staff including, now as always, leading Reds and atheists: Stefan Zweig of Austria, red Rabbi Louis L. Mann, Communist Romain Rolland of France, atheist Max Otto, atheist "humanist", Communist-supporter Eustace Haydon, etc.; exec. com. of B'nai B'rith's Natl. Conf. of Jews and Christians; radical "pacifist"; says he was "originator of movement for outlawry of war which resulted in Kellogg-Briand Treaty of 1928", which helped disable American defense until Jewry decided the U.S.A. must make war on Hitler; on red Sam Untermyer's anti-Nazi com.; etc.

LUDWIG LEWISOHN: German-born; eulogist of B'nai B'rith, which recommends his books to Jewry; Thelma Spear, as his common-law wife and mother of his child, loudly protested his marrying a young girl without regard to her claims (AP, 2/7/40, etc.), but this did not deter red Rabbi Edw. L. Israel from marrying him to the girl; in "Biographical Encyclopedia of American Jews, 1935", he stated he "married Thelma Spear 1924", and was "Assoc. Editor until 1924, and thereafter Contrib. Editor of the Nation" (revolutionary socialist); gives his Zionist activities; on edtl. bd. of Rabbi Wise' "Opinion" magazine; says he "has written and lectured a great deal on problems of Jewish nationalism".

LOUIS LIPSKY: v.p. radical Zionist Am. Jewish Congress; former pres. Zionist Org. of Am.; see under "Newspapers"; in his article in the revolutionary socialist New Republic, 6/21/39, on Palestine, he says the Socialist labor organization there now numbers over 100,000 members, and that "Jewish labor in Palestine has introduced social and economic methods that have evoked the admiration of the British Labor Party" (Marxist). "A large number of the agricultural colonies in Palestine are communal not individual"; pres. Eastern Life Insurance Co., N.Y., since 1930.

MAXIM LITVINOV (Finkelstein): Soviet Russian Commissar; Stalin's assistant bank robber, arms runner, etc.; jailed and exiled from various countries.

EMIL LUDWIG (Cohn): German-born; author; contrib. to communist "Soviet Russia Today" (USA), radical "Nation" magazine, etc.; said of Soviet Russia's fake "New Constitution": "It embodies all our hopes and desires" (Daily Worker, 8/27/36); author of "The Soviet Union: Defender of Democracy and Peace" (Soviet Russia Today, 11/38, p. 9).

JULIAN W. MACK: U.S. Circuit Judge; radical Zionist; exec. of Zionist Org. of Am., of World Jewish Congress and the leading org'ns. for Palestine; mem. bd. of Gov's. of Hebrew U., Palestine, headed by red Rabbi Judah Magnes; mem. Am. Jewish Committee since 1910; cited in N.Y. Kehillah's 1917-18 Communal Register as a Jewish leader since 1913; during World War was one of the Baruch-Frankfurter radical Jewish clique holding powerful positions on Pres. Wilson's War Labor Board, and "first chairman of Jewish Delegations in connection with Peace Conf., Paris, March-May, 1919" (Who's Who in Am. Jewry); "Overseer" of Harvard (Frankfurter's stronghold) 1919-25, 1927-33 and 1937-43; signer of the "Golden Book of Friendship for the Soviet Union", sponsored by the communist Friends of Soviet Union (Soviet Russia Today, 11/37); mem. bd. dir., communist American Russian Institute; mem. spons. com. for communistic Albert Einstein's 60th Birthday Anniversary (Jewish Frontier, 6/39); officer and bd. mem. socialistic Survey Associates; sponsor socialist Pioneer Youth of

Am., 1939; spons. socialist Consumers' Research; signer of Communist-aiding American Civil Liberties Union petitions for Reds imprisoned under Espionage Act (N.Y. World, 11/22/28) and sponsor of the A.C.L.U. national conference at Hotel Biltmore, N.Y., Oct., 1939, at which Earl Browder was a speaker; on Honor Roll of that "advocate of revolutionary Socialism", the "Nation" magazine (Nation, 1/1/38).

With a host of leading Reds, mem. bd. sponsors of "Am. Guild for German Cultural Freedom" (with Thos. Mann, Alvin Johnson of the red New School for Social Research, etc., officers). Its appeal letter (6/28/39) starts out with flowery eulogies of communist Ernst Toller (a leader of the bloody Bavarian Soviet) and dramatic pathos over his suicide, and begs funds for such "exiles" saying, "There are many like him who, if they can go on for just a little longer, can once more contribute most generously to our common civilization . . . we must help them".

JUDAH LEON MAGNES: chmn. exec. com. N.Y. Jewish Kehilla, 1909-22; former director of communist Garland Fund, supplying the principal Communist, Socialist, I.W.W. organizations bent on destruction of the American Govt.; since 1935, pres. Hebrew U., Palestine.

RABBI ZVEI HIRSH MASLIANSKY: "national Yiddish orator"; Russian-born; in Odessa, "he became the chief propagandist of Zionism"; in "1897 was appointed lecturer at Edu. Alliance, N.Y."; "taking an active part in Zionism he toured the U.S.A. a great number of times".

LORD MELCHETT: British Zionist; in cooperation with Socialist Histadruth presented to the united Palestine "kvutza" (Soviet-like Socialist cooperative) of Kfar Gileadi and Tel Hai a memorial statue in honor of Jews who died fighting Arabs (1936 Guide to New Palestine, p. 92). See pp. 187 and 189.

YEHUDI MENUHIN: violinist; mem., Musicians section "Coordinating Com. to Lift the Spanish Embargo" to aid the Communist-Socialist church burners of Spain.

JULIAN MORGENSTERN: pres., Hebrew Union College; mem., B'nai B'rith; mem., Central Conf. of Am. Rabbis which (N. Y. Times, 9/13/36) challenges America's **"present social system"**, demanding "a **socialization** of basic industries" and calling for "a thoroughly **socialized democracy"** (Socialism-Communism).

HENRY MORGENTHAU, JR.; Secy. of U.S. Treas.; his wife is honorary president of Argo Lodge of B'nai B'rith, Washington, D. C., which has a membership of some six hundred (B'nai B'rith magazine, 7/38, p. 390); foretold U.S. Recognition of Russia (N.Y. Times, 9/21/33); one of the com. of New Deal radicals (Harry Hopkins, Miss Perkins, Secy. Wallace, etc.) who presented a socialistic "comprehensive program of social insurance". Miss Perkins (former Socialist Party member) in a long description of its **ultimate comprehensiveness,** explained, **"It may be that we can only go part of the way at once"** (Phila. Inquirer, 8/14/34).

Master of the secret manipulations of America's **two billion dollar** mis-named "stabilization fund"; his buying of silver, "stabilizing" the red Chiang-Kai-Shek Chinese Govt. and anti-religious, red Mexican Cardenas Govt. (Daily News, 3/19/40, etc.), and his continual aid to the Soviets, **buying gold from Russia "at a premium price"** of $35 **an** ounce (to bury in Kentucky) assailed by anti-Reds; the "policy helps Russia", Sen. Townsend protested (Chgo. Tribune, 1/30/40).

"White House liason man with the British purchasing agents" (Herald-American, 2/19/40); his secret operations and betrayal of "American military secrets to an agent of France" created a scandal. "Morgenthau's activity was discovered as a result of the crash at Los Angeles last Monday of a Douglas light bomber. . . . Maj. Gen. Henry H. Arnold told the military affairs committee that the **army had refused permission** for the French agent to fly in the new experimental bomber but that Secy. Morgenthau **had ordered such permission"** (Chgo. Tribune, 1/27/39).

Morgenthau called for "additional taxes" and "an increase in the limit" on public debt (Chgo. Daily Times, 5/31/40); urged excess profits tax **(Chgo. Daily Times,**

8/9/40); announced **$5,700,000,000** federal **deficit** (Chgo. Daily News, 8/10/40).

"Employes of the U.S. Treasury are mighty careful these days about what they say while they're on duty. . . . They have learned that Herbert E. Gaston, press secretary for Secy. Henry Morgenthau, Jr., has installed a **listening device** in at least half a dozen offices. . . . There is some resentment at the snooping, but the workers don't know what they can do about it. They recall that the New Deal hasn't been hesitant about listening in on private conversations of business men, nor about searching the desks of senators who opposed the administration" (Chgo. Tribune, 3/12/39).

"When the so-called ship speed-up bill was sent to the White House for approval a short time ago it contained a provision authorizing the govt. **to take over, or confiscate, any industry that failed to take war contracts offered by the govt.** How this provision ever get into the bill is a mystery. Chairman Vinson, of the House Naval Affairs committee, knew nothing about it; neither did Rep. Maas of Minn., who is the ranking Republican member . . . one can only conclude that the proviso was slipped in while the bill was being engrossed. Secy. Morgenthau has long advocated such a provision. . . ." (Duluth Publicity, 8/10/40).

PAUL MUNI: Polish-born; real name Muni Weisenfreund; former Yiddish Theatre actor; sponsor of Soviet film "Alexander Nevsky" (communist "People's World", 5/19/39), of communistic Theatre Arts Com. (Daily Worker, 12/23/39); sponsor of (and his name painted on ambulance donated by movie stars to) communist "Medical Bureau to Aid Spanish Democracy" for Spanish Reds, 1937-9 (Daily Worker, 4/19/39, 2/2/40, etc.); featured in communist "Fight", 5/39, as member "Hollywood Committee of 56" whose "Declaration of Independence", a hymn-of-hate for Germany, demands severance of all U.S. relations.

ADOLPH SIMON OCHS: deceased head of N. Y. Times (see under "Newspapers"); son-in-law of the "liberal" Rabbi Isaac M. Wise (who "has well been called the master builder of American Judaism . . . a liberal in his entire outlook religious, social and political"), the founder, 1889, of the Central Conf. of American Rabbis, for which Ochs raised five million dollars, contributing a great sum himself; his son-in-law successor, A. H. Sulzberger, is nat. vice-chmn. of B'nai B'rith's radically controlled Nat. Conf. of Jews and Christians (1939) and was honorary pallbearer for the Socialist Party leader B. Charney Vladeck (Daily Worker, 11/2/38).

FRANZ OPPENHEIM: German-born; a radical single taxer; took active part in Palestinian colonization; upheld nationalistic "minority rights" for "Ost-Juden", or Eastern Jews, who flooded Germany after the World war (Encyl. Jewish Knowledge).

DAVID PINSKI: Russian-born Yiddish author; pres., Socialist Zionist "Jewish National Workers' Alliance"; mem. exec. com., Socialist Poale Zion Zeire-Zion; edtl. bd., Socialist "Jewish Frontier".

ARTHUR RUPPIN: Polish-born; Zionist; org. socialistic Palestine Land Develop. Co. Labor Bank; from 1929 dir. Zionist colonization work in Palestine.

PINCHAS RUTHENBERG: Russian-born; with Jabotinsky, organized illegal Jewish armed troops in Palestine; he controls the lucrative, far-reaching 70-year monopoly on all water power development, etc., in Palestine, which irks informed Britons bearing the burden of holding down by force of arms the resentful Arab majority of Palestine, which Arabs have occupied for over 1300 years, so that imported Jews may pour in and make it a Jewish State and collect the profits; "planner of large scale Palestine settlements"; "Ency. of Jewish Knowledge" says he "from his boyhood was an active member of the Russian Social Revolutionary Party and he played an important part in the upheaval of 'Bloody Sunday' Jan. 22, 1905," and saved Father Gapon's life until it was proved he was an "agent-provacateur" then was "ordered by his party to arrange the execution of the traitor", then had to leave Russia, returned and was a leader, with Kerensky, of the 1917 Russian Red revolution. See also under Sir Herbert Samuel.

110

SIR HERBERT SAMUEL: English politician and "a leading member of the Zionist org. as long ago as 1916 and was the channel of communication between them and the govt. of which he was then a member".

"The Alien Menace", by Col. A. H. Lane, Boswell Pub. Co., London, describes how Samuel had manoeuvered with the Zionists to get Palestine for Jewry at the expense of England, went to Palestine chosen by the Zionists as first British High Commnr. there, 1920-25, his "unpatriotic action" in almost immediately turning over the " 'white coal' or water power" and "the most complete monopoly of the future commercial position in that country that it is possible to conceive" to Pinchas Ruthenberg, Russian Jew (see his Red Revolutionary activities); how Samuel was both a member of the "National Govt." proposing tariffs while his "Samuelite Liberals" under Major Nathan opposed them. To quote (p. 3):

"This opposition is instructive. The Free Trade movement from its inception has always been well supported and financed by Jews. Karl Marx was a champion of Free Trade. Engels, the Prussian colleague of Marx, tells us in his introduction to Marx's 'Discourse on Free Trade' that Free Trade is 'the economic medium in which the conditions for the inevitable social revolution will be the soonest created—for this reason, and for this alone, did Marx declare in favour of Free Trade.' "

DAVID SARNOFF: Russian-born radio czar; pres. and dir. R.C.A. Communications, Inc., since 1930; chmn. bd. dir. Nat. Broadcasting Co.; dir. Motion Picture Producers & Distrib.; dir. Radio Keith Orpheum Corp.; dir. Metropolitan Opera Assn.; etc., etc.

One of those honoring Jacob Doletsky, Soviet Russia's head of "Tass" (Soviet News Agency) at a banquet (N.Y. Her.-Trib., 11/9/34) ; offered communistic Einstein $50,000 a year to broadcast (Chgo. Times, 8/8/38) ; mem. Am. Hebrew Medal Committee which has presented medals to such radicals as Pres. F.D.R., Mayor LaGuardia, Carrie C. Catt, executives R. W. Straus and Newton D. Baker of B'nai

B'rith's Nat. Conf. of Jews & Christians, for services to Jewry; his reported boast that if inquiry on the anti-trust case against R.C.A. could be delayed until after Pres. F.D.R.'s inauguration, "he would have little trouble in 'dealing' with Mr. Roosevelt", was cited before a Senate Com. (Chgo. Tribune 8/7/40).

RABBI ABBA HILLEL SILVER: Lithuanian-born; v.p. Zionist Org. of Am.; now and for years on nat. com. of the legal-aid and propaganda spearhead for the Red Revolutionary movement, the American Civil Liberties Union; speaker for communist Am. Lg. for Peace and Democracy (Civil Rights News, 5/39, p. 4); on communist-Garland-Fund-supported Com. on Militarism in Education for years (before Jewry decided for U.S. war against Germany); mem. Central Conf. of Am. Rabbis, which called for establishment in the U.S.A. of "a thoroughly **socialized** democracy" (N.Y. Times, 9/13/36).

Supporter of Spanish Red church-burners; sponsor communist North Am. Com. to Aid Spanish Democracy; urged U.S. recognition of Soviet Russia (Daily Worker, 9/23/27); upheld 1919 Steel Strike led by Communist Wm. Z. Foster; backer of Jewish-influenced League of Nations and World Court; urged help to England and France (Chgo. Trib., 9/28/39); sponsor, 1939, Am. Com. for Anti-Nazi Literature, which includes leading Communists and Socialists; on nat. coun. of Victor Berger National Foundation (to spread Berger's Red revolutionary Socialist doctrines).

PERCY SELDEN STRAUS: deceased pres. of R. H. Macy Co. and dir. N.Y. Life Insurance Co.; was pres. Jewish Agricultural Society, forming socialistic cooperatives, credit unions, bank, fire insurance co., etc., for Jews, and issuing Yiddish paper; was mem. coun. of the Am. Assn. for Labor Legislation, composed of leading Reds and New Dealers, Felix Frankfurter, Rabbi S. S. Wise, Felix M. Warburg, Leo Wolman (dir. communist Garland Fund), etc., devoted to securing passage of legislation "born of Revolutionary Socialism . . . to make room for advancing Communism" ("Reds in Am.", Whitney, p. 182); with leading Reds of all camps, formed "Provisional Council Against Anti-Semitism" (N.Y. Her.-Trib., 11/28/38).

HENRIETTA SZOLD: pioneer Zionist Org. exec. and founder of its women's branch, "Hadassah" in U.S.A.; living in Palestine for past years devoting entire time to socialistic Zionism.

ERNST TOLLER: a Communist Revolutionary from the time he led the bloody Soviet Revolution in Germany with Kurt Eisner and was chmn. of the Cent. Com. of the Bavarian Soviet and mem. Red Guard, 1918-19 (Am. Labor Who's Who) to his suicide in the U.S.A., 5/22/39; he was imprisoned by the German Republic, 1919-24.

He left his last article "Last Testament of Ernst Toller" to communist "New Masses" magazine (6/6/39); his book, "I Was a German", one of 50 books recommended to Jewry by B'nai B'rith Hillel Foundation director A. L. Sachar (B'nai B'rith magazine, 7/37).

Very active in behalf of Spanish Reds; signer of appeal in which "first aim is overthrow of Hitler" (Daily Worker, 1/28/37); his Red anti-Nazi play "Pastor Hall" is being put on by James Roosevelt with Mrs. F.D.R. taking part and Toller's estate is suing James for royalty fees. It is recommended as war "material" by Wm. Allen White's Com. to Defend Am. by Aiding the Allies according to the communist "People's World", 8/10/40; honored by Jewry as a "pacifist".

MENACHEM USSISHKIN: Palestine; Russian-born Zionist; pres. Jewish Nat. Fund, which buys Palestine land for socialistic Jewish colonies, etc., supported by B'nai B'rith, etc.

B. CHARNEY VLADECK: deceased; Russian-born; "Who's Who in Am. Jewry 1938-9" says he "joined Russian revolutionary movement 1903; fled to U.S. 1908, gen. mgr. since 1918 N.Y. Forward", largest Yiddish Socialist newspaper in the world (like the Communists, advocating the revolutionary socialization of the U.S. Govt.); was Socialist Party candidate 1934, etc.; was leader in principal Red organizations: bd. dir., Socialist-Communist "League for Industrial Democracy"; nat. com., Red-aiding American Civil Liberties Union; mem. Socialist-Communist American Labor Party; was nat. chmn. of Socialist Jewish Labor Committee (doing underground Red Revolutionary work here and abroad); etc.

LILLIAN WALD: deceased; mem. advis. coun. Am. Jewish Congress (Zionist); militant Red; exposed in Senate investigation of radicals, 1919; on the Dept. of Justice list of leading radicals, 1921; was vice chmn. of Soviet Russia's "Am. Soc. for Cultural Relations with Russia" organized at Henry St. Settlement, which she founded, 1893, and headed, with Felix M. Warburg of Kuhn Loeb & Co., Herbert H. Lehman and other Jews "with one foot in the bank and the other in the Socialist movement" (as Bakunin put it) supporting and directing her Settlement; Mrs. Jacob H. Schiff gave $300,000 to Henry St. Settlement (B'nai B'rith Mag., 4/33).

She was v.p. communist Am. Russian Institute of the above A.S.C.R.R.; mem. radical Am. Assn. for Labor (Red) Legislation; on communist Friends Soviet Union reception com. for Soviet Flyers (1929); was on Am. com. for communist World Congress Against War (for Red revolution); on Russian-Am. Industrial Corp., which raised money for Red Russia, headed by Sidney Hillman and praised by Lenin; eulogist of Soviet Commissar Litvinov in symposium on "The Soviet Union, Defender of Democracy and Peace" (Soviet Russia Today, 11/38); militant backer of Spanish Reds (N.Y. Times, 8/10/37, Nation, 7/8/39, Daily Worker, 10/28/38, etc.); contrib. to communist Lg. of Am. Writers pamphlet "Writers Take Sides" (for Red Spain); was petitioner for Reds imprisoned in World War (N.Y. World 11/22/28); on radical Am. Hebrew Medal Com. awarding Medals for services to Jewry to Pres. F.D.R., LaGuardia, etc.

She was greeted by the Communist Party on her 70th birthday (Daily Worker, 3/11/37); sponsor communist Am. Youth Congress; was mem. Civil Liberties Bureau which formed the Red-aiding American Civil Liberties Union;

sponsor radical Am. Com. for Anti-Nazi Literature, 1939; etc.

FELIX M. WARBURG: deceased; "Prince of Israel"; German-born; came to U.S. in 1894; with Kuhn Loeb & Co. from 1896 on; married to daughter of Jacob Schiff, Kuhn Loeb head who financed Russian revolution; was chmn. Joint Distribution Com. 1914-32, which has spent millions of dollars in Soviet Russia, also hon. pres. Am. Soc. for Jewish Farm Settlements in Russia; mem. exec. com. Am. Jewish Com. (see); on Hebrew U., headed by Judah L. Magnes of communist Garland Fund, and other Palestine activities; advis. com. Nat. Broadcasting Co.; mem. and financial supporter of socialistic Survey Associates; mem. exec. com. of N.Y. Kehillah, 1917-18.

OTTO H. WARBURG: former pres. of the World Zionist Organization.

MEYER WAXMAN: Russian-born; past exec. secy. Mizrachi Orgn. of Am. (devoted to socialistic Zionism and Hebrew); instr. in **Talmudics,** Hebrew Theol. Coll., Chgo., Ill.

CHAIM WEIZMANN: Russian-born; lives London and Palestine; pres. World Zionist Org.; agitated for establishment of Hebrew U., Palestine (headed by red Judah Magnes) and chmn. of its bd. of govs. since 1932; manoeuvered with Sir Herbert Samuel (see) and Lord Balfour to get Palestine for Zionists through British Govt.; feted in U.S.A. Jan.-Feb., 1940, when Jewry turned over $250,000 "salve" money to Catholics and Protestants for "refugees"; pictured with beaming Bishop B. J. Sheil (Chgo. Daily News, 2/1/40), who was decorated by B'nai B'rith for his services to Jewry (Chgo. Her.-Am., 1/3/40); preparing book on "the Jew" with radicals John Gunther, Thos. Mann, Pierre Van Paassen, and Jewry's protege Dorothy Thompson (Sentinel, 3/14/40).

FRANZ WERFEL: his books among Red literature burned in Germany 1933; in radical "pacifist" activities during World War; with Arnold Zweig hailed as attending radical world congress of writers, N.Y., participated in by communistic Theatre Arts Committee (its magazine "TAC", 5/39).

STEPHEN S. WISE: Hungarian-born; a founder and exec. of various Zionist organizations in America; pres. American Jewish Congress (Zionist) since 1924; backed every outstanding Red cause for years as member of committees of the Communist-aiding American Civil Liberties Union, communist American Lg. Against War and Fascism, for Anarchists Sacco and Vanzetti, Non-Intervention Citizens' Com. (to prevent interference with sovietization of Mexico), for Communist-dynamiter Tom Mooney, Nat. Religion & Labor Found. (which distributes Communist literature and Atheist Soviet cartoons); ardent backer of Spanish Reds and featured as such in the Communist Party's Daily Worker, 11/5/38, 1/30/39, 2/6/39, 2/15/39, etc. etc.

Opposed military training in schools as mem. of communist-Garland-Fund-financed "Com. on Militarism in Education", for years, until Jewry decided the U.S. should fight Hitler, then appealed for lifting arms embargo to aid England and France (N.Y. Her.-Trib., 10/30/39).

Was one of the Baruch-Frankfurter-Jewish clique in positions of power on Pres. Wilson's World-War Nat. Defense Council, and at Peace Conf.; married the niece of **Premier Molotov of Soviet Russia**, Gertrude R. Carp, to Martin Aronson (Chgo. Tribune, 5/28/40); his son, James Waterman Wise, a prominent Communist Party writer; sponsor **Leon Blum** Colony in Palestine.

EFREM ZIMBALIST: Russian-born; husband of the late Jewish singer, Alma Gluck (whose daughter married Russell Davenport, Fortune editor and author of B'nai B'rith propaganda); very active in support of Spanish Reds: mem. com. of communist North American Com. to Aid Spanish Democracy; appealer for lifting embargo for Reds (Daily Worker, 4/8/38, 1/26/39); participant in their aid (communist Midwest Record, 3/26/38); adopted orphan of Spanish Reds (Daily Worker, 4/10/39); at dedication of Soviet Pavilion, N.Y. World's Fair (Daily Worker, 6/30/-

116

39); hailed as one whose tours of Soviet Russia have endeared him to the Soviets attending banquet to honor Communist Anna Louise Strong (Daily Worker, 1/12/37).

ARNOLD ZWEIG: German-born author, ousted 1933 as a Red; went to Palestine; in Socialist "Jewish Frontier" (6/36, p. 21), he tells of his activities "in the Socialist wing of the Zionist movement", how "literary and radical activities claimed me" in association with "Arlosoroff" who "led the left wing in the Zionist movement", and bewails loss of Communist Einstein, etc. to "proud German Jewry"; contributor Communist "Daily Worker", 5/17/39; TAC (Theatre Arts Committee) magazine, 5/39, announced him speaker at radical PEN world congress, N.Y., 5/8/39, participated in by TAC; speaker with Communist Ernst Toller, red Sholem Asch, etc. (communist Daily Record, 5/15/39).

STEFAN ZWEIG: Austrian-born author exiled as a Red; as a Jewish internationalist, "He asserted that the 'inevitable fusion of world affairs' would make necessary a world planning that would develop a higher community" (Boston Herald, 1/12/39); Austrian representative of communistic John Haynes Holmes' magazine "Unity" 1937-40; was member of communistic International Committee sponsoring publication of "The Letters of Sacco and Vanzetti", the Anarchist murderers for whom Frankfurter agitated and Reds of the world rioted; was associated 1919, with Red, free-love, Bertrand Russell, communist Henri Barbusse, etc. (p. 56, "American Writers Congress" issued by Soviet's "Intl. Pub.").

CHAIM ZHIDLOWSKI: "joined the Russian revolutionary forces and in 1888 was forced to leave Russia . . . later became the theoretician of the Russian Revolutionary Party and was first to publish its program in his study 'Socialism and the Struggle for Political Freedom' 1898 . . . his concept a Jewish nationalism on a Socialistic basis with Yiddish as its national language. He thus laid the foundation for the autonomy idea which in the hands of **Dubnow** became the minority rights program. He was an active participant in the revolution of 1905 and came to the

117

U.S.A. . . . As early as 1885 he organized Teschuat Israel, a Jewish socialist revolutionary group which . . . supported Zhidlowski's concept" (Encyl. of Jewish Knowledge).

## In Addition

Closely linked to the above, is SIMON MARKOVITCH DUBNOW: Russian-born; "regards the Jews as a nation but a nation within the nations . . . the man who gave the theory of Jewish national autonomy its most thorough development . . . spread the philosophy for minority rights for Jews at the Peace Conf." (Encyl. of Jewish Knowledge").

Also SELIG BRODETSKY: Russian-born; Cambridge Senior Wrangler; World Zionist Org. executive.

Also MARTIN BUBER: Jewish nationalist and "re-discoverer of Hasidism in Western Europe". Hasidism had been a system of "physical ecstacy", dancing, singing and merrymaking in the name of religion. Its works were burned in Prague. Its followers were charged with immorality and were anti-Czarist plotters (Encyl. of Jewish Knowledge).

Also Russian-born ISRAEL DAVIDSON, and JOSEPH KLAUSNER and SHOLOM SPIEGEL, "Hebraists", and RABBI HERZOG, Chief Rabbi of Zionist socialist Palestine Jews.

Also MAX REINHARDT (Goldmann): Austrian-born exiled theatrical producer, now with Warner Bros., Hollywood, whose "first presentation of" Soviet Communist "Maxim Gorky's Night Refuge was a commercial success"; put on radical Franz Werfel's play, "The Eternal Road", etc.

Also MEIER DIZENGOFF: (deceased) Russian-born; active in Zionism since 1882; was Mayor of the all-Jewish Zionist town of Tel Aviv, where all varieties of Communist literature from the U.S.A. and Europe are sold on the public news stands.

Also DR. SIMON FLEXNER: trustee of, and his office at, the Rockefeller Foundation which has financed the Univ. of Chicago, the Intl. Houses, etc., with millions of dollars used to spread Red propaganda which has soaked thousands of students with Marxism.

Also MOSES GASTER: "expelled from Rumania for participating in political affairs in the interest of his fellow Jews"; active leader of Zionism since 1896. "It was at Gaster's home that the British and French officials held the conference with Zionists which was the preliminary to the Balfour Declaration" (Encyl. of Jewish Knowledge).

## JEWRY'S 120 LEADERS

There are most of them!

World Jewry's 120 leaders, chosen to hold up **"living ideals to Jewish youth"**, are largely a mass of Jewish Nationalists, Marxian Revolutionists and industrialists "with one foot in the bank and the other in the Socialist movement". To quote Nahum Goldman, one of the above 120:

"There is no such thing as a special privileged fate for one part of the Jewish people as compared with other parts. **We are one people** with the same past, and we must all be free or all be enslaved; the destiny of one part will finally be the destiny of all" (Jewish Sentinel, 9/5/40, p. 27).

## SOVIET-LIKE ZIONISM

Red Rabbi Edward L. Israel (who married Ludwig Lewisohn to his girl friend despite the outcries of the deserted common-law wife and child), writing on "Children in Collectives" in the socialist Jewish Frontier (Sept.-Oct., 1936, issue), said:

"To learn that there is no such thing as family life (in the traditional sense) in the kvutzot or agricultural collectives of Palestine will be a shock to many Jews and quite a few Zionists. . . . First we must understand the physical organization of a kvutza. It is a group of people living a completely **collectivized** economic life on a stretch of ground usually leased from the Keren Kayemet, the Jewish National Fund. The group is of both sexes, usually in their twenties or early thirties. . . . In our badly disorganized capitalistic society, youths with little or no financial resources are usually forced to postpone marriage. . . . The opportunities for marriage in a truly cooperative economic society such as exists in the kvutzot are practically without these grim material obstacles. . . . There is no private property over which to worry, and except for the necessity of endeavoring to provide the married couple with a room of their own as living quarters, the community is no better or worse off financially as a result of this marriage. For, be it clearly understood there is no such thing in the kvutza as the occupational classification, 'housewife'. The girl, when married, continues at her regular work which she performed before marriage, whether in the community kitchen, stable or fields. . . .

"In some of the poorer and newer kvutzot, however, it is essential for the married couple to retain their separate and **separated sleeping** quarters in the general men's and women's dormitories. . . . Despite a completely enlightened knowledge of contraceptives, the desire for progeny is strong among these halutzim. The girl becomes pregnant. What now is the course of events. . . . She, as a member of the Histadrut, is entitled to the hospital benefits. . . . When she is able, and the medical attendants have so specified, she returns to her work. She resumes her place in the kitchen, stable or fields as before. . . . **Her child remains in the community nursery.** . . . When you drive into a kvutza even of the poorer sort, there is one building which stands out as superior to the rest. This is the children's house. . . .

"Doesn't this system which **removes the child practically at birth from the parental fireside** . . . destroy the filial affection which we usually associate with family life?"

Israel defends the system and quotes a kvutza leader as saying, "We love them undisturbed by the complications of child-training which should be taken care of by specialists." This is the Soviet system exactly, the system of the Marxian collectivist **herd** state.

## DIFFERENCE BETWEEN ZIONISM AND COMMUNISM—PALESTINE

"Not Fighting Communism" (in the same issue, p. 38) heads a heated denial by the Social Workers Chapter of the League for Labor Palestine that it was organized to combat "the influence of communism among Jewish social workers". It says: **"We deny this categorically and emphatically. . . .** It might even be pointed out that members of the Chapter are **sympathetic to much of the communist program,** but take serious issue with its stand regarding **Palestine** and the Jewish question."

## JEWRY IN GERMANY AS IN U.S.A.

While B'nai B'rith, to delude Gentile suckers, denies that Jewry was radical in Germany, itself said of "B'nai B'rith's Role in Germany" before it was dissolved as subversive by Hitler:

"Jewish history in Germany will forever be inextricably bound up with the B'nai B'rith movement. . . . Every Jewish community head, every Jewish party leader, every Jewish club and society president was a member of B'nai B'rith. . . . The **Zionist** movement attracted most of the Jewish youth. But at the same time the **Socialist** and the **Communist** movements also increased and they, too, won to their ranks many of the Jewish youths" (B'nai B'rith magazine, 1/38, p. 164).

### British Tools of Jewry

The British, French and American people, dragged in by skillful propaganda, are now engaged in another world war for Jewry. How the British people have long been **used** by world Jewry is strongly and resentfully set forth by a British patriot, Col. A. H. Lane, who is aware of the inconsistency, during the World War, of Britain having promised the Arabs of Palestine National independence if they helped Britain oust the Turks, at the same time that they were promising the Jews Palestine if they enlisted the U.S.A. in the war. He says:

"Millions of British taxpayers' money were spent during the War in driving the Turks out of Palestine. Since the War ended British taxpayers have provided many more millions to make this rather barren and desolate land a National Home for the Jews. The British people have gained nothing out of this effort and expenditure except the hostility of the Arabs—who feel that we have betrayed them—

and the contempt of the Jews. The English have been ousted out of anything that might be profitable to the Jews. We find the money; the Jews take the profits, if any" (p. 161, "The Alien Menace", Boswell & Co., Pub., London).

The usual Jewish interpretation of what constitutes "persecution" of the Jews (?) in Palestine is this report: "The violence in Palestine from June 1, 1938, to June 30, 1939, took the lives of 1,967 persons and wounded 1,643 more. Of the total killed 1,529 were Arabs, 320 Jews, and 55 British" (The American Hebrew, 9/29/39).

## JEWS IN MOVIES

Sometimes peddlers of B'nai B'rith propaganda, like Keith Brooks, outdo their source in making a story good.

While Keith Brooks flatly asserts "In Movies Jews control 3 of 8 principal companies", his source (p. 9 of the B'nai B'rith pamphlet, "Jews in America, By the Editors of Fortune", stating it is a "slightly condensed version" of the 2/36 Fortune magazine article) says:

"Three of the eight principal companies are owned and controlled by Jews, two are probably owned and controlled by non-Jews, and in three management and ownership are divided. But though Jews do not monopolize the industry moneywise they do nevertheless exert pretty complete control over the production of pictures".

The uncondensed version (p. 144, Fortune, 2/36) however, made a droll struggle to give these Jewish-controlled Movie companies a Gentile-looking face that is a masterpiece of futility. Russel W. Davenport, managing editor of Fortune, is married to the daughter of the late Rumanian-born Jewish singer, Alma Gluck, who was married to the Russian-born Jew, Efrem Zimbalist.

The eight major film companies covered are: (1) Warner Bros., (2) Loew's, Inc. (which owns Metro-Goldwyn-Mayer), (3) Columbia, which are admitted to be Jewish-controlled; (4) RKO and (5) United Artists, claimed to be "divided" in control; (6) Twentieth Century-Fox, (7) Paramount, (8) Universal, supposedly Gentile-controlled.

122

### How They Do It!

UNIVERSAL is classified as "Gentile" controlled by stating that its president, admittedly a Jew, "Carl Laemmle is the **largest stockholder** at present but . . . it is understood" a Gentile group were considering buying it! This might be called speculating in "futures".

### Another "Gentile" Company

To quote in full: "PARAMOUNT is non-Jewish in **management** and **probably** in control. After a complicated and exciting history winding up in a reorganization the controlling group is now Lehman Bros. (Jewish), Electrical Research Products, Inc. (an A.T.&T. subsidiary), Royal Liverpool Insurance group, Public Natl. Bank & Trust of N.Y. (Jewish), and Floyd Odlum's Atlas Corp. Directors and executive committee are predominantly non-Jewish."

### Is Control Gentile?

Note above that in **control** are: Lehman Bros. and the Pub. Nat. Bank & Trust of N.Y., **both labeled Jewish,** plus the Atlas Corp., and the Jewish tie-up of Atlas is complete.

### Atlas Corp. Jewish Tie-Ups

Floyd B. Odlum, pres. of Atlas Corp., is dir. of the United Fruit Co., controlled and headed by the Jew, Sam Zemurray, and Zemurray, in turn, is dir. of the Atlas Corp. Atlas Corp. acquired control of the Jewish Goldman Sachs Trading Corp., 4/33 (Fortune, 9/35) and **Atlas** underwrote the reorganization of **Paramount** in 1935 (same source). The Jewish-appearing L. Boyd Hatch, vice pres. of Atlas Corp., is dir. of the Jewish firm of Franklin Simon Co., and Oswald Johnson, also vice pres. of Atlas Corp., is also a dir. of the Jewish firm of Franklin Simon Co.

### "Managing" Officers All Jewish

Let us see how "Gentile" the "management" of Paramount is. In "Who's Who in American Jewry, 1938-9", are listed:

Barney Balaban as **pres.** of both Paramount Pictures, Inc.

and its subsidiary, Balaban & Katz Corp.; **Emmanuel Cohen** as **vice-pres.**, not only of Paramount Pictures, but of Paramount Productions, Inc., Paramount 43rd St. Corp., Paramount Laboratories, Inc., Paramount Film Corp., also vice-pres. and gen. mgr. of Paramount Ins., Inc., and dir. of Paramount Pictures Distrib. Corp. and Paramount Intl. Corp; **Adolph Zukor** (Hungarian-born) as **chmn. of the bd.** of dirs. of Paramount; his son, Eugene James Zukor, **asst. to chmn. of bd.**; B. P. Schulberg, formerly of Paramount, as making independent pictures for Paramount; Samuel Katz (Polish-born) as former vice-pres.

With Jewish finances controlling it, a Jewish pres., vice-pres., chmn. of the bd., asst. to chmn. of the bd., etc., managing it—page the "Gentile" control!

### Do-Three-Fourths Jews Make it "Gentile"?

To quote them: "UNITED ARTISTS: here ownership and control are **partially** Jewish. The active owners are Mary Pickford, who is now President; Charles Chaplin, Douglas Fairbanks, and Sam Goldwyn. The last two are Jews and Chaplin is **claimed** as a Jew by other Jews."

The last is weasel-worded, for Chaplin lists himself plainly as a Jew in "Who's Who in American Jewry", his real name as "Thonstein" and his family as having "emigrated from Eastern Europe" to England. But with **three out of four,** all but **one,** avowed Jews in control, United Artists is classified as a Gentile firm only "partially" controlled by Jews. (The Fairbanks family name was Ullman.)

### More "Gentile" Data

RKO seems to be even less "divided" than United Artists. To quote in full on RKO:

"RKO: here management and control are divided. Control is in **Atlas Corp.** and **Lehman Bros., a Jewish banking house.** Management was until recently under **David Sarnoff** but, as is also true in other Sarnoff enterprises, the Jewish influence did not dominate. **Leo Spitz, a Jew, is now President,** but Sarnoff's **Jewish bank affiliations, Lehman Bros., Lazard Freres, J. & W. Seligman, and Speyer**

& Co., are still represented on the Board. Some of these houses may be eliminated but **Herbert Swope and Louis E. Kirstein,** both prominent Jews, will certainly remain as Directors."

The only RKO control mentioned and not labeled **Jewish** in the above is the Atlas Corp., whose Jewish tie-up is complete, as previously noted. David Sarnoff still lists himself as dir. of RKO, as well as dir. of Motion Picture Producers and Distributors of Am. ("Who's Who in Am. Jewry, 1938-9").

Get the microscope to find the "Gentile" control!

### Of Course Not! It's Gentile Too!

Of TWENTIETH CENTURY-FOX FILM CORPORATION, to quote: "Joseph Schenck is Chairman of the Board, but control is nevertheless definitely not Jewish."

Joseph Schenck (Russian-born Jew) was founder of Twentieth Century Pictures Corp., and after the merger with Fox Film Co., became **vice-pres. and chmn. of the bd.,** and lists himself (1938-9) as **executive head of production of it.** (Also pres. of the Assn. Motion Pictures Producers, Inc., and former pres. United Artists Theater Circuit and United Artists Corp., etc.)

Another "Gentile" motion picture concern!

In addition, Harry Cohn lists himself as President in charge of **Columbia** Pictures Corp.; Jack Cohn as vice-president and chmn. of its bd. of directors and also editor and producer of **Universal** Weekly (Who's Who in American Jewry, 1938-9), for this previously mentioned "Gentile" concern.

To quote from "International Events" magazine, 1/33:

"The name of America, supposedly a Christian country, is being made a stench throughout the world by means of corrupt film industry centered in this country. Do you know who the men are that put vice on a pedestal, represent lust as virtue and drag all the decencies of life into the gutter? There are **eight major film companies.** We take the names of their officers and leaders from the American Hebrew:

125

" 'Paramount Publix—Adolph Zukor, Eugene Zukor, Sam Katz, B. P. Schulberg, Emmanuel Cohen, A. L. Mayer, and the three Balaban brothers. **Metro-Goldwyn-Mayer**—Nicholas M. Schenck, Louis B. Mayer, I. G. Thalberg, J. R. Rubin, A. M. and David Loew, D. Bernstein, U. Rapf. **First National**—Harry, Jack and Albert Warner. **United Artists**—Joseph M. Schenck, Samuel Goldwyn. **Universal Pictures**—Carl Laemmle, L. J. Schlaiffer, Samuel Bergerman, Sam Jacobson, Herman Stern. **Fox Film Co.**—Sol M. Wortzel, Albert Lewis, Jack Cohn, Walter Wanger. **Columbia Pictures**—Harry Cohn (successor to Joe Brandt). **Radio Pictures**—Joseph Schnitzer, Lee Marcus, David O. Selznick, David Sarnoff'.

"These are the men who are educating millions of our American children to be criminals and to scoff at the Christian religion. They are the men who pocket millions of dollars earned by church members who do not feel they can afford to give a tithe of their income to the work of the church."

## JEWISH DEPT. STORES CONTROL NEWS

How B'nai B'rith, which **"serves Jewry"**, controls editors and the news you read by forcing newspapers to knuckle to pressure exerted by Jewish advertisers, is proudly told by them in their own reports, some of which are quoted later in this article.

A Chicago newspaper executive personally related, in confidence, how after a certain truthful paragraph relating to Germany, had been printed in his paper, a large Jewish department store, because of it, cancelled its $400,000 advertising contract with his paper and waited silently a week for the punitive effect to sink in. Then the Jewish head came to see the Gentile publisher to dictate the conditions on which he would (and did) renew the contract. This executive said "We **have** to run anti-Nazi cartoons from time to time to show we are friendly to the Jews".

### On Germany and Spain

Can one get the truth in the press about Germany under

126

such conditions? Did Americans get a truthful impression from the press about the Communist-Socialist-Anarchist church-burning Spanish Govt. strongly favored by Jewry? It did not. It was habitually referred to in the press as the "legitimate", "Loyalist" or "Republican" Govt. of Spain, while Gen. Franco, fighting with Spain's decent element for Christianity and order against typical Bolshevist atheistic murder and chaos, was referred to as a horrible "Fascist" and slurred in countless ways.

So many Jews served in the Communist Intl. Brigade in Spain that a paper was issued in Yiddish for them (Jewish Life, 1/38, p. 16).

### B'nai B'rith on Dept. Stores

B'nai B'rith (parroted by its stooges) says: "Department stores are largely Jewish-owned in New York. . . . But in Chicago the two leading stores are Marshall Field and Carson Pirie Scott & Co., one of Yankee origin and the other Scotch" ("Jews in America", p. 7).

B'nai B'rith's echo, Keith Brooks, snaps this up a bit by saying: "Department Stores of N.Y. City largely Jewish, but in Chicago the largest stores are non-Jewish".

### What Are the Facts on Chicago Dept. Stores?

In Chicago's "loop" shopping district are Chicago's leading dept. stores and its largest clothing store, all on State Street—Marshall Field & Co.; Carson, Pirie, Scott & Co.; The Fair, operating one other Chicago store; Netcher's Boston Store (Jewish); Goldblatt's (Jewish) which operates seven other large Chicago dept. stores; Mandel Bros. (Jewish); Sears Roebuck & Co. (now, as always, controlled by the Jewish Rosenwalds) which operates six other Chicago dept. stores (plus hundreds of retail branch stores all over the U.S.A., and a mail-order business); Maurice L. Rothschild (Jewish), largest clothing store.

**Five** of the **eight** largest State Street stores are known as Jewish. The three which possibly could be assumed to be Gentile-controlled, operating **four** Chicago dept. stores, as against **eighteen** operated by the five Jewish-owned dept. stores.

Smaller Chicago loop State Street stores are overwhelmingly Jewish in management and personnel: Red Robin, Lerner Shops (2 State St. stores), Three Sisters, Mangel's, Gaylard's, Baer's, Page, all women's clothing stores; Berland's, Maling, Wise, "Kitty Kelly", Burt, all shoe stores; Marks Bros. Credit Jewelers, Katz Exclusive Millinery (2 State St. stores); etc., etc.

### Chicago Dept. Store Advertising Affects Newspapers

According to official sources, in 1939, for advertising in the three Chicago newspapers—Chicago Tribune, Herald-American and the Times, **Goldblatt's (Jewish)** spent $1,-162,272. Over a million dollars. Money enough, if withheld, **to ruin any paper,** bold enough to print news unpleasing to Jewry. **Mandel's (Jewish)** spent **$919,525.** Nearly a million dollars. **Sears, Roebuck and Company (Jewish)** spent **$643,179.** Over a half million dollars. **Netcher's Boston Store (Jewish)** spent **$602,309.** Over a half million dollars. **Maurice L. Rothschild's (Jewish)** spent **$615,602.** Over a half million dollars.

The above five Jewish stores alone spent nearly four million dollars with the three above named Chicago newspapers, in addition to what all the lesser Jewish State St. stores spent, for advertising.

What newspaper could afford to be deaf to such a golden jingle of Jewish advertising? Advertisers, not readers' pennies, keep newspapers going.

DUPLICATE THIS SITUATION IN ANY AMERICAN CITY WHERE STORE OWNERS ARE LARGELY JEWISH AND CAN MAKE OR BREAK NEWSPAPERS THROUGH GIVING OR WITHHOLDING ADVERTISING.

## JEWS IN NEWSPAPERS

Jewish advertising, Jewish financial interests, along with B'nai B'rith's prowling army of snoopers, suppressors and hirelings, effectively muzzle newspapers that are Gentile-owned.

In seeking to show that Jews have little influence in newspapers, B'nai B'rith propagandists emphasize the Hearst papers being supposedly "Gentile". Not only do both B'nai B'rith-Fortune "research" versions and their echo, Keith Brooks, stress this, but the Jewish Sentinel (9/12/40 p. 14) says:

"We're pretty tired of hearing the truth kicked around about 'Jewish control of press, radio and movies' ". Whereupon the **Hearst** papers are dragged out to be paraded again as Gentile, and, to quote, "In Chicago, with the second largest Jewish population, none of the dailies are owned or controlled by Jews. The Tribune is owned by Bertie McCormick" (whose principal editorial writer is Leon Stolz, son of a Rabbi executive of the socialistic Cent. Conf. of Am. Rabbis, etc.), "the News by Col. Frank Knox" (dir. Max Epstein, a Jew, and Kuhn Loeb & Co., heavy owner of its stock, according to the press, also hooked up with the N.Y. Post, owned by Jewish George Backer, son-in-law of a Kuhn Loeb partner), " . . . and the Herald-American **by Hearst**". "Hearst" again.

Are these vociferous authorities unaware that by looking in "Editor and Publisher, 1940", the year book of all U.S.A. newspapers (p. 111), they can see that the **general manager of all Hearst papers** is J. D. Gortatowsky, who lists himself as a **Jew** in "Who's Who in America"?

Are they unaware that Solomon Solis Carvalho lists himself as "chairman of the **executive committee** of **Hearst Enterprises Inc.**" in Who's Who in American Jewry, 1938-9?

That Carl Dreyfuss lists himself as **publisher** of Hearst's Boston American, Boston Sunday Advertiser; also v.p. New England Newspaper Pub. Co., in Who's Who in American Jewry, 1938-9?

That Arthur G. Newmyer lists himself as the **publisher** of Hearst's N.Y. Journal; also that Jerome J. Karpf lists himself as **managing editor** of Hearst's N.Y. American since 1933, and that a swarm of Jews, such as Eugene B. Block,

**news editor** since 1925 of Hearst's San Francisco Call-Bulletin, Bruno Lessing, **columnist** for all Hearst papers, etc., etc., are in key positions in the Hearst Newspapers and thus listed in Who's Who in American Jewry?

That Benjamin De Casseres lists himself as **"editorial writer, N.Y.** American and allied Hearst papers since 1934", in Who's Who in American Jewry, 1938-9?

De Casseres boasts also that he is "collateral descendant of Benedict de Spinoza" and author of "Spinoza". B'nai B'rith says Spinoza was one of the only two Jews ever expelled from a Jewish Synagogue "and we are still apologizing for it" (Article VI, p. 6). Spinoza's first biographer, Colerus, described Spinoza's philosophy as "the most pernicious atheism that ever was seen in the world". Bayle, a fellow philosopher, called him "the systematizer of atheism". Jewry, generally, proudly calls him "blessed Spinoza".

Jews do not mind Hearst attacking Stalinist Communism, one splinter of Marxism, providing the **bulk of Marxism,** which is in Jewish Socialist, Zionist and other organizations, is not touched. And it **is not.**

It is one thing to let Harry Lang and Eugene Lyons, Socialist Jews, attack Soviet Russia, another to attack Jewish Socialism.

Nothing appears in the Hearst papers reflecting on Jewry. Despite their full knowledge of the play and that Jewish Ernst Toller was a Revolutionary Communist to the day of his suicide, the Chicago Hearst paper for days built up opposition to the police ban on Toller's war-propaganda film against Germany, "Pastor Hall", giving the play a **full page puff spread** (9/15/40 Her.-Am.) until the ban was lifted.

Keith Brooks again outdoes his B'nai B'rith sources saying **"Associated Press** with 1,300 papers, not a single Jew. Intl. News Service owned by **Hearst".**

### Heart's Intl. News Service Headed by Jew

Moses Koenigsberg lists himself in Who's Who in Am. Jewry, 1938-9, as **pres. and gen. mgr. of Hearst's Intl. News Service,** pres. Universal Service, pres. Premier Syndicate, pres. Kay Features Inc., pres. King Features, pres. Cosmopolitan News Service.

## The Associated Press and Jewish Ochs

The late Adolph S. Ochs tells in Who's Who in Am. Jewry how he organized the Southern Associated Press and was director and member of the exec. com. of the Associated Press from 1901 on.

## Comparing Jewish Owned Papers with Hearst's

B'nai B'rith's "Jews in America" represents the daily circulation of four Jewish newspaper chains (Adolph Ochs, J. David Stern, Paul Block, E. P. Adler's Lee Syndicate) as **1,368,816** (1,614,491, Ed. & Publr. Yr. Book, 1940). They contrast this figure, as though it were all of the Jewish press influence, with "the 5,500,000 daily of Hearst who is not a Jew". (4,472,336, Ed. & Publr. Yr. Book, 1940).

No mention is made of such Jewish newspaper publishers as **Eugene Meyer** (former gov. Federal Reserve Bd., etc.), publisher of one of the largest Washington, D. C., papers, the Post, or **Moe Annenberg**, racing-service czar, now in prison. He was, until 1926, cir. dir. **in charge of all Hearst papers and magazines, and mem. Hearst exec. council**; now publisher of the Phila. Inquirer with a Sunday circulation of **1,021,666**; owner of the Daily Racing Form Pub. Co.; pres. of the Cecelia Co. which operates the Nationwide News Service, N.Y. Morning Telegraph, Miami Tribune, also Radio Guide, Screen Guide, Official Detective Stories, and other magazines; pres. Interstate Brokerage Co., private banking and insurance co.; principal stockholder of Am. Bank & Tr. Co., Chicago, etc. (Who's Who in Am. Jewry, 1938-9).

## Omits Host of Others

Nor is mention made of the host of lesser Jewish newspaper publishers and editors listed in Who's Who in American Jewry, such as:

**B. P. Alschuler,** dir. of the Aurora Beacon-News, and Elgin Courier-News (newspapers) and Joliet Pub. Co., and v.p. of the Copley Press, I. C. Copley, pres., publisher of the S. Calif. Associated Newspapers, a chain of **ten newspapers**; **Meyer Jacobstein,** who lists himself as publr. Rochester (N.Y.) Evening Journal and Sunday American since 1933; **Louis Benjamin,** publr. Erie (Pa.) Dispatch-Herald since 1925, pres. Erie Dispatch-Herald Broadcasting Corp.; **Irving Abraham Brody,** pres. and ed. of the N.J. Shield and political commentator over radio station WHOM, Jersey City, N.J.; **Michael Leopold Goodman,** publr. of the Scrantonian, Scranton. Pa., with a circulation of 40,222 and v.p. and dir. of the Scranton Nat. Bank; **Leon Lowengard,** publr. Harrisburg (Pa.) Courier since 1912; **Charles Homer Joseph,** asst. publr. Pittsburg Sunday Telegraph since 1933; **Howard Kahn,** St. Paul (Minn.) Daily News since 1919; **Abraham Bennett Kapplin,** mng. ed. Duluth (Minn.) News-Tribune since 1934; **Cosman Henry Eisendrath,** city ed. Biloxi (Miss.) Daily Herald; **Albert Y. Aronson,** mng. ed. Louisville (Ky.) Times since 1921; **Bernard Aaron Bergman,** an ed. Phila. Record since 1935; **Aaron Blum Bernd,** an ed. since 1922 Macon (Ga.) Telegraph; **Eugene Benjamin Block,** an ed. San Francisco Cali-Bulletin since 1925; **David Cramer,** publr. Litchfield Enquirer and Woodbury Reporter (Conn.); **David (Henry) Dietz,** an ed. Scripps-Howard newspaper chain since 1921 and mem. edtl. staff Cleveland Press since 1915; **Alexander Fried,** an ed. San Francisco Examiner since 1934; **Edwin Samson Friendly,** bus. mgr. **N.Y. Sun** since 1922; **Morris Edmund Speare,** dir. edtl. dept. Funk & Wagnalls Co., publrs.; **Myer Agen,** Paris agent, Bell Syndicate, Inc., newspaper features, since 1927; **Myron S. Blumenthal,** pres. Universal Trade Press Syndicate, intl. news agency for business and technical papers (mem. various Red organizations); **Stanley Howard Brams,** ed. Ward's Automotive Reports, Detroit mgr. Transradio Press Service, Inc.; **Wm. Feigenbaum,** who lists himself as a Socialist Party worker since 1902, and edtl. writer for the Brooklyn Standard Union, Brooklyn Times Union, Newark (N.J.) Ledger; etc., etc.

It is a commentary on former German conditions that

132

Julius Klein lists himself in Who's Who in Am. Jewry, 1938-9, as editor-in-chief of the Leicht Syndicate, publishing 42 consolidated German newspapers in U.S., 1930-33, and **"resigned as protest against Hitlerism"; news editor RKO-Radio Picture Corp. Am.** since 1936; mem. B'nai B'rith.

No Gentile who has not paged through Who's Who in Am. Jewry could imagine the magnitude of the strictly Jewish press or the legion of Jewish writers.

### Sidney Hillman's Editor

In addition, take the sketch Jacob Benjamin Salutsky Hardman gives of himself as "editor since 1925 of Advance, organ of the Amalgated Clothing Workers Union" (headed by the red Russian Jew, Sidney Hillman, of FDR's **National Defense Council!**). "Born Vilna, Russia. Was active on revolutionary councils of Social Democratic Labor Party in Vilna, Borisov, Homel and Kiev; was jailed, then exiled (1908) by Czarist Govt. Came to U.S. 1909. Mem. cent. exec. com., 1927-34, Conf. for Prog. Labor Action" (Abraham J. Muste's revolutionary group with which the Trotskyite Communist Party combined, and later the combination went into Norman Thomas' Socialist Party). Now "mem. Am. Labor Party" (Communist-Socialist).

And one could go on with: **Montefiore Moses Harris,** ed. San Antonio (Tex.) Express and San Antonio Evening News since 1918; **George Hechter,** pres. George Hechter Publications, Inc., publrs. Broadway News, Greenpoint Home News, Astoria Times, Woodside Herald, **The Leader,** N.Y.; **Abraham Hurwitz,** ed. Reading (Pa.) Times since 1924; **Louis Isaac Jaffe,** ed. Virginian-Pilot, Norfolk, Va., since 1919, and dir. Norfolk Newspapers, Inc. All are listed in Who's Who in American Jewry.

### McFadden Whoops It Up!

Bernarr McFadden is a Jew, according to Samuel Roth, a Jew, in his book "Jews Must Live" (p. 105).

No periodical prints more lurid, rabble-rousing, war-inspiring, dime-thrillers, pleasing to Jewry, against Hitler and

Germany, than "Liberty" weekly. Coupled with some Trotskyite and other "anti-Communist" articles, it parades its "Americanism", "democracy", sex-muck and "hate-Hitler" material, draped in the American flag with bands playing and the Liberty Bell ringing.

### Jewish Heatter Palpitates—For Jewry

Melodrama rings in the voice of Liberty's Jewish commentator, Gabriel Heatter, as he palpitates over England, **Jewry's** present tool. Only **German** bombs, according to him, strike little children. Heatter lists himself in "Who's Who in Am. Jewry, 1928" as former pres. of the Jewish Forum magazine.

McFadden lists himself as publisher of Liberty Weekly, Physical Culture, True Story, True Romance, Dream World, Love and Romance, True Detective Mysteries, Master Detective, Photoplay, Movie Mirror, and True Detective (magazines), and as pres. and chmn. bd. McFadden Pub., Inc. (Who's Who in America.)

### Hires Red Jewish Lawyer

In McFadden's dispute with Lucien Koch of Commonwealth College, McFadden employed the Jewish law firm of Hays, St. John, Abramson & Schulman, N.Y. The two red Jews, Arthur Garfield Hays (of the above firm) and Morris Ernst are the two national legal heads of the Communist-aiding American Civil Liberties Union, busy for years fighting stubbornly in Court in aid of every phase of the Red Revolutionary movement in the U.S.A.

### "Keyhole" Winchell Sleuths

Walter (Keyhole) Winchell, another ardent Jew, posing as a self-appointed F.B.I. agent, gloatingly loves to drag forth into the limelight as a "Nazi" any American who mentions the word "Jew" without swinging an altar censer of praise before it.

### In the Entertainment Limelight

Among American performers listed in Who's Who in Am. Jewry, 1938-9, are the following:

134

Stella Adler; Jack Benny (Kubelsky), mem. B'nai B'rith; Binnie Barnes (Gittel), English-born; George Burns (Birnbaum); Fanny Brice (Borach); Bobbie Breen; Artur Bodanzky, Austrian-born; Leo Braun, German-born; Benny Baker (Benj. Michael Zifkin); Chas. Chaplin (Thonstein); Eddie Cantor (B'nai B'rith booster); Sue Carol (Evelyn Lederer); June Clayworth (Cantor); Ricardo Cortez (Jacob Krantz), Austrian-born; Bette Davis; Parkyakarkus (Harry Einstein); Harry Green (Henry Blitzer); Benny Goodman; George Jessel; Al Jolson (Asa Yoelson), Russian-born; Bertha Rachel Kalich, Polish-born; Sergei Koussevitzky (Alexandrovitch), Russian-born; Ted Lewis (Theo. L. Friedman); Francis Lederer, Czecho-Slovakian-born; Noel Madison (Moscovitch), mem. B'nai B'rith; Marx Bros.; Kenneth MacKenna (Mielziner), divorced from Kay Francis; Fania Marinoff, Russian-born; Paul Muni (Weisenfreund), Polish-born; Eugene Ormondy, Hungarian-born; Irene Pavloska; Molly Picon (Mrs. Jacob Kalich); Harry Richman (Reichman); Edward G. Robinson, Rumanian-born; Luise Rainer, Austrian-born; Rosa Raisa (Burchstein), Polish-born; Gregory Ratoff, Russian-born; Dave Rubinoff, Russian-born; Lazare Saminsky, Russian-born; Ludwig Satz, Polish-born, Socialist, mem. B'nai B'rith; Ted Shapiro; Jos. Schildkraut, Austrian-born; David Warfield; Sophie Tucker (Abuza), Russian-born; Ed Wynn (Israel Edwin Leopold). Also Douglas Fairbanks (Ullman).

It is not by accident that Hollywood is a hot bed of radicalism!

## "ANTI-COMMUNIST" JEWISH WRITERS

"DISTINGUISHED AMERICAN JEWS WHO HELP TO FORMULATE PUBLIC OPINION . . . ARE ALL VIOLENTLY OPPOSED TO COMMUNISM", says B'nai B'rith (Article XXII, p. 1), and then proceeds to name some of these "brilliant writers", thus supplying Gentile echoes like Rembert G. Smith with parroting material (See p. 16).

Among B'nai B'rith's "anti-Communists", for example, is the staunch Communist Party "fellow traveler" George

Seldes. Let us take George's "pulse" to record how "violent" he is.

His endorsement of "The Soviet Union: Defender of Democracy and Peace" appears in the Soviet's magazine "Soviet Russia Today", 11/38.

He has long been a contributor of Red articles to the New Republic, classified by the N.Y. State Lusk Com. as an "advocate of revolutionary Socialism", by radical Benj. Stolberg as a "Stalinoid weekly".

When **demanding** an embargo on Nazi goods was part of the Communist Party "line", he was a **"demander"** (Communist Party's Daily Worker, 11/18/38). When fighting Germany and Italy as "aggressor" nations was part of the Party "line", he was one of the nat. com. of the "Am. Boycott Against Aggressor Nations" (7/7/39). After the "line" changed with the Nazi-Soviet pact (9/39), he was praised by the Communist Party's Daily Worker (2/3/40) for exposing the "war mongering" lies of the capitalist press!

When the farcical Moscow "trials" (Stalin's murder purges) had shocked all but the hardest of Communists, Seldes signed a statement **upholding** the trials (Daily Worker, 4/28/38), saying that the Moscow "trials have by sheer weight of evidence established a clear presumption of the guilt of the defendants" (Communist Party's Midwest Daily Record, 4/26/38).

He is head of the N.Y. branch and was elected a vice-pres. (Daily Worker, 6/6/39) of the Lg. of Am. Writers, organized, backed and controlled by the Communist Party whose "line" it follows to the letter. Seldes ardently endorsed its affiliation with the celebration of the Communist May Day (Daily Worker, 4/20/40), which he praised as "Peace Day".

To describe his activities for **Red Spain** would require a chapter. He has been on the jump: as backer of the rally for the Communist Party's Abraham Lincoln Brigade (Daily Worker, 6/22/37); sponsor of a dinner for Red Spain (New Masses, 9/28/37); speaking to raise funds for the communist N. Am. Com. to Aid Spanish Democracy,

136

along with Communist Ernst Toller (Daily Worker, 3/16/39) ; denouncing the French Govt. for ordering Spanish Reds to return to Spain (Daily Worker, 3/22/40) ; defending the communist Abraham Lincoln Brigade (Daily Worker, 3/11/40).

His books "Lords of the Press", "You Can't Print That", "Sawdust Caesar", are puffed by the Communist Party press and their loyal aide, the American Civil Liberties Union. Praising his book "Lords of the Press", the Daily Worker (11/25/38) said that Seldes **pays tribute to the Daily Worker** and to the organ of the **Communist unit** of the N.Y. Times, called the "New Times"; he has sent eulogies to other Communist papers.

His article condemning Donald Day's anti-Soviet Chgo. Tribune articles was printed in New Masses and reprinted in the Communist Party's "Record Weekly" (2/3/40, p. 11). He was one of those at the dedication of the Soviet Pavilion at the N.Y. World's Fair (Daily Worker, 6/30/39). He was one of those headlined in the Daily Worker, 5/13/40, as **blasting** the Dies Committee and demanding that it be **dissolved** and **investigated** by Atty. Gen. Robt. Jackson.

He was: scheduled lecturer for the pro-Communist sex-filth-purveying New School for Social Research starting Feb. 7 (Daily Worker, 1/31/39) ; also sponsor of the communistic Am. Com. for Prot. of Foreign Born (3/40), which fights for admission and retention of alien Reds of all nations in the U.S.A.; signer of the American Civil Liberties Union telegram to Gov. Lehman urging him to **repeal** the Devany Civil Service bill **barring Communist advocates of overthrow of the U.S. Govt.** from holding civil service positions (ACLU Bulletin, 5/27/39).

His article, "Hero Loyalist Vets Held for Deportation", calls for floods of protests to free these Reds, in the organ of the Communist Party's Intl. Labor Defense (11/38), the Russian section of this world-wide organization being "M.O.P.R." He outdid himself, we are told, as a speaker at the Communist Party's defense rally for its New Masses magazine (Daily Worker, 3/7/40) and was at the reception when a portrait of Communist John Reed was presented to New Masses (Daily Worker, 6/6/39).

He contributed (1937-8) to "Fight", magazine of Moscow's treasonable Am. Lg. Against War and Fascism, which Dies' publicity forced under cover. He was a speaker with Communist Party leaders at the convention of the "Intl. Workers Order", Communist fraternal insurance society (Daily Worker, 6/12/40). The Daily Worker, 5/29/40, announced his new weekly news letter "In Fact" and Mike Gold, in his Daily Worker column, recently, again mentioned it, giving Seldes' address.

If Seldes is "anti-Communist", Earl Browder is a member of the Dies Committee!

### Gilbert Seldes

Gilbert Seldes, another of B'nai B'rith's "violent" anti-Communists, is George's brother. Their father (says Jewish Communist Joseph Freeman in his "American Testament") was one of the organizers of the Anarchist-Communist colony at Stelton, N.J., named in honor of the Spanish Anarchist, Francisco Ferrer, whose unappreciative govt. executed him for treason. The communist Garland Fund donated to it and tales of conduct there make scandalous reading.

Gilbert was one of the scheduled "bright lights" of the Communist Party's Unity Campers' New Year Ball, in N.Y., after their lease on the 71st Infantry Armory for the ball was cancelled by the Colonel, who had to call a special drill in order legally to prevent the Communists from using the Armory (Daily Worker, 12/24/37). His Hearst articles "Communists in Russia Are Happy Radicals" (4/3/34, etc.) puffing Soviet Russia, are opposite to the truth about that dreary graveyard, and his "Is Communism a Religion" (6/10/32) is a glowing eulogy of the murderous Communist creed. He was long an editor of the New Republic, "Stalinoid" weekly.

### Emil Lengyel

Emil Lengyel (Hungarian-born), another of B'nai

B'rith's "violent" anti-Communist Jews, lists himself (Who's Who in Am. Jewry) as being a member of the "History Dept., Brooklyn (N.Y.) Polytechnic Inst. since 1935" and as member of the **Intl. Com. for Political Prisoners,** a communist-Garland-Fund-aided organization which fights for Reds all over the world!

His activities for Red Spain are chronicled in the Communist Party's Daily Worker of 2/7/38, 6/2/38, 11/12/38, 2/1/39, etc. In the Communist Party's Daily Worker appears his denunciation of Bertrand Russell's ousting and his petition that the N.Y. City College professorship be given this militant exponent of free love, immorality and Marxism (Daily Worker, 4/10/40). His assault on the Dies Committee for its anti-Communist activities and demand that it be **halted** is featured by the Daily Worker, 1/8/40.

He is one of the board of sponsors of the Am. Guild for German Cultural Freedom (headed by red Thos. Mann), whose release (6/28/39) pleaded for funds for exiles like the Communist Jew, Ernst Toller, saying "There are many like him. . . . We must help them!"

His misleading article "Germany's Fifth Column" (Nation, 10/14/39) wishfully represents Germany as full of "torrential" discontent and tells of his contact with underground Communist activities there at the outbreak of the 1939 war, claiming "The Communists found unexpected strength in the offer of **left-wing** Catholics to cooperate with them". Just how he managed to get inside Germany to do his Red snooping, if he did, is a mystery.

### Paul Block

Newspaper publisher Paul Block, another of B'nai B'rith's "violent" anti-Communists, is one of the Am. Hebrew Medal Committee which be-medaled the roaring radical Jewish Mayor LaGuardia and Pres. F.D.R., the most potent "fellow traveler" and "Angel" the Communist Party ever had, furthering the Marxist program 100%.

When it was proposed that someone of the Jewish faith be run for Gov. of N.Y. in 1928 when Gov. Smith ran for

President, Block in a signed editorial, instead, urged running F.D.R., saying "Leading Democrats . . . so far as the vote of the Jewish citizens of Greater N.Y. is concerned, believe that every man and woman voting for Gov. Smith will vote for Franklin Roosevelt who has so ably championed the Governor for a number of years" (N.Y. World, 9/28/28). Incidentally, to "look at the record" during those years when Al Smith was in his heyday of political favor, he was completely subservient to and surrounded by Jewish interests, with Belle Moscowitz, his right hand, Secy. of his Labor Bd., etc. He obediently served on the Reds' Russian "Famine Fund", 1922, and opposed the anti-Red N.Y. State Lusk laws which were repealed, etc. On F.D.R. fell Smith's Jewish mantel.

After Sacco and Vanzetti, the Anarchists for whom the Reds of the world rioted, were executed for murder, Harry Canter was arrested for picketing the threatened Gov. Fuller with an incendiary sign "Fuller, Murderer of Sacco and Vanzetti". Paul Block's signed editorial defending and appealing for Canter not only appeared in his own chain of papers but as paid advertisements in leading newspapers (6/3/29, N.Y. Times, Herald-Tribune, N.Y. World).

When part of the Communist Party program was the enactment of the Federal anti-lynching bill to give the Federal govt. power over all local police depts., according to the Daily Worker, 12/18/37, Block joined in backing the bill along with John L. Lewis, red Rabbi Stephen S. Wise, Virginius Dabney of the American Civil Liberties Union, Cyrus Adler, J. E. Spingarn (Jewish head of the communist-Garland-Fund-supported Nat. Assn. for Advancement of Colored People, aimed to radicalize Negroes), etc.

### Walter Lippmann

Walter Lippmann, another of B'nai B'rith's "violent" anti-Communists, is an old time Marxist as well as writer for the "carriage trade" conservatives. He organized the Socialist Club at Harvard; was secy. to America's first Socialist Mayor; was formerly assoc. editor of the revolutionary socialist New Republic; was one of the very core of Pres.

140

Wilson's radical Jewish group in power during the World War as secy. to Edward Mandel House preparing data for the Jewish-controlled Peace Conference. House in his book "Philip Dru, Administrator" laid out the plan of U.S.A. dictatorship under a Socialist hero, since followed by the New Deal. Lippmann was also secy. to Newton D. Baker, who called himself a "practical" Socialist working in the Democratic Party "to get things done".

The American Hebrew, which "be-medaled" Baker, F.D.R., La Guardia, etc., for their services to Jewry, praises Lippmann as a great American Jew (12/30/38).

Illuminating Lippmann's activities in the Wilson War Dept., is a letter cited in the N.Y. State Lusk Report on Revolutionary Radicalism (p. 1087) which was written to a radical by Anarchist-Communist Roger Baldwin of the American Civil Liberties Union, then working for Red "conscientious objectors", bemoaning that **"Lippmann and Frankfurter** are of course out of that particular job now (war office), and I have to depend entirely upon Keppel".

Possibly because of some of Lippmann's cracks at the New Deal, the Daily Worker, 6/2/38, asked: "Here's a question we have been wanting to ask for some time. Is it true that Columnist Walter Lippmann wrote a letter to Professor Felix Frankfurter back in 1933 requesting the professor to intercede for him to secure the position as private secretary to one Franklin Delano Roosevelt, president-elect of the U.S.?"

Along with the nation's leading Reds, Lippmann was one of the Am. Com. Opposed to Alien Registration (headed by Alvin Johnson of the red New School for Social Research) protecting Jews and radicals by opposing registration of aliens (N.Y. Times, 5/22/30). He was lecturer for the red New School for Social Research, 1936-7.

When Mayor Hague was endeavoring to keep Communists and Socialists from agitating trouble in Jersey City, the Communist Party's Daily Worker (12/21/37) announced that its communist Am. Lg. Against War and Fascism had organized a committee of 67 to defy and fight Hague, with Lippmann as member. The communist Am. Lg. Against War and Fascism organ ("Fight" 4/28) cited how Lippmann had defended the Soviets, writing "A Test of the News", "to show how colored, perverted and false were almost all the reports about the Soviets in the American press".

Lippmann closed his column praising the TVA, the Socialists' dream, saying, "TVA is by all odds the best vision of the New Deal" (Chgo. Daily News, 2/25/36).

Faithful to Jewry is his stand in his 6/4/40 column that "the successful resistance of the Allies is a vital interest of the whole American hemisphere", and his support of **conscription** (8/5/40) ; and faithful to the radicals is his anti-Japanese warmongering urge to the State Dept. (Common Sense, 3/39) and his haranguing the Dies Committee 1/11/-40) charging that "the procedure of the Dies committee is itself a violation of American morality: it is a pillory in which reputations are ruined, often without proof and always without the legal safeguards that protect the ordinary criminal", and that "the committee needs to be reformed", while he plays to the "carriage trade" conservatives in this same column by saying that of course the Dies committee "cannot be abolished". Lippmann's present dual role is well summed up in the following letter:

"To the Editor of The Inquirer: Dec. 11 Lippmann critizes the 'Civil Liberties Union' for the pro-leftist lopsidedness of its activities. Dec. 20 Lippmann publishes letter from three C.L.U. members citing six gestures in defense of non-radicals as proof of the union's 'nonpartisan disinterestedness,' and Walter is 'much reassured.' The next day Lippmann joins the C.L.U. in demanding that Jersey City be made safe for C.I.O.-ism. What a build-up! I cannot help wondering if Walter and Comrades Ward, Baldwin and Hays 'planned it that way?'" (Phila. Inquirer, 12/29/37).

## JEWRY'S PROTEGE, "DOTTIE" THOMPSON

Literary "soulmate" of Lippmann's, in the chameleon-conservative-radical technique of public befuddlement, is

"Dottie" Thompson, Jewry's protege, limelighted from the unknown after publicity gleaned by getting herself ousted from Germany. She knew, she wrote in 1932, when she saw Hitler that he would never gain power in Germany. To quote the Jewish Sentinel (8/29/40, p. 15): "Dorothy Thompson became a newspaper woman **thanks to American Zionists.** On the way to Europe many years ago she ran into Felix Frankfurter and other Zionist leaders who filled her full of information on Zionist ideals, history and politics. When she got to London she sold the International News Service on letting her cover the Zionist Congress. Once she borrowed $500 from the late Sigmund Freud to finance a quick trip to Warsaw to cover Pilsudski's coup d'etat".

### And So They "Made Her What She Is Today"

How they push their Dottie! They gave her the Jewish Gottheil Medal for services to Jewry (Am. Hebrew, 4/7/-39). B'nai B'rith magazine (July-Aug. 1940 issue) featured her picture on the front cover. The American Hebrew magazine (1/13/39) includes her name on its front cover list "WHO'S WHO AMONG AMERICAN JEWS AND CHRISTIANS **NOTABLE IN MUTUAL ENDEAVOR** DURING THE YEAR 1938", along with the names of Jewry's faithful old Gentile Red-front, Wm. Allen White, communistic Einstein, Felix Frankfurter, Max Lerner (former nat. organizer of the Communist Party), and radicals of every hue.

### Aiding Jewish Murderer

The American Hebrew specifically extols her for her 1938 money-raising to defend Herschel Grynzpan, the young Jew who picked himself a German Embassy secretary in Paris to murder, in order to express Jewish feelings about "anti-Semitism".

After Dottie went out to get herself more publicity heckling a German-American Bund meeting until they had to usher her out, her radical, Soviet-praising, atheistic (second) husband, Sinclair Lewis, said "I am extremely proud of my wife, Dorothy Thompson, for having denounced the speaker. . . . Jews and liberals are among our most noble and valuable American citizens" (Communist Party's Daily Record, 2/22/39). She was divorced from her first husband, a Hungarian, Josef Bard.

### She Echoes For Them

While gnashing at Hitler and upholding radical "Refu-jews" are Dorothy's star specialty, she also gets around to support leading Red causes. When the Communists were organizing "Save Czechoslovakia" meetings from coast to coast, she was the principal speaker for the red "Save Czechoslovakia" mass meeting at Madison Sq. Garden, chairmaned by the nat. chmn. of the Communists' Am. Lg. for Peace and Democracy (Daily Worker, 9/24/38).

When the Communist and Jewish forces were whooping up aid for Red Spain, she valiantly "whooped", signing Red pamphlets and appeals, etc., from 1937 on, her activities in this line being chronicled in the Communist Daily Record 9/6/39, Daily Worker 4/8/38, etc.

When Communists and Jews unitedly were roaring for a U.S. embargo against all Nazi goods, she loaned her "cult-chah-d" accents (developed since Chicago high school days) as "speakah" for a big red Madison Sq. Garden embargo rally of 20,000, the chief speaker being William Weiner, the Russian Jewish financial secy. of the Communist Party (now parked in jail). Lesser fellow speakers were the pro-Soviet H. V. Kaltenborn and the red Jewish authoress, Dorothy Parker (Rothschild), to whom "Keyhole" Winchell throws "orchids" in his column when he is not chasing anti-Reds as "Nazis" and distributing Communist John L. Spivak's libelous writing to Congress. (Chgo. Daily News, 11/18/38).

When the Reds and Jews were denouncing the Munich pact, her denunciation of the Munich pact was praised in the Communists' "Soviet Russia Today" (11/38). Her book "Anarchy or Organization", was recommended by Chas. Recht (legal representative of the Soviet Govt. in the U.S.) in the communist "New Masses", 9/27/38.

144

Along with the bright Reds, Einstein, John Dewey, Heywood Broun, Lillian Wald, Mary Woolley, she was on the nat. advis. council of the Women's Intl. Lg. for Peace and Freedom (long communist-Garland-Fund-supported), when it was a section of the Comintern's Am. Lg. Against War and Fascism, later called Am. Lg. for Peace and Democracy, which had to go under cover recently as a result of Dies Com. publicity.

## Silencing Father Coughlin

Backed by the Communist Party and its American Lg. for Peace and Democracy, she was speaker for a rally of 15,000 (3/7/39) to protest the anti-Communist activities of Rev. Gerald Smith and Father Coughlin. Her speech was broadcast and later rebroadcast (Civil Rights News, 3/39, 4/39, Communist Party's Sunday Worker, 3/12/39).

Naturally, she urged the Federal Communications Commission to investigate and silence Father Coughlin's radio talks as some of his facts reflect on atheistic and radical Jews, and he **has** been silenced, as B'nai B'rith promised. The president of the Nat. Assn. of Broadcasters announced that "arousing racial bigotry is 'not to be tolerated' " (N.Y. Her.-Trib., 12/22/38), meaning that anything distasteful to Jewry was not to be tolerated.

Other of her many radical activities include being: lecturer for the red New School for Social Research, 1936-7; fellow speaker with the bloody Communist Ernst Toller (later a suicide), and sponsor of the red American Guild for German Cultural Freedom soliciting funds to aid others like him (1939); a member of the Communist-controlled (C.I.O.) Am. Newspaper Guild (Chgo. Daily Times, 11/25/38). She presented a "Golden Book of Remembrance" to the Red author, Thos. Mann, at a banquet in his honor (N. Y. Her.-Trib., 5/10/38) and wrote an article eulogizing him.

She upheld Secy. Perkins in her refusal to deport the alien Jewish Communist Harry Bridges (12/2/38 column).

## Dies Committee

One can see why, with personal cause, she fearfully said

"The Dies Com. might easily develop into . . . our own little Gestapo" (Am. Hebrew, 3/22/40). The Am. Hebrew added that "The Jewish members of Congress are unenthusiastic about the Dies Com. because they realize . . . the committee has **fostered** class and racial prejudice" (By exposing Red activities! What an admission!).

Following the Nazi-Soviet pact, she hewed to the strictly Jewish side, and after Finland was invaded by Russia, spoke at a "Help Finland" meeting (Daily Worker, 12/21/39).

To quote Time, 6/12/39: "Her chief advisor on economic problems is Alexander Sachs who works for the Lehman Corp." (He lists himself in Who's Who in Am. Jewry as Russian-born, dir. of research and v.p. of Lehman Corp. since 1936).

### The Kuhn Loebs Like Her

To quote, "Her present companions consist largely of intellectual Jews, refugees and otherwise, who assist her in writing her columns, among whom is **Lewis Strauss** of Kuhn Loeb & Co. A story carried in Town and Country magazine last year of a tete-a-tete Thompson-Strauss luncheon in Biarritz, France, stands as a classic of society reporting" (Curtiss' Weekly Am. Bulletin, 3/19/40). She was speaker for the United Jewish Appeal for Refugees and Overseas Need with Mrs. Felix M. Warburg (widow of late Kuhn Loeb & Co. partner) as hon. chairman (N.Y. Her.-Trib., 4/7/39).

### Dosing Americans

A German-American paper called her taking from "Mein Kampf", Hitler's description of mistreatment dealt Germany under the Versailles Treaty and misrepresenting it as Hitler's own program, a "swindle", easily verified by reading Chapter 15 of "Mein Kampf".

### The War Mongering "D.T.'s"

She was called a "pro-war pundit" by Gen. Johnson (Chgo. Her.-Am., 10/20/39). To quote another writer:

"Another amusing thing about D.T. is her lack of originality. She is the only columnist on the American scene today who dares to make wholesale use of the adjectives and catchwords that got us into the last war, in her frantic efforts to get us into this one.

"The British and French Empires, she writes, are fighting on the side of 'Western civilization, Christianity and democracy'. Hitler is a 'beast, barbarian and butcher'. The tyrants of London are 'good'; the tyrants of Berlin are 'bad'. The 400 million people of Europe will be 'enslaved' if Hitler wins the war. The 400 million enslaved people of British India are not mentioned.

"Of course something that is not funny, in fact something that is very unfunny, is that Miss Thompson's rantings are leading the United States directly toward involvement in the present European bloodfest with the consequent slaughter of two million of our best young men.

"And, most important, neither she nor her ten-year-old son will be called upon to die in the front-line trenches when her crusade finally materializes." (Styles Thomason, 3/19/40.)

### Pearl Buck Likes Dottie

Dorothy Thompson received the "achievement award" (Chgo. Daily News, 11/15/38) the American Women's Assn. previously awarded to the radical "birth-controller" Margaret Sanger, Socialist Francis Perkins, etc., the award jury including the radical Jewish writer Fannie Hurst (see elsewhere), Margaret Bourke-White (photographer for Communist periodicals), and Pearl Buck (Sydenstricker), whose paid position as a "missionary" for Christianity, which she frankly admitted she disbelieved, caused a row resulting in her severance from the missionary payroll. Her divorce, remarriage and open contributions to the Red press followed.

"Pearl Buck after spending twenty years as a Christian missionary to the heathen Chinese, confesses blushingly to being a Galician Jewess", says Jewish Samuel Roth, in his "Jews Must Live", p. 103.

## Jewry Molds American Opinion—"F.P.A.", Fadiman, etc.

According to American Hebrew of 6/18/37, "The proper legal name of Sinclair Lewis, husband of Dorothy Thompson, is Sinclair **Levy**".

Molding public opinion, occupying the public spotlight in radio, press and screen features, are a host of Jewish radicals like **Clifton R. Fadiman,** author of "How I Came to Communism" in communist New Masses (9/32, p. 7), backer of Spanish Reds, 1939, eulogist of the revolutionary socialist Nation (1/20/40), listed in the Communist Party's Daily Worker, 2/5/40, as a participant with the nation's leading Reds in a Broun Memorial Meeting.

"F.P.A.", Franklin P. Adams (son of Moses), who served on a Socialist Party campaign committee, 1929, supported the Spanish Reds, 1939, praised the revolutionary socialist Nation (1/20/40) as follows:

> "I prefer to express in versification
> My candid notion of The Nation:
> Some people idolize, some abhor it;
> In a word, I am all for it."

Adams and Fadiman are listed in Who's Who in American Jewry.

## JEWS IN BANKING

B'nai B'rith-Fortune "research" and its stooges represent (See p. 11) the power of Kuhn Loeb & Co., "the highest Jewish concern", as 2.88%, in contrast with J. P. Morgan's 19.87% and the "Gentile" (Jewish) Dillon, Read & Co.'s 11.44%. They say there are "no Jews at all" in the largest N.Y. banks, that few directors in the N.Y. Clearing house are Jews and only 18% of the N.Y. Stock Exchange members are Jews.

### Dillon (Lapowski) the "Gentile"

Keith Brooks "improved" on his B'nai B'rith source (p. 6, "Anti-Semitism in the U.S.? by Russell W. Davenport, mng. ed. of Fortune", distributed free by B'nai B'rith) when he copied from the following: "Kuhn Loeb & Co., Speyer

148

& Co., J. & W. Seligman & Co., Ladenburg, Thalmann & Co. and Lehman Bros. are the best known though they do not compare in power with the great houses owned by non-Jews".

Brooks saw, in this source following the above last word, "non-Jews", these weasel-words: "Dillon of Dillon, Read & Co., **is considered a Jew** by other Jews, but he is not, as his name suggests, an **active** member of his race".

## Silly Talk

When is a Negro, Jew or Oriental an "active" or inactive member of his **race?** When he is running or sitting still? When he changes his name? Clarence Dillon lists himself as a Jew in "Who's Who in Am. Jewry, 1938-9" and as pres. of Dillon, Read & Co. since 1921; also as one of the Baruch-Frankfurter Jewish group in power during the World War as asst. to chmn. Barney Baruch on the War Industries Board.

To quote "In Fact" (8/12), issued by Jewish George Seldes:

" 'Clarence Dillon, head of Dillon Read, was born Clarence **Lapowski,** son of a poor storekeeper, Sam Lapowski, in Victoria, Texas. . . . Dillon got $100,000,000 to reorganize Goodyear, outbid Morgan for control of Dodge Bros., wrote the famous $146,000,000 check, became head of Dillon Read.

" 'Biggest loans to German firms: $70,000,000 Vereignegte Stahlwerke; $48,000,000 Siemens u. Halske; $25,000,-000 Rheinelbe Union; $15,000,000 Gelsenkirchen . . .

" 'One of the biggest swindles in Italian history was the theft of $30,000,000 by Belloni, podesta, or vice-dictator, of Milan . . . the stench was so strong the Duce had to send Belloni to the penal islands. This $30,000,000 was the proceeds of the Milan 7's floated in America by Dillon, Read & Co.' " (Quoted in the Arbitator, 9/40.)

## Power of Dillon Read

To quote another comment: "Just what are we to think about the appointment of Mr. James Forrestal as one of . . .

149

the $10,000-a-year assistants of Mr. Roosevelt? . . . Until his appointment to the White House secretariat, he was head of Dillon, Read and Company, Wall Street banking firm **whose influence is surpassed only by that of Morgan and Kuhn, Loeb"** (New Republic, 7/8/40).

### Dillon, Read Maneuvers Aired

In connection with James V. Forrestal's strange move from acting as head of **Dillon, Read & Co.** to being **Secy. to Pres. Roosevelt,** Senator Holt dragged out the 1933 Senate investigation of Dillon Read & Co's smelly practices (Congressional Record, 7/11/40, pp. 14360-1), saying that, despite F.D.R.'s public denunciation of tax evasions through holding companies, **"This** is the man whom the President has appointed to be his secretary".  He proceeded to quote the following:

" 'A Dillon Read & Co. member told Senate investigators how he paid no income tax in 1929 on a stock profit of $864,000 by means of setting up a personal company in Canada.  James V. Forrestal the banker testified between puffs on a pipe that the tax would have been far in excess of $95,000 if he had made the sales direct' ".

A long report on various Dillon, Read deals follows, and then, " 'Paul M. Streiffler an employee of Dillon, Read & Co. is pres. of both the Delaware and Canadian Companies, **the** witness said, and John Vincent, a personal friend, is vicepres. and secy. . . .' " (Forrestal's son Frank Vincent is v.p. of the Commercial Nat. Bank & Tr. Co., N.Y.)

" 'Into a tale of pyramiding profits to Dillon, Read & Co. from Brazilian and Bolivian bonds, Pecora yesterday interjected a charge of pegging prices by market operations and **concealment of impending defaults.**

### Leading Suckers On To Ruin?

" 'Evidence to show payment of **interest** on some of the Brazilian securities was made by Dillon Read from a special fund created **from the bonds,** instead of a remittance from Brazil, and that bond holders were not apprised of whence the money came, was put before the market inquisitors. During the day's hearing he developed that the New York banking house'" (Dillon, Read & Co.) "'and associated bankers realized approximately $6,000,000 in profits from handling about $130,000,000 in bonds of the two South American republics virtually **all of which now are in default.'"**

## Is Kuhn Loeb a 2.88% Power?

What are the facts? Take a friendly New Deal source (U.S. Govt. National Resources Com., June, 1939, report, entitled "Structure of the American Economy, Part 1", issued by the Govt. Printing Office, Wash., D.C., price $1.00).

It takes up the power of "eight principal interests groups and their assets". (1) J. P. Morgan, First Nat. Bank, (2) Kuhn Loeb, (3) Rockefeller, (4) Mellon, (5) duPont, (6) Chicago, (7) Cleveland, (8) Boston.

It rates Kuhn Loeb second in importance and **first** in railroad power. To quote (p. 162): "The **second** interest group **in importance** has been named the Kuhn Loeb group and consists primarily of railroads whose financing has for many years been handled by Kuhn-Loeb & Co. It includes **13** major railroads or railroad systems . . . Western Union Telegraph Co. and one bank".

Interests in the U.S.A. controlled by **Kuhn Loeb & Co.** are listed at **10** billion, 843 millions of dollars; by Rockefeller interests, **6** billion, 613 millions; by eleven Chicago companies, 4 billion, 266 million; by Mellon, 3 billion, 332 millions; by the duPont family, 2 billion, 628 million; by seven Cleveland companies, four of which are underwritten by **Kuhn Loeb & Co.**, 1 billion, 404 million; by seven Boston companies (including the United Fruit Co. of which Sam Zemurray, a Jew, is mng. dir. and a footnote, p. **317,** states "Zemurray retains the old directorate unchanged"), **1** billion, 719 million. In all these City groupings of companies, Jews exert influence.

## The Kuhn Leob Method of Control

(Pp. 306-7): "**Control** is the central issue around which the study must turn . . . some individuals are perfectly will-

ing to act as directors in a purely ornamental capacity. . . .
For example it was the general policy of Kuhn Loeb & Co.
under the leadership of Jacob Schiff to eschew formal representation on the boards of its clients . . . he preferred that
his firm should not be so represented. He felt that by personal conference and advice he could do as much as through
formal representation. When relations are of the kind preferred by Schiff, they can only be recognized and evaluated
by knowledge of the history of the companies involved".

To quote (p. 311) : "In financing, reorganizing, rehabilitat-
ing and advising railroads, Kuhn Loeb & Co. has since the
1890's been the peer of J. P. Morgan & Co. As previously
noted, it has never been the policy of Kuhn Loeb to main-
tain more than a few of its contacts by means of director-
ship but the reality of the community of interest between
the firm and its clients is certainly not open to question on
that account. The peculiarly intimate connection which
exists between a railroad and its banker is very clearly set
forth and vigorously defended in a statement prepared by
Kuhn Loeb & Co. for the Interstate Commerce Commn. in
1922. . . . Only those contacts which have been very close
and of long duration have been admitted as evidence of
membership in the Kuhn Loeb interest group".

### Between Kuhn Loeb and Cleveland

To continue the analyses (p. 315) : "Between Mellon
and Kuhn Loeb.—Westinghouse Electric & Manufacturing,
certainly under Mellon influence and probably under Mellon control, has had long and close relations with Kuhn,
Loeb. The late Jerome Hanauer, former Kuhn, Loeb partner, was a director of Westinghouse until his death. Between Kuhn, Loeb and Du Pont.—One of the few large companies in which Kuhn, Loeb partners hold directorships is
United States Rubber, and in this case two Kuhn, Loeb
partners are directors. United States Rubber is controlled
by minority ownership by the Du Ponts".

### du Pont "Anti-Communism" Tempered by Jewish Blood?

Informed persons have wondered why, with unlimited

resources, the du Ponts' ineffective American Liberty League, neither in 1936 nor since, has unearthed any biting facts on radicalism, has done nothing real to stem the Red tide it ostensibly was set up to fight, why it was kept under the direction of Jouett Shouse, married to Catherine Filene, daughter of the Boston Jewish radical. The business hook-up with Kuhn Loeb & Co. might induce the somnolence of the presumably "anti-Red" du Pont family. Also, Pierre, Lammot and Irenee du Pont are sons of **Mary Belin** and Lammot du Pont, and, to quote: "When Lammot in Oct., 1865, married Mary Belin, daughter of Henry H. Belin, bookkeeper at the mills, there were those who expected the walls to fall. For Mary Belin was one quarter Jewish" ("The duPont Dynasty", by John H. Winkler, p. 120).

### Morgan Jewish Alliances

The Morgan-First National interests are listed as controlling assets of 30 billion, 210 million dollars (p. 317 of above Government report). "The House of Morgan" by Lewis Corey (1930) details the Jewish financial alliances of Morgan & Company with Kuhn Loeb & Company, the Guggenheims, Rothschilds, etc. To quote (p. 199): "In its reorganizations the House of Morgan was helped by its international financial affiliations (particularly the Rothschilds, now a Morgan ally), since considerable blocks of American railroad securities were owned in Europe."

To quote from the chapter "Government Financing" (p. 125): "The Morgan Rothschild syndicate secured an issue of $30,000,000 4½ per cent bonds . . . an issue of $25,000,000 4 per cent bonds was sold in London by the Rothschild-Morgan syndicate in order to prevent the shipment of gold from this country to Europe."

(Page 328): "During the war with Russia, Japanese loans aggregating 130 million dollars were floated in the United States by Kuhn-Loeb syndicates in which Morgan's Bank of Commerce participated. . . . In 1905 the House of Morgan intervened in the Chinese situation by acquiring control of the American China Development Company."

In view of Morgan's Jewish alliances at home and abroad, it is not strange that we read of his powerful position in and tremendous loans to England, where he even now keeps two homes.

## No Power in Banking?

The following are a few of the Jewish bankers found in Who's Who in American Jewry, 1938-9, who have power in U.S.A. banking and industry:

FRANK ALTSCHUL: mem. nat. Republican Program Com.; chmn. bd. dir. intl. banking firm of Lazard Freres Co.; pres. Gen. Am. Investors Corp.; dir. Commercial Investment Trust.

HAROLD L. BACHE: partner of J. S. Bache Co., bankers; Gov. of N.Y. Coffee Exchange, Inc.; Gov. Commodity Exchange, N.Y.; Gov. Produce Exchange.

JULES SEMON BACHE: now yelling for war; head of intl. banking firm of J. S. Bache Co.; his granddaughter married to Gen. Pershing's son; has other great interests in autos, transportation, etc.

PAUL BAERWALD: Jewish "communal" leader; German-born; treas., Am. Soc. for Jewish Farm Settlements in Russia; succeeded Felix M. Warburg as chmn. Joint Distribution Com., 1932 (active in Russia); partner Lazard Freres, intl. bankers, since 1907; dir. Gen. Am. Invest. Corp.

EDGAR SIGMUND BARUC: mgr. foreign dept., Goldman Sachs & Co., bankers, since 1933; partner Wertheim Co., bankers, 1930-2.

EDGAR H. BAUMAN: commercial banker; org. and pres., Madison Industrial Corp.

JACOB BLAUSTEIN: banker and oil magnate; dir. Union Trust Co. of Md., U.S. Fidelity & Guaranty Co.; dir. of Jewish Telegraph Agency.

SAMUEL MATTHEW BOMZON: v.p., Nat. Safety Bank since 1929.

BENJ. J. BUTTENWEISER: partner **Kuhn Loeb & Co.**; on faculty of red New School for Social Research since

154

1934; numerous Jewish org.; wife is daughter of Arthur Lehman, brother of **Gov. Herbert Lehman**.

WM. B. CARDOZO: dir. and sr. v.p., City Bank Farmers Trust Co.; v.p., Wyoming Land & Realty Co.; dir., Rogers Peet Co.

SAUL COHN: "engaged in banking business since 1929"; mem. B'nai B'rith; "Pres. City Stores Co., operating dept. stores in Phila., New Orleans, Memphis, Birmingham, Louisville, Miami".

CLARENCE DILLON (Lapowski): pres., Dillon Read & Co., bankers, N.Y.

VICTOR EMANUEL: partner Emanuel & Co., bankers, N.Y.; public utilities executive and aviation czar.

MAX EPSTEIN: chmn. indust. loans dept. of Chicago **Federal Reserve Bank**; dir. of **Chicago Daily News,** published by FDR's warmongering "Republican", Frank Knox; see under Industry.

MAURICE FALK: dir., Farmers Deposit Natl. Bank, Farmers Deposit Trust Co., Pitts.; see under Industry.

HAROLD E. FOREMAN: exec. v.p. Am. Nat. Bank & Trust Co., Chicago, of which Moe Annenberg is principal stockholder.

S. H. GOLDEN: Russian-born; commercial banker since 1907; pres. Golden Co., Inc.; on radical Mayor LaGuardia's com. for "relief" of home owners; mem. Alliance Israelite Universelle, the radical intl. org. to which B'nai B'rith is affiliated; pres., Textile firm of S. H. Golden.

MENDEL GOTTESMAN: Hungarian-born; pres., Credit Utility Banking Corp., N.Y.C.

J. J. HANAUER: partner Kuhn Loeb & Co. until recent retirement; dir. of Westinghouse Electric, of various railroads of U.S.A. and Mexico, of great coal, oil companies, etc.

RUDOLPH HECHT: German-born; pres. since 1918 Hibernia Nat. Bank, New Orleans; dir., **Federal Reserve Bank**, New O.; pres., New O. Clearing House Assn.; past pres. Am. Bankers Assn.; dir. Miss. Shipping Co., New O. Pub. Service Co., etc.; pres. Bd. of Port Commnrs., New O. since 1921.

ADOLPH HELD: Polish-born; v. p. Amalgamated Bank, N.Y.; pres. Socialist "Forward Assn.", which issues Yiddish Socialist Daily Forward; chmn. bd. dir. Socialist radio station WEVD (named for Eugene V. Debs); mem. Workmen's Circle; etc.

WALTER E. HELLER: pres. since 1919 Walter E. Heller Commercial banking firm, Chicago.

ISAIAS WARREN HELLMAN: dir. Farmers & Merchants Nat. Bank, Los A.; v.p. Wells Fargo Bank & Trust Co., San F.

JOHN D. HERTZ: born Czechoslovakia; partner Lehman Bros., bankers, since 1934; v.p. Lehman Corp; transportation magnate, with power also in oil, movies; mem. exec. com. Paramount Pictures; dir. Hialeah race track, Madison Sq. Garden Corp., etc.

DAVID MELVILLE HEYMAN: formerly with Kuhn Loeb & Co.; partner banking firm Adolph Lewisohn & Sons since 1933; committeeman Am. Jewish Com.

SIDNEY HILLMAN: Russian-born Red; chmn. bd. Amalgamated Bank, N.Y.C.; mem. Workmen's Circle, etc., etc.; on FDR's Nat. Defense Council.

MAX L. HOLTZ: pres. Columbia Banking Assn.; pres. Monroe Co. Lg. of Savings & Loan Assns., Rochester, N.Y.

HENRY R. ICKLEHEIMER: partner Heidelbach, Ickleheimer & Co., private bankers; dir. Fifth Ave. Bank; dir. Commercial Nat. Bk. & Tr. Co.; dir. S. H. Kress & Co. chain stores.

GILBERT WOLFF KAHN: partner Kuhn Loeb & Co., bankers.

DAVID KASS: pres., Empire State Mercantile Co.; pres. Overland Trading Co.; secy. and dir. Park Ave. Improvement Co., Fifth Ave. and 30th St. Corp.; dir. Trade Bank of N.Y.; dir. Astor Financial Corp; active in United Jewish Campaign.

ROBERT LEE KEMPNER: pres. U.S. Nat. Co.; v.p. U. S. Nat. Bank; pres. Texas Prudential Ins. Co.; pres. Imperial Sugar Co.; "active in drives for Am. Jewish Com. and Jt. Distribution Com." (active in Russia).

SIGMUND KLEE: banker, pres. Klee Corp. of N.Y.C.

ARTHUR S. KLEEMAN: investment banker; pres. Arthur S. Kleeman Co., Ltd.; pres. Home & Foreign Securities Corp., and Oils & Industries, Inc.; chmn. bd. Colonial Trust Co., N.Y.; dir. Morris Plan Industrial Bank; dir. Kirby Petroleum Co., Houston, Texas.

HENRY H. KOHN: German-born; pres. Morris Plan Ins. Soc.; dir. Industrial Finance Corp.; dir. Industrial Acceptance Corp.; dir. Morris Plan Bank in several New England cities.

PHILIP LEHMAN: since 1887 partner Lehman Bros., bankers; chmn. bd. of dir's. Lehman Corp.; dir. F. W. Woolworth Co.

HERBERT H. LEHMAN: partner Lehman Bros., bankers, from 1908-32 when he was elected Gov. of N.Y.; married Edith Altschul, sister of Frank Altschul (see); was dir. Abraham & Straus, County Tr. Co. of N.Y., Studebaker Corp., Jewel Tea Co., Van Raalte Co., Kelsey-Hayes Wheel Corp., Pierce Oil Corp., Spear & Co., Franklin Simon & Co. Robt. Reis & Co., Gen. Am. Investors Inc., the Knott Hotels, Fidelity Tr. Co.; is and has been v.p. Jewish Joint Distribution Com. (active in Russia); v.p. Palestine Econom. Corp.; trustee Henry St. Settlement (red Lillian Wald's); dir. of communist-Garland-Fund-financed Natl. Assn. for the Advancement of Colored People.

JACOB LEICHTMAN: Polish-born; pres. since 1924 Modern Indust. Bank; treas. radical Zionist American Jewish Congress since 1925; v.p. Fed. Polish Jews since 1932; dir. Keren Hayesod (fund for buying cooperative Palestine land).

JEROME LEWINE, SR.: member H. Hentz & Co.; dir. Ryan Consolidated Petroleum Corp.; org., first pres., Commodity Exchange, Inc.; org., past pres., Nat. Raw Silk Exchange; Gov., N.Y. Cotton Exchange; Gov., N.Y. Coffee and Sugar Exchange; Gov., Assn. of Stock Exchange Firms.

WALTER LICHTENSTEIN: v.p. since 1933 First Nat. Bank, Chgo.; secy. advis. coun. Federal Reserve System since 1926.

CARL M. LOEB: German-born; sr. partner Carl M. Loeb & Co., intl. bankers and brokers, since 1931; connected with War Dept. under Pres. Wilson.

HOWARD ADLER LOEB: pres., later chmn., Tradesmen Nat. Bank & Tr. Co.

M. J. MANDELBAUM: partner Mandelbaum & Wolf Co.; dir. Cleveland Trust Co., etc.

JACOB MARKEL: Russian-born; org. and pres., Merchants Bank, N.Y.; mem. Mizrachi Org. of Am., Soc. for Advancement Judaism; etc.

OTTO MARX: org., Otto Marx & Co., banking and bonds; dir., Lord & Taylor (a "Gentile" concern); dir. Electric Boat Co.; dir. James M. McCreery Co.; dir. Southern Investors Corp.; dir. Am. Writing Paper Co.; dir. Asso'd. Dry Goods Corp.; dir. Hahne Co.; dir. U.S. Realty Co.

DEWITT MILLHAUSER: partner, Speyer & Co., investment bankers; dir. Radio Corp. of America; Mexican-American Steamship Co.; mem., N.Y. Stock Exchange and Intl. Com. of Bankers of Mexico.

ARTHUR J. MORRIS: established Morris Plan banks, Fidelity Savings & Tr. Co.; pres., Industrial Finance Corp.; pres., Industrial Acceptance Corp.; pres., Morris Plan Industrial Bank, N.Y.C.

GEO. WASH. NAUMBURG: mem. firm E. Naumburg Co., 1899-1932; was on Baruch's War Industries Bd. under Pres. Wilson; married d. Henry Morgenthau; dir. Refugee Econ. Corp.; chmn. exec. com. Parents' Magazine since 1930; banking & currency com., N.Y. Merchants' Assn. since 1928.

JACOB KIEFER NEWMAN: pres. Newman Saunders

Co., bankers; pres. City Utilities Co.; pres. Investment Asso's., Inc.; dir. St. Louis Public Service Co.; dir. Nat. Power & Light Co.

C. Y. PALITZ: Russian-born; pres. Credit Alliance Corp.; pres. First New Amsterdam Corp.; v.p. Commercial Credit Corp.; pres. of a B'nai B'rith lodge; mem. Bankers' Club; past chmn. Young Judea; trustee Palestine Endow. Fund, etc.

EUGENE HUGO PAUL: gen. secy. Kuhn Loeb & Co.; pres. Wilpin Corp.; pres. Mogmar Realty, Inc.; pres. Bedapawa Co., etc.

HARDWIG PERES: Memphis, Tenn.; mem. firm Jacob J. Peres Co.; dir. First Nat. Bank; mem. B'nai B'rith, Zionist Org. of America.

CARL HOWARD PFORZHEIMER: org. firm of Carl H. Pforzheimer & Co., specialists in oil securities; pres. Petroleum & Trading Corp.; treas. Purchase Community, Inc.

GEORGE PICK: pres., investment banking firm Geo. Pick & Co., Chgo.; dir. Am. Radiator Co.; dir. Gen. Am. Investors Co.; dir. Gen. Realty & Utility Corp., etc.

JOS. PULVERMACHER: pres. Sterling Nat. Bank & Tr. Co.; dir. Noma Electric Corp.; dir. Jewish Conciliation Court; mem. Soc. of Tammany; com. 42nd St. Bd. Trade; etc.

HAROLD CHAS. RICHARD: dir. Mfrs. Trust Co.; dir. Gen. Bronze Corp., Madison Sq. Garden Corp., etc.

CHAS. RICHTER: chmn. bd. dir. Nat. Safety Bank & Trust Co.

L. N. ROSENBAUM: Hungarian-born; pres. Newman Corp. of Wash.; partner L. N. Rosenbaum & Son, private financing company; exec. v.p. Donahoes, Inc., 31 chain grocery stores; etc.

LOUIS F. ROTHSCHILD: mem. banking firm L. F. Rothschild & Co.; dir. Worthington Pump & Machinery Corp., one of the largest firms in the heavy industry; dir. New River Collieries Co. (coal mines).

MELVILLE NELSON ROTHSCHILD: pres. Nat. Trust & Credit Co.; Nat. Bond & Invest. Co.; mother, Gusta Morris; began with Nelson Morris & Co., **Packers,** Chicago.

ALFRED H. SACHS: mng. dir. Mfrs. Trading Corp., Commercial Bankers, regional counsel Keeshin Transcontinental Freight lines.

WALTER E. SACHS: mem. firm Goldman Sachs & Co., bankers; dir. of **Jewel Tea Co.** (chain stores); dir. **Lehn & Fink Products Co.** and **Merck & Co.** (both drugs); mem. Bankers' Assn. of America; dir. May, also Kauffman, Dept. Stores; etc.

JOS. W. SALUS: Phila. banker; pres. Broad St. Trust Co.; mem. exec. com. Sup. Grand Lodge B'nai B'rith; pres. A. Salus & Son; etc.

KARL SCHENCK: Czechoslovakian-born; exec. v.p. and cashier Trade Bank of N.Y.; dir. Trade Bank Safe Deposit Co.; dir. Astor Financial Corp.; dir. Standard National Corp.; dir. Century **Transportation** Co., Inc.; etc.; mem. Rothschild Soc.

HENRY LEO SCHENK: pres. Trade Bank of New York; dir. Astor Financial Corp.

JOHN M. SCHIFF: grandson of Jacob H.; partner **Kuhn Loeb** & Co.; dir. Western Union Telegraph Co., dir. Los. A. & Salt Lake R.R.; mem. N.Y. Stock Exchange; dir. Westinghouse Electric & Mfg Co. (heavy industry).

MAX J. SCHNEIDER: Austrian-born; pres. Nat. Safety Bank & Tr. Co.; active in Keren Hayesod (Palestine fund) and Jewish orgns.

EUSTACE SELIGMAN: mem. Nat. Pub. Housing Conf., of socialist-communist Lg.. for Industrial Democracy; dir. Marine Midland Trust Co. of N.Y.; dir. Am. Bemberg Corp.; dir. N. Am. Rayon Corp.; dir. Allied Stores Corp.; dir. **Fed. Home Loan Bank,** N.Y.; dir. Simms Petroleum; treas. radical Foreign Policy Assn.

JOSEPH SINGER: asst. v.p. Public Nat. Bk. & Tr. Co.

JOS. JACOB SLONIM: Russian-born; asst. v.p. and head

Bowery office Mfrs. Trust Co., N.Y.; mem. advis. bd. radical (Zionist) Am. Jewish Congress since 1936; officer of Zionist Org. of Am.; treas. E. Side Chamber Commerce, etc.

PHINEAS SONDHEIM: mem. firm Heidelbach Ickelheimer & Co., bankers.

JAMES SPEYER: edu. in Germany and transferred to Paris and London branches of Speyers, intl. bankers; sr. partner Speyer & Co., N.Y., since 1899; has been trustee Central Savings Bank, Central Trust Co., Union Trust Co., Title Guarantee & Trust Co., mem. bd. mgrs. Gerard Trust Co., Phila.; dir. Mutual Life Insurance Co., N. British & Mercantile Insurance Co., Gen. Chemical Co., Guaranty Trust Co., Underground Electric Railways Co. of London, Ltd., Rock Island Co., Pacific Mail Steamship Co., Md. Trust Co. Citizens' Savings & Trust Co. of Cleveland, Industrial Trust Co. of Providence, R.I., Mexican Bank of Industry of Mexico City, Baltimore & Ohio R.R. Co., Nat. R.R. of Mexico, Corn Products Refining Co., Pacific Ry. Co., St. Louis-San Francisco Ry. Co., Mo., Kans. & Texas Ry. Co., Chgo. Rock Island & Pacific Ry. Co., Pitts. Steel Co.; past pres. Provident Loan Society of N.Y.; was trustee of radical **Teachers' College of Columbia Univ.**, 1900-32, and donor of Speyer School to Columbia Univ.; a founder 1912, v.p. and mem. of council since, of the **Pan-American Society**; very active against prohibition; mem. advis. bd. **Salvation Army** since 1922; mem. **Pilgrims Club.**

### The Pilgrims

This club, said to be closely aligned with the Jewish-controlled "English Speaking Union", for British propaganda, has long had Nicholas Murray Butler, internationalist front, as pres., and as N.Y. members, the J. P. Morgans, the Jews Henry Morgenthau, Jr., intl. bankers Jules S. Bache, Kuhn-Loeb's Mortimer L. Schiff, James Speyer, etc. The Jews Otto Kahn, Paul M. Warburg and Julius Ochs Adler were "Pilgrims" when alive.

HERBERT TELLER SPIESBERGER: v.p. Am. Nat.

Bank & Tr. Co., Chgo., since 1931; treas. Jewish Charities; etc.

FRED M. STEIN: treas. radical Am. Indian Defense Assn., financially aided by the communist-Garland-Fund; dir. Molybdenum Corp. of Am.; was mem. Simon Borg & Co., bankers; active in Jewish orgns.

DAVID BECKER STERN: pres. A. G. Beeker & Co., investment bankers, Chgo.; dir. Alfred Decker & Cohn, Domestic & For. Investors Corp., Gillette Safety Razor Co., Nat. Bond & Invest Co., etc.

WILLIAM STERN: pres. Dakota Nat. Bank; dir. Northern & Dakota Tr. Co.

ROBT. ELI STRAUS: v.p. Am. Nat. Bank & Tr. Co. since 1932; mother, Mattie Horner; "aide to Gov. Horner"; Col. in Ill. Nat. Guard; dir. Jewish Home Finding Soc., etc.

LEWIS L. STRAUSS: partner **Kuhn Loeb** & Co.; dir. and mem. exec. com. U.S. Leather Co.; dir. and mem. finance com. **U.S. Rubber Co.;** dir. Susquehanna & N.Y. Ry.; dir. Gen. Transportation Co.; dir. Commercial Investment Trust; chmn. **Jewish Joint Distribution Com. Relief Work for Russia;** trustee radical Inst. Pacific Relations; trustee Jewish Theological Sem. of Am.; exec. com. **Am. Jewish Com.;** trustee Palestine Develop. Council; etc.

S. A. TELSEY: Polish-born; pres. American Title & Guarantee Co.; dir. Merit Mortgage Co.; dir. Marshall Mortgage Co.; dir. Hebrew Edu. Soc.; v.p. HIAS (Hebrew **Immigrant** Aid Society).

RUFUS M. ULLMAN: secy. and treas. Ullman & Co., investment bankers.

CLARENCE E. UNTERBERG: investment banker, mem. firm C. E. Unterberg & Co.; dir. Unterberg Realty Corp.; dir. Merchants Sq. Corp.; pres. Belise Securities Co.; Gov. of N.Y. Security Dealers Assn.; mem. Commodity Exchange, Inc.; exec. com. Jewish Theol. Sem. Am.; etc.

FREDERICK M. WARBURG: grandson of Jacob Schiff; partner **Kuhn Loeb** & Co.; dir. Los A. & Salt Lake Ry. Co.

JAMES PAUL WARBURG: German-born; mother Mina Loeb, her father Soloman Loeb founded intl. banking house of Kuhn Loeb & Co., paternal ancestors founded banking house M. M. Warburg, Hamburg, 1798; dir. Bank of Manhattan Co.; pres. Bydale Co.; pres. Kara Corp.; pres. Cosmopolis Securities Corp.; dir. and mem. exec. com. Union Pacific, Los A. & Salt Lake R.R.; dir. Ore.-Wash. R.R.; dir. Ore. Short Line R.R.; etc.; advisor at World Econ. Conf., London, 1933; mem. radical For. Policy Assn.

PAUL FELIX WARBURG: banker; grandson of Jacob Schiff; v.p. Bank of the Manhattan Co.; dir. County Trust Co.; Coordinating Com. for Aid to (Jewish) Refugees Coming from Germany; nat. coun. Boy Scouts of Am.

MAURICE WERTHEIM: dir. **"The Nation"** (advocate of revolutionary Socialism); dir. radical **New School for Social Research**; a founder radical Theatre Guild, N.Y.; founder Wertheim & Co., investment bankers; dir. Underwood-Elliott Fischer Co.; dir. Hat Corp. of America; dir. Franklin Simon & Co. Inc.; married Alma Morgenthau; dir. Axton-Fisher Tobacco Co.; dir. Cuban Atlantic Sugar Co.

SIDNEY JAMES WEINBERG: partner Goldman Sachs & Co., bankers; dir. Cluett Peabody & Co.; dir. Continental Can Co.; dir. General Cigar Co.; dir. B. F. Goodrich, **rubber**; dir. General Foods Corp.; dir. McKesson & Robbins Co., **drugs**; dir. Nat. Dairy Products Corp.; dir. Pierce **Petroleum** Co.; dir. **Sears Roebuck & Co.**; Gov. of Bankers Assn. of Am. since 1934; mem. N.Y. Stock Exchange; was mem. adv. bd. **NRA**; now mem. of five or more coms. of **U.S. Dept. Commerce.**

Then there are Maurice Gusman, pres. Merchants Tr. & Svgs. Bank, Cleveland, O., Edwin M. Berolzheimer, mem. adv. bd. Chemical Bank & Tr. Co., and so on, and on.

## WHAT IS BANKING CONTROL?

### New York Clearing House

Regardless of the truth or falsity of B'nai B'rith figures on percentages of Jews in the N.Y. Clearing House and

Stock Exchange, as one financial expert states: "Director-ship of the **New York Clearing House** merely administers the mechanics of transferring deposits from one account to another and as between and among banks throughout the country. It exercises no control over business policies or economic trends.

"Membership on the **New York Stock Exchange** has nothing to do with the control of American industry. Membership merely entitles the owner to certain rights in buying or selling securities for the accounts of others.

"Actual control of the banking system is the power to force movements of gold in and out of countries, force the uses, expansion and contraction of bank credit, to change ratios at which money of one country is exchanged for that of another, which is a power to juggle price levels preventing exchange of goods between countries or entry of competitive goods imported from lower wage-scale countries. This power can cause business stagnation and depressions.

"As Secy. of the **U.S. Treasury, Henry Morgenthau, Jr.,** a Jew, has absolute control over the operations of what is mis-called the 'Stabilization Fund'. This is control over foreign exchange ratios. His power is absolute and his decisions final. The Federal Reserve Board and the Federal Deposit Insurance Corporation **dominate** the **policies** of all domestic banks. Thus, these Boards are able to control granting or withholding loans to private industries and thus dominate the state of trade and determine who may take an important part in American industry."

### Some World Banking Mysteries

Rather than wade through the complexities and mountains of boring figures usually used to explain banking, the average brain lies down cold and simply skips it. Perhaps they "planned it that way". The clearest explanation of our Jewish-inspired banking system and its world controls is given by the British patriot A. N. Field (P. O. Box **154**, Nelson, New Zealand) in his book "All These Things". How booms and slumps are "created to order", the close tie-ups between our illegal N.R.A. and other Socialist New

164

Deal legislation and Israel Moses Sieff's similar Marxian "P.E.P." (Political, Economic Planning) program, in part already in action in England, is set forth in various chapters.

Lady Reading (Isaacs), one of Israel Moses Sieff's "P.E. P." satellites, is now (9/40) whooping up aid in America for Britain, Jewry's stronghold. Lady Marley, another Jewish "noblewoman", is here, and so is Lady Mendl (Elsie de Wolf), also Sir Geo. Paish, who openly boasted, according to Sen. Wheeler, that he will get us into this war as he did the last one (I.N.S., 8/26/40).

To quote Mr. Field: "The similarity between the British economic policies and those of the U.S. has been remarked in many quarters. . . ."

Describing the P.E.P. Potato Control law in England, he says: "Here is one of the many examples of the results of unintelligent Jewish economics in application to the enterprising Aryan British farming industry. In America, under Pres. Roosevelt's Jewish A.A.A. . . . the equivalent of P.E. P. in this country, they actually paid farmers out of tax-payers' money not to grow crops or rear stock. The steps taken to limit and restrict the supply to the people of Britain of this staple food are almost identical with American Potato Law described in the preceding chapter. As under the New Deal in the U.S., so under Planned Economy in Britain, the State now stands between the nation and the bounty of the soil. No more complete negation of Christian principles can be conceived."

## Bank of England, Private, Secret

(P. 198): "With respect to the eulogistic reference in the Israel Moses Sieff document to the Bank of England, it is sufficient at the moment to point out: (1) that the Bank of England is a **private corporation** open to **foreign ownership** and with a **secret share list**; (2) that according to evidence before a British Parliamentary Committee many years ago its constitution imposes no obligation on it to consider the public interest in its operations; (3) that its board is strongly representative of **international finance**; and (4) that it pressed for the policy of **currency and credit contraction**

165

which plunged British industry into difficulties from 1920 onwards and **demoralized a large section of the population by the consequent prolonged unemployment**".

## A Peculiar Set-Up Like Ours

"In 1930 two emissaries of the Bank of England visited New Zealand to advise its Government on monetary matters. Their names were not distinctively British. One was Sir Otto Ernst Niemeyer; the other was Professor Theodor **Emanuel Guggenheim** Gregory, a member of the teaching staff of the London School of Economics, a nursery of Socialism" (The leading light of its many Red Jews is Harold Laski, Felix Frankfurter's close friend).

"Sir Otto Niemeyer made a report advising the Govt. of New Zealand to establish a private corporation to control the volume of currency and credit in the country. He also proposed that this privately owned central reserve bank should be given a permanent monopoly of all the Govt's 'money, remittance, exchange and banking transactions.' He further proposed that the Government should find a **million** sterling for the working capital of the bank, in respect of which sum it would **hold no shares and have no voice in the management**; and that **half a million** should be obtained by the issue of shares to the public, the holders of such shares to be the **owners of the bank**. In the original Bill as introduced it was left open to foreigners to own the bank, though only shareholders who were British subjects resident in New Zealand had votes at bank meetings. Furthermore, the share list was not open to inspection and **ownership of the institution was thus secret**.

"It was not easy to see what advantages the Government was to gain from an institution set up as recommended in this report. Sir Otto Niemeyer certainly pointed to no outstanding benefit to the people of New Zealand. The terms on which the Government banking account was secured were distinctly unfavourable terms. The bank was given a monopoly of the account; the Government was given no right to so much as a pennyworth of accommodation from the bank; the bank might give accommodation to a limited

166

amount if it chose, but need not if it did not so choose. No private concern would dream of giving a monopoly of its banking account on such terms, nor would any private person ever consider finding two-thirds of the capital for any venture without having a voice in its control. . . .

### "Internationalism in Excelsis"

"**The parent** of the new model central reserve banks **is the U.S. Federal Reserve Board** and its twelve regional Federal Reserve Banks set up about six months before the European War broke out. These banks are **privately-owned institutions with very complete control over the volume of currency and credit** in the U.S., and thus over the prevailing level of wages and prices. The principal prime mover in creating the Federal Reserve system was the late Mr. Paul Warburg (1868-1932), who with his brother, Mr. Felix Warburg, was a partner in the international banking-house of Kuhn, Loeb & Co., N.Y. The head of that firm at this time was Mr. Jacob H. Schiff (1847-1920). . . . He was born in Frankfort-on-the-Main, where his father was a broker for the Rothschilds. . . .

"Mr. Paul Warburg was brother-in-law to Mr. Schiff, and was also a Jew of German birth, becoming naturalized as an American citizen in 1911, three years before the war. His brothers conduct the powerful German banking-house of M. Warburg & Co., Hamburg, financing the German shipping industry and controlling the Hamburg-American and North German Lloyd lines" (before Hitler). "Herr Max Warburg, head of this banking-house, played an important part in German politics, particularly at the time the Kaiser fled to Holland. Dr. Carl Melchoir, a partner in it, was one of the five German delegates-in-chief at the **Peace Conference at Versailles,** and in later years was prominent in the founding of the **Bank for International Settlements,** the central bank of the central banks established in Switzerland, which has been internationalized in peace and war alike, pays no taxes, and is above and beyond all law".

(Dr. Per Jacobsson, representing the Bank of Intl. Settlements, Basle, Switzerland, lunched with Barney Baruch in

New York, 6/30/39.)

"Provision was made in the New Zealand Reserve Bank Act for our reserve bank to join up with the Bank for International Settlements (B.I.S.) A message from Basle, Switzerland, published in the London 'Times' of 4/9/34, in reporting a meeting of this institution, said: 'The newly-established (Reserve) Bank of Canada and Bank of New Zealand are empowered by their Governments to buy B.I.S. shares and to make deposits at the bank as soon as the stabilization of the respective currencies will allow.' This shows that these reserve banks were established as part of the **network of an international money trust.**"

## When Paish Was Here Before

"Of the war-time activities of Mr. Paul Warburg, promoter of the Federal Reserve, we find Sir Cecil Spring-Rice, British Ambassador to the U.S. from 1912 to the end of 1917, writing as follows under date of 11/13/14: 'He practically controls the financial policy of the Administration, and **Paish** and Blackett had to negotiate with him. Of course it was exactly like negotiating with Germany. Everything that was said was Germany property.' In various books on war-time espionage the Hamburg-American offices in New York are referred to as the centre of German espionage in the U.S." (This was when Germany **was** Jewish property and before Jewry switched from Germany to the Allied side to get Palestine; it is now on the Allied side to "get" Hitler.)

"Mr. McAdoo, Pres. Wilson's son-in-law and Secy. of the Treasury during the war, was a former partner with Mr. Warburg, and the 'Dictionary of National Biography' records that the late **Sir Ernest Cassel,** the Jewish friend and financial adviser of King Edward VII, was associated in former years with Mr. Jacob Schiff in effecting some of the great American railway combines in which his firm specialized. . . ."

## Slumps and Crises Prepare for Dictatorship

"As to the mode of operation of the great American

168

money-controlling machine established under the above auspices, we have the fact that it was created for the ostensible purpose of preventing financial crises, and there have been greater and **more violent** crises since it was established than were ever previously known. Prof. J. R. Commons, of the University of Wisconsin, testified in evidence before the U.S. House of Repr. Banking and Currency Committee in 1927 that a member of the Federal Reserve Board had told him that the **great inflation of 1919 was deliberately created by the Federal Reserve Board.** Minutes of a **secret Federal Reserve** conference of 5/20, ordering immediate **contraction of credit** have been freely quoted in Congressional documents as direct evidence of the **cause of the depression which brought disaster all over the world at that time.** Former Sen. Robert L. Owen, who as chairman of the Senate Banking and Currency Committee, piloted the Federal Reserve Bill through the Senate in 1913, testified before the House Banking Committee on 3/18/32, that the **great world depression** beginning in Nov., 1929, was brought about by deliberate contraction of credit by the Federal Reserve system, specifying in detail the actions which led to the disaster. . . ."

## A World System

"Soon after the war was over the international financiers decided that the time was ripe to establish reserve banks **all over the world.** Whatever other people might think of the Federal Reserve system in the U.S., it satisfied the financiers. In 1922 there was held a great international conference at Genoa at which was Herr Walter Rathenau, the **Jewish Foreign Minister of Germany.** . . . Simultaneously another conference was sitting in Genoa attended among others by Mr. Montagu Norman, Gov. of the Bank of England, the Gov. of the Bank of France, the Gov. of the Federal Reserve Bank of New York, and other international bankers. This conference resolved that central reserve banks should be set up in all countries where they were not already in existence. This work was thereafter steadily proceeded with and such banks have been established through-

169

out the whole world.

"A prominent part in the establishment of these banks was played by Mr. Montagu Norman, Governor of the Bank of England. . . .

"Of the doings of this internationalist picnic party, Mr. Einzig, conductor of London's 'Financial Review,' proceeds to tell us that: 'Another condition on which Mr. Norman and his collaborators insisted was that the central banks should be independent of their governments.' It is emphasized that on this 'they insisted rather dogmatically.' In other words, the State was not to govern in the sphere of money, which was to be left to the **Normans, Siepmanns, Niemeyers, Strakosches,** etc., ad lib. Despite the audacity of these proceedings they were entirely successful". (Their Jewish blood and connections are cited.)

### Queer Gold Movements

"Furthermore, we were told that we would be benefited by having our Reserve Bank ship away all or most of the gold by the Banks in New Zealand. It was pointed out that this gold did not bear interest and it was thus a dead loss to hold it when we might exchange it for interest-bearing paper. It thus appeared that Sir Otto Niemeyer and his friends, on purely philanthropic grounds, were willing to carry off our gold, bear the dead loss on it themselves, and hand us over valuable paper for it. Nobody in the Government of New Zealand ever paused to think whether there might be any drawback to this admirable arrangement. It was swallowed whole". (Whereas in the U.S.A. the Jew Deal mysteriously keeps buying unneeded gold from Red Russia to bury in Kentucky and stabilizes the Red Mexican Government by unneeded silver purchases.)

"Immediately it was established the New Zealand Reserve Bank took over the gold in the trading banks and duly shipped about three-quarters of it away in return for exchange paper. It also took over from the trading banks something in the neighborhood of 16 millions of sterling in London. Large sums were thus made available for dealing in bills of exchange in the short-term money market in

London. If it were possible to uncover the actual facts it might be instructive to see exactly who has been financed by the internationalists with these millions belonging to the people of New Zealand. . . . The London moneylenders, as everybody knows, have long had much greater interests in the Argentine than in this quarter of the world. . . ." (Now U.S. taxpayers are to subsidize buying Argentine and South American exports.)

### Ivar Krueger Swindle

"The Reserve Bank Act was passed in 1933. It so happened that in the preceding year advantage had been taken of a similar, but not so sweeping, provision in the U. S. Federal Reserve law by one Ivar Kreuger" (Swedish Jew) "with the assistance of aiders and abettors in America. . . .

"Speaking in Congress on 6/10/32, Mr. Louis T. McFadden, long chairman of the House of Repr. Banking and Currency Committee, said: 'Every dollar of the billions Kreuger and his gang drew out of this country on acceptances (bills of exchange) was drawn from the Government and the people of the U.S. through the Federal Reserve Board and the Federal Reserve Banks. The credit of the U.S. Govt. was peddled to him. . . .'

"Among the fiercest and most trenchant critics of the Federal Reserve system have been Mr. Louis T. McFadden, for many years chairman of the Banking and Currency Committee of the House of Repr., and a former pres. of the Bankers Assn. of Pa., and former Sen. Robert L. Owen, for twelve years chairman of the Senate Banking and Currency Committee, and who actually piloted the Federal Reserve Bill through the Senate in 1913.

"Congressman McFadden, 6/10/32, referred in Congress to the Federal Reserve Bank as: 'one of the most corrupt institutions the world has ever known,' which had 'impoverished and ruined the people of the U.S.; has bankrupted itself, and has practically bankrupted our Govt.' . . . Mr. McFadden was detailed and specific in his numerous charges of mal-administration, declaring among other things, that money had been drained wholesale out of the U.S. for the

171

purpose of **financing Russia** by means of loans through German financiers. He especially denounced the operations of **Kuhn, Loeb & Co. . . .**" (Even Sen. Carter Glass, its faithful champion, attacked the lawless and "outside meddling" of the Federal Reserve Board before the American Bankers' Assn., 9/26/40.)

"Mr. Owen, like Mr. McFadden, is a banker. In 1890 he established the first national bank in Oklahoma, was its president for ten years, and has been a director for 45 successive years. In 1907 he entered the U.S. Senate and served there for 18 years, and from 1913 to 1925 was chairman of the Banking and Currency Committee. . . . In the Bill as originally framed was an instruction that the powers of the system were to be used to promote a stable price level, but, states Mr. Owen, 'I was unable to keep this mandatory provision in the Bill because of the **secret hostilities** developed against it, **the origin of which I did not at that time fully understand.**' "

## Our Gold??

(P. 129) "On March 5, Pres. Roosevelt by proclamation took the U.S. off the gold standard, relieving the Federal Reserve of its obligation to pay out gold to U.S. citizens, but still permitting international financiers to withdraw gold and ship it abroad. At the same time the people were ordered, under heavy penalties, to hand into the banks all gold in their possession in return for bank paper. In condemning these proceedings as unconstitutional, Mr. McFadden said in his speech of 5/4/33:

## Kuhn Loeb Again

". . . 'Pres. Roosevelt has brought with him from Wall Street, James Warburg, the son of Paul M. Warburg. Mr. Warburg is head of the Bank of Manhattan Co. Mr. Warburg, alien born and the son of an alien who did not become naturalized here until several years after this Warburg's birth, is a son of a former partner of Kuhn, Loeb & Co., a grandson of another partner, a nephew of a former partner, and a nephew of a present partner. He holds no office in

172

our Govt., but I am told that he is in daily attendance at the Treasury, and that he has private quarters there. In other words, Mr. Chairman, Kuhn, Loeb & Co. now control and occupy the U.S. Treasury.'"

## Henry Morgenthau, Jr.

(Pp. 155-6) "Of Mr. Henry Morgenthau, Jr., Pres. Roosevelt's Secy. of the Treasury, Mr. Louis T. McFadden spoke in Congress as follows on 1/24/34: 'Mr. Chairman, understanding that Henry Morgenthau is related by marriage to Herbert Lehmann, Jewish Governor of the State of New York, and is related by marriage or otherwise to the Seligmans, of the international Jewish firm of J. & W. Seligman, who were publicly shown before a Senate committee of investigation to have offered a bribe to a foreign government; and to the Lewisohns, a firm of Jewish international bankers; and to the Warburgs, whose operations through Kuhn, Loeb & Co., the International Acceptance Bank, and the Bank of Manhattan Co., and other foreign and domestic institutions under their control, have drained billions of dollars out of the U.S. Treasury and the bank deposits belonging to the U.S. citizens; and the Strauses, proprietors of R. H. Macy & Co., of New York, which is an outlet for goods dumped upon this country at the expense of the U.S. Govt., which is compelled to issue paper money on the said foreign goods of the Strauses; and that Mr. Morgenthau is likewise related or otherwise connected with the Jewish banking community of New York and London, Amsterdam, and other foreign financial centres, and that he has as his assistant, presiding over public funds, Earl Bailie, a member of the firm of J. & W. Seligman, bribegivers as aforesaid, it seems to me that Henry Morgenthau's presence in the U.S. Treasury, and the request that Congress now give him a $2,000,000,000 "kitty" of the people's money for gambling purposes is a striking confirmation of the statement made by me on the floor of the house on 5/29/33. . . .'"

## Secrecy in England and Here

"This secret fund, to be used in a manner unexplained,

was on the lines of the British Exchange Equalization Fund of 350,000,000 pounds voted by Parliament soon after the abandonment of the gold standard in 1931. Of this mysterious British fund Prof. Gustav Cassel, the European monetary expert, said in 'The Crisis in the World Monetary System' (Oxford, 1932): 'In England a huge fund has been voted for what is described as "the protection of the pound," but nobody seems to have a clear conception even of the fundamental principles on which this fund is to be used.' Thus two huge secret funds have been abstracted from the public Treasuries of Britain and America for unexplained financial manipulations."

## Some Jewish Federal Reserve Officers

Pres. Wilson appointed Paul M. Warburg to the Federal Reserve Board 1914-18, and he was also chmn. bd. Intl. Acceptance Bank, Inc. and of the Intl. Acceptance Securities & Trust Co., N.Y.

Eugene Meyer (Jew), former partner of Lazard Freres, intl. bankers, and mem. gov. com. N.Y. Stock Exchange, another of the Jewish Baruch-Frankfurter War Industries Bd. attaches during the World War, and dir. War Finance Corp. for four years, appointed by Pres. Wilson, was made Gov. of the Federal Reserve Bd., 1930-33, by Pres. Hoover.

J. David Stern, Jewish radical newspaper owner, was F.D.R. appointee to the Federal Reserve Bd., Phila., etc., is also an executive of the N.Y. Post owned by George Backer, son-in-law of Kuhn Loeb Co. partner, Mortimer Schiff. Max Epstein bosses the industrial loans dept. of the Chicago Federal Reserve Bank; Rudolph Hecht is dir. New Orleans Federal Reserve Bank; Walter Lichtenstein is secy. advis. council Federal Reserve System, since 1926; Eustace Seligman is dir. Federal Home Loan Bank; etc., etc.

The Kuhn Loeb type of control by personal pressure, avoiding open directorships, as before cited from the Govt. Report, is noticeable by glancing at names of "Jew Deal" stooges in the Federal Reserve System. For example, the supreme head, "Chmn. and Fed. Reserve Agent", of the Federal Reserve District of Chicago (Fed. Reserve Bulletin, 9/40) is **Robt. E. Wood,** manager and front for the Jewish Rosenwalds, one of them, Wm. Rosenwald, being fellow executive with Kuhn Loeb partner L. L. Strauss of the Jewish Joint Distribution Com.

ERNEST G. DRAPER, FDR's New Deal Asst. Secy. of Commerce, 1935-8, and Gov. Fed. Reserve System since 1938, is member of the socialistic Am. Assn. for Labor Legislation (pres. 1930-2) and member of the socialistic, predominantly Jewish, Survey Associates. CHESTER C. DAVIS, FDR's administrator of the radical AAA, 1933-6, since 1936 is Gov. Fed. Reserve System.

However, on the Nat. Bd. of Governors of the Fed. Reserve System, of which Henry Morgenthau, Jr., is automatically the leading voice, is E. H. GOLDENWEISER, Russian-born Jew (teacher at the red New School for Social Research, 1919-26, and at the socialist Rand School, 1912-29, etc.) He is the Fed. Reserve System's natl. "Director of Division of Research and Statistics", and Economist of its "Federal Open Market Committee".

WALTER LICHTENSTEIN, German-born Jew, is secy. of the System's natl. Federal Advisory Council, and its v.p. is HOWARD A. LOEB (son of Mathilde Adler), listed in Who's Who in Am. Jewry as chmn. Tradesmens Nat. Bank & Tr. Co. since 1938 and dir. in many big interests, mem. radical Foreign Policy Assn., etc. BENEDICT J. LAZAR (son of Rebecca Feldman) is managing director of the Fed. Reserve District of Cincinnati. MAX B. NAHM, dir. of the Fed. Reserve Bank of St. Louis, is also listed in Who's Who in Am. Jewry as v.p. Citizens Nat. Bank and Bowling Green Tr. Co., and pres. Mammoth Cave Park Assn.

## NO POWER IN INDUSTRY?

Jews have no power in transportation, oil, steel, communications, rubber, utilities, drugs, autos, aviation, heavy industry, and Sears Roebuck is a Gentile concern, says B'nai B'rith and its stooges.

## Transportation

On the contrary, the control of 41% of all U.S. railroad transportation by Kuhn Loeb & Co. has already been cited from the Govt. report.

We find FREDERICK MARCUS WARBURG: dir. Los Angeles & Salt Lake R.R. Co.; JAMES PAUL WARBURG: dir. and mem. exec. com., Union Pacific, Los Angeles & Salt Lake, Oregon & Wash., Oregon Short Line Rys.; J. MORTIMER SCHIFF: dir. Los Angeles & Salt Lake R.R.

In addition, listed in Who's Who in Am. Jewry, for example, are:

JACOB ARONSON: v.p. N.Y. Central R.R. and dir. R.R. Federal Savings & Loan Assn.; JULES S. BACHE: dir. Ann Arbor R.R. Co., Interborough Rapid Transit Co., Manhattan Ry. Co.; MURRY GUGGENHEIM: dir. Nevada Northern Ry. Co.; JEROME J. HANAUER: dir. Hudson & Manhattan, Ill. Cent., Yazoo & Miss. Valley R.R. Co's., Nat. Rys. of Mexico; RUDOLPH S. HECHT: dir. Miss. Shipping Co.; DANIEL W. KEMPNER: dir. Port Isobel & Rio Grande Ry. Co.; LEWIS L. STRAUSS: married daughter of Jerome J. Hanauer; dir. Susquehanna & N.Y. R.R., Gen. Am. Transportation Co.

The largest trucking freight line is the Keeshin Transcontinental Freight Lines, which is under Jewish control, with A. H. Sachs (regional counsel), John D. Hertz (director), etc. In transportation note the power of JOHN D. HERTZ alone who is: founder Yellow Cab Co. and Chgo. Motor Coach Co. merged with 5th Ave. Coach Co. of N.Y.C. forming Omnibus Corp. of Am. (1924), of which he is chmn. of bd. and dir.; founder of Yellow Cab Mfg. Co. (1926); founder People's Motorbus Co., St. Louis (1926); dir. and chmn. exec. and fin. com. N.Y. Rys. Corp.; dir. Keeshin Transcontinental Frt. Lines, Inc., Seaboard Freight Lines, Inc.

HAROLD E. FOREMAN: dir. Omnibus Corp (N.Y. and Chgo. busses); DAVID COPLAND: v.p. Gen. American Transportation Co.; MAX EPSTEIN: chmn. bd. Gen.

American Transportation Co. (which manufacturers tank cars) and its affiliated companies; trustee U. of Chgo., where radicalism flourishes.

## Autos

In automobiles, for example, we have JOHN D. HERTZ: dir. Studebaker Corp.; JULES SEMON BACHE: dir. Chrysler Corp.; MEYER LEON PRENTIS: Russian-born; treas. Gen. Motors Corp., Detroit, since 1919, and dir. numerous subsidiary companies; active in Zionist and Jewish activities; mem. nat. coun. Joint Distribution Com., of which L. L. Strauss of Kuhn Loeb is a head; A. E. BARIT: pres. Hudson Motor Car Co.; pres. and sales dir. Hudson & Terraplane Sales Corp.; etc.

## No Power in Aviation?

The following concerning the Aviation Czar, VICTOR EMANUEL, who is now cleaning up in war profits (listed in Who's Who in Am. Jewry also as senior partner Emanuel & Co., bankers), is of interest.

"Victor Emanuel rules a vast business empire—right here in the United States. Only 42, he is already a veteran in the utilities industry, where he heads the $760,000,000 Standard Gas & Electric Co. In addition, through purchase of a portion of the holdings of E. L. Cord in 1937, he directs enterprises in a variety of other fields as chairman and president of the Aviation & Transportation Corp. (formerly the Cord Corp.) and as president of the Aviation Corp. (28 percent owned by A. & T.).

"Aviation & Transportation is essentially a holding company, having a controlling interest in such firms as the New York Shipbuilding Corp., the Columbia Axle Co., makers of automobile axles, and the Auburn Central Manufacturing Corp. (formerly the Auburn Automobile Co.—Newsweek, July 22/40). On the other hand, the Aviation Corp. sticks more closely to the industry after which it is named. Among its subsidiaries and their manufacturing divisions are Vultee, which makes military planes; Stinson, which until last year concentrated on private planes but now also builds observation craft for the Army, and **Lycoming,** which produces engines and propellor blades. . . .

"Meanwhile, directors of Aviation Corp. and Aviation & Transportation Corp. met to discuss, among other matters, expansion plans necessitated by Vultee's **$80,000,000 in unfilled orders,** mostly contracts under the national defense program. . . .

"Emanuel and his associates hope that the rush of military business **(Stinson has $2,800,000** in unfilled orders and **Lycoming** approximately **$15,000,000)** will enable them to simplify the somewhat tangled corporate structure of the two holding companies and to play an important role in commercial aviation after the defense program is completed". (Newsweek, 10/7/40.)

## Rubber

Whether B'nai B'rith-Fortune research claims, that Kelly-Springfield Rubber Co. is no longer in Jewish hands, are true or not, LEWIS L. STRAUSS is dir. and mem. fin. com. U.S. Rubber Co., and SIDNEY JAMES WEINBERG is dir. B. F. Goodrich & Co., and MILTON ROSEN is mem. advis. coun. bd. of dir. U.S. Rubber Co.; owner Milton Rosen Tire & Rubber Co.; mem. B'nai B'rith, etc.

"U. S. Rubber is controlled by minority ownership by the DuPonts" (part Jewish) in connection with Kuhn, Loeb and Company, as cited in the Government report.

## Heavy Industry

Take the power of the Swopes alone as listed in Who's Who in American Jewry:

GERARD SWOPE is not only pres. Gen. Electric Co., and chmn. bd. of dir.'s Internat. Gen. Electric Co., but also dir.: Compagnie Francaise Thomson-Houston (Paris, France), Compagnie des Lampes (France), Societe Financieres pour la Developpement de l'Electricite (Paris), Societe d'Electricite et de Mecanique (Brussels, Belgium), Allgemeine Elektricitats Gesellschaft (Berlin, Germany), Internat. Power Securities Co., Nat. City Bank, Gen. Electric Supply Co. During the **World War,** asst. dir. purchase, storage and traffic.

HERBERT BAYARD SWOPE, brother of Gerard; was asst. chmn. to Barney Baruch on War Industries Bd.; chmn. official American press delegation at **Paris Peace Conf.;** "mem. Internat. Press Com. successfully advocating publicizing the Conf.; 1st to publish secret **League of Nations** Covenant and **full text of reparations clauses".** A founder and a gov. Am. Soc. of Newspaper Editors; chmn. bd. of dir.'s Polo Magazine, Inc. and Keewaydin Corp.; dir. and mem. exec. com. Bklyn. Manhattan Transit Corp (mem. com. to negotiate subway unification, N.Y.City); dir. Bklyn. & Queens Transit Corp.; Columbia Broadcasting System, Inc., N.Y. Rapid Transit Corp.; chmn. com. of sponsors Jewish Telegraphic Agency. Active in councils of Democratic Party and in Democratic Admin. since 1933; appointed by Pres. Roosevelt to accompany Asst. Secy. of State Moley to London Econ. Conf., 1933; presidential elector, 1936. Mem. advisory bd. Nat. Pub. Housing Conf. (sponsored by the socialist-communist League for Industrial Democracy); mem. Pilgrims Club; etc.

### In Steel & Metal

PHILIP BLOCK is pres. of Inland Steel Co., also dir. of Jos. T. Ryerson & Sons, Inc. MELVIN LLOYD EMERICH: dir. Fansteel Metallurgical Corp.; MAURICE FALK: v.p. Fed. Metals Corp. (now Am. Smelting & Refining Co.) since 1924; dir. Nat. Steel Corp., Edgewater Steel Co., Blaw-Knox Co.; pres. Falk Products Co.; dir. three banks and of Reliance Insurance Co.; CARL M. LOEB: v.p. Climax Molybdenum Co., DAVID STRAUSS: pres. Continental Iron & Steel Co., N.Y.; ROGER W. STRAUS: v.p. since 1923 Am. Smelting & Refining Co.; married daughter Daniel Guggenheim; Nat. Conf. Jews & Christians; received American Hebrew Medal; JULES SEMON BACHE: pres. Dome Mines, Ltd.

### Guggenheim Copper and Smelting Kings Aid Reds

SIMON GUGGENHEIM: pres. American Smelting & Refining Co.; mem. firm Guggenheim Bros. He established

179

the John Simon Guggenheim Foundation which has aided such leading Reds as communist Chas. R. Walker who got a Guggenheim Fellowship in 1938 to study "the effects of radical political movements on American culture from 1917 to the present", and the rampant red Lewis Mumford, author of "The Day Before the Revolution", who got his second Guggenheim fellowship at the same time (N.Y. Her.-Trib., 4/4/38).

MURRY GUGGENHEIM: one of the Guggenheim American Smelting & Refining capitalists; dir. Utah Copper Co., Yukon Gold Co., New River Collieries Co., Kennecott Copper Corp., Keno Hill, Ltd., Braden Copper Co., Minerec Corp., Pacific Tin Corp.

SOLOMON R. GUGGENHEIM: mem. firm Guggenheim Bros.; dir. Braden Copper Co., Utah Copper Co., Kennecott Copper Corp., Pacific Tin Corp., Carecoles Tin Co. of Bolivia, New Consolidated Copper Co.; married daughter Henry Rothschild, one child Eleanor is Countess Castle Stewart, England.

CHAS. S. GUGGENHEIMER: mem. law firm Guggenheimer & Untermyer; dir. Miami Copper Co., Warner Bros. Pictures, etc.

### In Addition

To quote: "since the beginning of 1935 Kuhn Loeb & Co. has been the leading underwriter for the four steel companies in the Cleveland group, namely, Republic, Youngstown Sheet & Tube, Inland, and Wheeling, also for the two of the other large steel independents, Bethlehem and National" (p. 315, 6/39 Report of U.S. Govt. Nat. Resources Com.).

Even B'nai B'rith-Fortune "research" admitted that the scrap iron and steel industry, which provides the steel industry with half its metal requirements, "is owned 90% by Jews", with such Jewish firms as Luria Bros. & Co. of Phila. (Russian Jews), Hyman Michaels Co., Chicago (Portuguese Jew), Chas. Dreifus Co., Pitts., Luntz Iron & Steel Co., Canton, O.

## Oil

In oil, there is, for example: JACOB BLAUSTEIN: (son of Louis) pres. since 1933 of merger of Am. Oil Co. and Pan Am. Petroleum & Transport Co., pres. Mexican Petroleum Corp. (Me.); exec. v.p.: Mexican Petroleum Corp. (Ga.), Pan Am. Refining Corp., Pan Am. Petroleum & Transport Co., Pan Am. Pipe Line Co., Am. Trading & Product Corp., Lord Baltimore Filling Stations; dir. Union Tr. Co. of Md., U.S. Fidelity & Guaranty Co.

LOUIS BLAUSTEIN: Russian-born; founder and pres. Am. Oil Co.; pres.: Pan Am. Refining Corp., Pan Am. Pipe Line Co., Mexican Petroleum Corp. (Ga.), Pan Am. Production Co., Am. Trading Corp.; initiator Oil Tanker Fleet; JEROME J. HANAUER: dir. Mid-Continent Petroleum Corp.; JOHN D. HERTZ: dir. Tide Water Asso'd. Oil Co., Inc.; ARTHUR S. KLEEMAN: pres. Oils & Industries, Inc.; dir. Kirby Petroleum Co., EUSTACE SELIGMAN: dir. Simms Petroleum Corp.; ALVIN UNTERMYER: dir. Consolidated Oil Corp., Pierce Petroleum Corp., Gen. Development Co.

## Communications

Jewish control of radio is undisputed. WM. S. PALEY, a Jew, is pres. Columbia Broadcasting Co., and the Russian-born DAVID SARNOFF is pres and dir. R.C.A. Communications, Inc. and chmn. bd. of dir. National Broadcasting Co. **Kuhn Loeb** control over Western Union Telegraph was before cited and J. MORTIMER SCHIFF is dir. Western Union Telegraph Co. WALTER LICHTENSTEIN lists himself as official delegate to the Telecommunication Conference abroad, as well as mem. bd. of gov's. Rockefeller's radical Intl. House and gen. secy. orgn. com. Bank for International Settlements, 1929, and secy. federal advis. coun. Federal Reserve System since 1926.

## Furniture

The B'nai B'rith-Fortune research, aimed to show the smallness of Jewish influence, nevertheless states that "in furniture making a particular Jewish affinity for the upholstered field gives Jewish manufacturers like Artistic in Detroit, Angelus in Los Angeles, and S. Karpen in Chicago almost half the total".

## Liquor and Tobacco

Hedging, it says "not even in the liquor business . . . nor in the tobacco business in which many a rich Jew has made his start, are Jewish interests dominant", yet, admits **"Jews have practically blanketed the tobacco** buying business where Jew and buyer are synonymous words, and control **three of the four** leading cigar-manufacturing concerns including Fred Hirschhorn's General Cigar, which makes every seventh cigar smoked in America". (Note that the red banker, Maurice Wertheim, is dir. of the Axton-Fisher Tobacco Co. and Jules S. Bache is dir. of Cuba Distilling Co., and Sidney Weinberg is dir. General Cigar Co.) "As for the liquor business **about half the important distilling concerns are Jewish"**.

It says Daniel K. Weiskopf is vice president of "the largest U.S. concern National Distillers (1934: sales $50,000-000)", and "The second, Schenley (1934 sales: $40,000,000) is controlled by Jews though with Grover A. Whalen as Chairman of the Board. The third, Seagrams (sales figure not published), is owned, controlled, and managed by the Bronfman brothers who are Jews". (Willkie's brother is manager of their Kentucky plant.) **"These three companies do about 50 percent of the business"**. Since they admit, in addition, that Continental, another of the largest distilleries, is under Jewish management, thus giving Jews more than half of the distilling business, the actual percentage is probably nearer to the 90 percent claimed by others.

## Sears Roebuck, "Gentile"

Sears Roebuck, which Keith Brooks "improved" to pure Gentile ownership status when he copied, is referred to in this slippery manner ("Jews in America", B'nai B'rith pamphlet, p. 8): **"Sears, Roebuck has a** Jewish history (Julius Rosenwald) but active management of Sears, Roebuck now is in the hands of General Robert Wood". So Brooks, generously, gave the whole works to Wood.

Wood, Rosenwald's Gentile front, is trustee of the Rosenwald Foundation headed by Lessing J. Rosenwald, son of Julius and **chmn. of bd. of dirs.** of Sears. (W. W. Alexander, Edwin R. Embree, Howard W. Odum, Chas. S. Johnson and M. O. Bousfield, the last two colored, and all radicals, serve the foundation.) S. J. Weinberg, Jewish banker, and Edgar B. Stern, son-in-law of Julius Rosenwald, are other directors of Sears.

Wm. Rosenwald, another son of Julius, lists himself in Who's Who in Am. Jewry as nat. co-chmn. Joint Distribution Committee (active in Russia); vice chmn. Nat. Co-ordinating Committee for German Refugees since 1936; mem. exec. com. **American Jewish Committee**; treas. Julius Rosenwald Foundation, and dir. of Sears Roebuck, which is just as Jewish and as "Rosenwald" as it ever was, despite silly attempts to make it look "Gentile".

### More "Gentile" Firms

Jews have no influence in drugs, according to the B'nai B'rith-Fortune research which mentions McKesson & Robbins (Sidney J. Weinberg, Jew, is dir. of McKesson & Robbins) as "non-Jewish". Jewish Walter Sachs is dir. of Lehn & Fink, also of Merck & Co., M. L. Emerich is dir. of Katz Drug Co., and Harry Goldstine is v.p. of the Walgreen chain, all great drug firms.

McCreery (Jewish Otto Marx, dir.), Lord & Taylor (Otto Marx, dir.), S. H. Kress (H. R. Ickleheimer, dir.), F. W. Woolworth (Philip Lehman, dir.) and food chains are listed as non-Jewish. Herbert Lehman and Walter Sachs list themselves as directors of the Jewel Tea store chains. Sidney Weinberg is dir. Gen. Foods Corp., Nat. Dairy Products Corp.; etc., etc.

# JEWS IN ENGLAND

### War for Jewmocracy

As the international Jewish control is being unseated from one European nation after another, leaving England and

183

America as Jewry's greatest remaining strongholds, it is not strange that world Jewry becomes ever more hysterically attached to "Democracy" (but not to the American Republic with its checks and balances, now largely destroyed by the "Jew Deal"), and is now commercializing American flags and whipping up "patriotism" for war, and that Hore-Belisha, Jewish ex-war minister of England, is calling for a union of the U.S.A. and Great Britain, "a common citizenship" (U.P. 9/19/40).

### Onward Christian Soldiers!

A leaflet issued in England after the war started is headed:

### "THE ARMY OF TODAY'S ALRIGHT?"

**"IT'S LED BY A JEW**—Leslie Hore-Belisha, Minister of War.

**"IT'S FED BY A JEW**—Sir Isadore Salmon, M.P., Hon. Catering Advisor to the Army with an office at the War Office.

**"IT'S CLAD BY A JEW**—Montague Burton, Vide Daily Express, May 2, 1939, 'Montague Burton and Prices Trust shares improved on reports that the Companies may receive large orders for uniforms for the Regular and Territorial Army.'

"IT'S PAID FOR BY YOU!—John Citizen. Onward Christian Soldiers! Join the Navy."

### Where Jewry Rules, "Anti-Semitism" is Criminal

Already the London periodical, "World Jewry", 3/8/35, was "urging amendment of the British libel laws to make expression of anti-Semite opinion a criminal offense" ("All These Things" p. 217), and British patriots like Capt. Ramsay now languish in prison, while Reds have unbridled liberty in England. A similar law was enacted in France, 4/21/39, when Jewry was at the height of its power, and many Christian patriots were jailed under it.

Before that, as B'nai B'rith magazine had said (5/34, p. 282) : "Russia is the only country in the world where anti-Semitism is a crime. If someone calls a Jew 'Zhid' which is the equivalent of 'Sheeney', he is immediately arrested and punished, sometimes by fine, sometimes by imprisonment".

## When England Banished Jews

To quote: "the Jews were banished from the realm on All Saints Day, 1290. The banishment endured until the year 1655. There was never any formal re-admission of the Jews. The Jews of Amsterdam, in pursuit of their own ends, sought permission of Oliver Cromwell to enter Britain. Cromwell, for reasons of his own . . . desired to admit them. He was quite unable to obtain any approval of his project from the councils he called to consider the matter. . . . Cromwell dismissed his counsellors and then turned a blind eye upon the semi-surreptitious influx of the Jews. . . ."

## England's Glory

". . . English achievement during the period of 365 years in which the Jew was absent compares favourably with that during the periods before and after. The Elizabethan Age, for example, has always shone in English annals with a lustre of its own, even though almost the only known Jew in the kingdom was the physician Roderigo Lopez, said to be the original of Shylock, and hanged for attempting to poison England's Queen. The Elizabethan authors and poets, with Shakespeare at their head; the voyagers and discoverers, including Raleigh, Drake, Hawkins, and Gilbert; the statesmen; and the companies of merchant adventurers, were each in their respective spheres fully as competent as those of later and earlier ages.

"Nor did the commerce of the country suffer with the Jew no longer on the scene. Picking up an old school history, the eye lights upon the following passage: 'The greatest and most rapid expansion of English trade took place in the reign of Elizabeth. . . .' "(p. 215, "All These Things".)

185

## Marconi Scandal and Jewish Power

One reads, in the above, the details of the Jewish manipulation of Marconi Telegraph shares, the great scandal and Parliamentary inquiry (1912) into charges of huge profits shared with the Jewish promoters by British high officials, the hushing up of this inquiry followed by the bestowing of powerful government positions on Jews, also the connection formed between the Marconi Company and the U.S.A. Western Union Telegraph Company. To quote: "Its stock issues were floated by Kuhn Loeb and Company and Mr. Jacob H. Schiff, senior partner in that firm, was a director of it up to the time of his death in 1920. The Marconi Company thus became linked with the enormously powerful **Kuhn Loeb** interests" (p. 22).

One may reflect with interest on how the Russian-born Jew David Sarnoff came to be the Czar of the Radio Corp. of America and allied interests. He lists himself as **"With Marconi Wireless Tel Co. of Am. from 1906 until its absorption by Radio Corp. of Am. in 1919".**

## Lord Reading, Lloyd George

Reverting to the report of the Marconi scandal: "The managing director of the Marconi Company at this time was Mr. Godfrey Isaacs, brother of Sir Rufus Isaacs, at the time Atty. General in the Asquith Cabinet. Immediately after the inquiry into the Marconi transactions Sir Rufus Isaacs was appointed Lord Chief Justice of England and presently raised to the Peerage as **Lord Reading,** Associated with Sir Rufus Isaacs in the Marconi transactions was **Mr. Lloyd George, destined soon to play an even greater part in guiding British destinies"** ("All These Things", p. 20).

"Jewish influences in British politics became pronounced after the rise of Mr. Lloyd George. In the days when he followed his profession Mr. Lloyd George had been solicitor to the **Zionist Association** (vide 'Patriot', 9/21/33), which position would naturally bring him into close contact with the powerful Jewish interests behind that movement".

## Chemical King Melchett

"Sir Herbert Samuel" (listed in Who's Who in **American** Jewry, 1938-9) "was Postmaster-General and then Home Secretary in the war years, in the latter post having control of aliens. **Sir Alfred Mond, afterwards Lord Melchett**" (also listed in Who's Who in **Am.** Jewry) "was First Commnr. for Works in the Lloyd George War Ministry, and as head of the Mond chemical works (afterwards converted into Imperial Chemical Industries) **dominated the chemical resources of the British Empire.** Mr. **Edwin Samuel Montagu,** cousin of Sir Herbert Samuel, was appointed Secy. of State for India by Mr. Lloyd George, and, as will be related in a later chaper, in 1917 set out to awaken the masses of India from their 'placid, pathetic contentment' by launching them into democratic politics. In 1922 Mr. Lloyd George sent Lord Reading to India as Viceroy to continue this work. Jews were to be noted also in many minor positions and in important advisory capacities.

"In his book 'The Jews' (Constable, 1922) Mr. Hilaire Belloc said: 'The Great War brought thousands upon thousands of educated men (who took up public duties as temporary officials) up against the staggering secret they had never suspected—the **complete control** exercised over things absolutely necessary to the nation's survival **by half a dozen Jews. . . .** ' The 'Spectator' was constrained to write in a leading article in its issue of June 20, 1920: 'We are convinced that at the present moment the professors of the Jewish faith are far too numerous in our Govt. . . . We have got a great many more Jews than we deserve, and the wrong kind of Jew at that!" (p. 104).

## The "Tribes" of Monds, Sassoons, Isaacs

"For some years a group of financiers whose families, for the most part, are of German-Jewish origin, has assumed control of political power and exerts a predominant influence over Mr. Lloyd George. The Monds, Sassoons, Rufus Isaacs, those known as the representatives of the international banking interests, **dominate Old England, own its** newspapers, and control its elections. . . .

"The close solidarity existing between Mr. Lloyd George and Jewish high finance is easily shown by the brief biographical sketches of some of the influential personages by whom he is surrounded. . . . Each of these names represents not only an individual, but also **a veritable tribe** and head of **immense financial interests.**

"Sir Philip Albert Gustav David **Sassoon,** secretary to Mr. Lloyd George and his constant companion, whose famous estate of Lympne is so frequently used as a meeting-place by the Supreme Council, is the son of **Edward Sassoon,** one of the richest financiers in the world. On his mother's side he is a grandson of Baron Gustave de **Rothschild** (the Sassoons are Asiatic Jews coming originally from Bagdad). Sir **Philip Sassoon** and his cousin, **D. R. Sassoon,** are at the head of the banking house of David Sassoon and Co. He is likewise closely related to Sir **Jacob Elias Sassoon,** head of E. D. Sassoon and Co., one of the most powerful commercial and financial establishments in India and the Far East, and is a near relative of a score of other Sassoons in England and India. The House of Sassoon, with all its affiliations and ramifications, is considered from a financial standpoint as holding the same position in Asia as that held by the **House of Rothschild in Europe.** Sir Philip Sassoon, Mr. Lloyd George's secretary, being a Sassoon on his father's side and a Rothschild on his mother's, is without question one of the most important financial personages in the world".

## Wilson, Isaacs, and League of Nations

"**Lord Reading** . . . is now Viceroy of India. Toward the close of the war he was sent as High Commnr. and Ambassador Extraordinary from Great Britain to the **United States.** As such he possessed tremendous influence with **President Wilson** and his intimate associates, **among whom were a great number of Jews.** He played a prominent part in the drawing up of the peace terms and in the creation of the **League of Nations.** . . . He belongs to the world of

188

Jewish high finance, in which his two brothers play very important parts".

### Isaacs Chemical and Wireless Kings

"One of them, **Godfrey Charles Isaacs,** is general manager of all the **Marconi Companies,** and could justly lay claim to the title of the **Wireless King.** The other, **Harry M. Isaacs,** manages and controls the **British Cellulose and Chemical Mfg. Co., the largest manufacturers of chemical products in England.**

"The **Samuels** constitute a vast tribe, exceedingly numerous, influential and complex. Besides two of Mr. Lloyd George's intimate associates—**Edwin Samuel Montagu,** member of the Privy Council and Secy. of State for India, and **Sir Herbert Samuel,** Viceroy (High Commnr.) of Palestine, there is a host of other Samuels belonging to the world of Jewish high finance. For instance, there is **Sir Harry Samuel,** who controls the **Shell Transport and Trading Co.,** and the **Anglo-Saxon Petroleum,** as well as the **Royal Dutch Co., the Mexican Eagle Co., and Balaafsche Petroleum Maatchaaoij.**

### Nickel King Mond (Melchett)

"Last comes **Sir Alfred Mond,** member of the Privy Council, Minister in the present British Cabinet and head of the Economic Council of the **Zionist movement.** This man, son of a naturalized German, is one of the **nickel kings, the supreme master of international commerce in chemical products,** and proprietor of the 'Westminister Gazette'. . . . Associated with Sir Alfred Mond in all his enterprises is his brother, **Robert Ludwig Mond.** Sir Alfred's daughter married the son of **Lord Reading (Rufus Isaacs),** Viceroy of India".

### They Control and Misrepresent British People

"**This group,** of which Mr. Lloyd George is the very eloquent mouthpiece, **is by no means the British people,** but Jewish international finance, whose headquarters are the London Stock Exchange. If it is beyond all question that

189

Jews of German origin occupy most of the influential positions in England; it is equally true that **they do not present real British public opinion, in spite of the fact that they are often able to make it appear so, by means of the newspapers they control**" (pp. 105-6).

## More About British Jewry

A British group in **July, 1938,** issued a leaflet entitled "His Majesty's New Sub-Government" concerning Jewish influences in the British Govt. Referring to "P.E.P." (Political and Economic Planning), founded and headed by "Israel Moses Sieff of Marks and Spencer stores", it says: **"Its object is the same as that of the New Deal in the United States of America,** i.e., to increase Jewish **control over industry** and to induce the normal Briton (or American) to believe that the cause of industrial depression is insufficient organization and not the Jewish control by **virtual monopoly and planned restriction** of the national credit and currency".

## Like Red Einstein

"The Jew Money Power **disarmed Britain** because the latter, having been the principal instrument by which worldwide control by Jews has been established, had now to be removed as a rival power.

"**But the Jews had not reckoned upon Hitler; in disarming us, they now find they have disarmed themselves, and so we are to be re-armed** to deal with our blood-brothers across the North Sea and fight the Jew's battles all over again". (This reminds one of all our vociferous Jewish Red "pacifists", like Einstein, now yelling for war.)

"His Majesty's Privy Council is being packed with real Jews and with 'synthetic' Jews and with strongly pro-Jew Gentiles.

"**PRIME MINISTER**—Mr. Neville Chamberlain. His father owed his career to Jewish support. . . . Mr. Joseph Chamberlain's aunt by marriage was Jewish (Andrade), and it is believed that there was Jewish blood from the mother's side (Harben). Sydney Dark in his 'The Jew Today' lists Sir H. Harben, Joseph Chamberlain's first cou-

190

sin, as Jewish. Whilst Andre Spire, a Jew, in 'Quelques Juifs', Mercure de France, 1913, says that Jos. Chamberlain was of Jewish blood. Sir Austen Chamberlain was considered by the Jews to be a veritable champion of Jewry. Mr. Neville Chamberlain's son has an appointment in Imperial Chemical Industries, the great Jew-controlled monopoly. The Chamberlains, like the Churchills, seem to have dedicated themselves to the service of Jewry.

"Financial Secy. to the Treasury—Capt. D. E. Wallace, who married the daughter of the Earl of Lytton who is Pres. of the Jewish Palestine Potash Co., Ltd.

"Lord President of the Council—Viscount Hailsham. His brother, Sir Malcolm Hogg, married the granddaughter of a Jewish Gompertz.

"Lord Chancellor—Baron Maugham. Has a Jewish sister-in-law. His Permanent Secy. is the Jewish Sir Claud Schuster.

"Secy. of State for Home Affairs—Sir Samuel Hoare. His Parliamentary Private Secy. is Mr. W. W Astor, whose uncle is a Director of the **Jewish Bank of Hambros**; his mother is sister-in-law of Hon. R. H. Brand, Managing Director of the Jewish Bank, **Lazard Bros.** in London". (Note U.S.A. connections.)

"Secy. of State for Foreign Affairs—Viscount Halifax. His heir married the granddaughter of a Rothschild. One of his two Parliamentary Under-Secretaries is Viscount Cranbourne, married to the great granddaughter of the Jew Bernal Osborn, M.P.; . . .

"Secy. of State for Dominions—Lord Stanley. His sister married the son of a Rothschild. His Under-Secretary is the Duke of Devonshire, who is mixed up in the Alliance Assurance Co. Directorate with the Jews Rothschild and Bearstead, and the half-Jew **Lord Rosenbery**; he was a member of the Management Committee for the 1936 Exhibition in aid of the Jewish National Fund.

"Secy. of State for the Colonies—Mr. Malcolm Macdonald. His father, Ramsay Macdonald, employed for years a Jewess Rosenberg as his Private Secy. Father and son were closely associated with Jew Sieff's 'P.E.P.' It was Ramsay Macdonald who in 1917 exhorted the workers to follow the example of Russia.

"**First Lord of the Admiralty**—Mr. A. Duff Cooper. The late Otto Kahn, of the firm of Kuhn Loeb & Co., Jewish Bankers who financed the Russian Revolution, was god-father to his child. Mr. Duff Cooper's great grandmother was a Stein" (said to be Jewish). "His sister married a Jewish Levita. Mr. Duff Cooper's Parliamentary Private Secy. is Mr. H. W. Kerr, an enthusiast for Sieff's 'P.E.P.' The Fourth Sea Lord and Chief of Supplies and Transport is G. S. Arbuthnot, whose mother was a Jewish Schomberg.

"**Secy. of State for War**—Mr. L. Hore-Belisha. A Jew. His parliamentary Under-Secy. is Lord Strathcona, whose brother is a Director of the Trading Investment Co., Ltd., on the Directorate of which are several Directors of Helbert, Wagg & Co. (real name of Helbert was Israel). The Deputy Under-Secy. is the Jewish Sir F. C. Bovenschen. The Catering Advisor for the Army is the Jew Sir I. Salmon.

"**Secy. of State for Air**—Sir Kingsley Wood. On 23rd Feb., 1937, at Manchester, he described the Jews as 'a race whom we value in this country and whom we always desire to have with us'. Strong supporter of the Retail Trading Standards Association of 'P.E.P.' The Under-Secy. is Capt. H. Balfour, who is brother-in-law to one Jewish Oppenheimer and nephew by marriage to another. The Permanent Under-Secy. is Sir Donald Banks, who married a Jewess and was 'guest of honour' at a B'nai B'rith dinner in 1937.

"**Pres. of Board of Trade**—Mr. Oliver Stanley. His sister married the son of a Rothschild. It was Mr. Stanley who unveiled a portrait of Mr. Ernest Schiff in January, 1933, a Jew of the family of Schiff of **Kuhn Loeb & Co.** . . . The Chief Economic Adviser is the mystery-man Sir F. W. Leith-Ross, who supports international finance.

"**Pres. of Board of Education**—Earl Stanhope. His Parlia-

mentary, Secy. is Mr. Kenneth Lindsay, Secy. of the Jew
Sieff's Political Economic Planning Organization ('P.
E.P.') and once Secy. to the Jew Schwelm's Victoria
Colonization Co., which encouraged British people to settle
in a South American 'El Dorado'. . . . Mr. Lindsay's Parliamentary Private Secy. is Miss Thelma Cazalet, whose
brother is an ardent Zionist M.P.

"**Minister of Health**—Mr. W. Elliot. An original member of Israel Moses Sieff's 'P.E.P.' organization. . . . His
Parliamentary Secy. is the Jewish R. H. Bernays.

"**Minister of Labour**—Mr. E. Brown. His Deputy Secy.
is the Jewish Humbert Wolfe.

"**First Commissioner of Works**—Sir P. Sassoon. A Jew,
and a Rothschild on his mother's side.

"**Minister of Pensions**—Mr. H. Ramsbotham. Who married a Jewish De Stein. His Permanent Secy. is Sir Adair
Hore, step-father of the Jew Hore-Belisha (Secy. of State
for War).

"**Chancellor of the Duchy of Lancaster**—Earl Winterton.
Lord Winterton's Parliamentary Private Secy. is Mr. C. I.
C. Wood, married to a granddaughter of a Rothschild.

"**Postmaster General**—Major G. C. Tryon. On his Council
is the Jew and Zionist pioneer, L. Simon, Comptroller of
the Savings Bank.

"**Secy. of State for India and Burma**—The Marquess of
Zetland. The Assistant Under-Secy. is the Jew Sir Cecil
Kisch, whilst Sir H. Strakosch, Jew, sits on his Council.
The Economic Advisor to the Indian Government is the
Jew T. E. Gregory, real name Guggenheim."

### Winston Churchill, Prime Mover for War

The record of Churchill's Jewish great-grandmother is of
interest. Pallycarpus von Schneidau in Sweden fell in love
with Froecken Jacobson, Jewess, and had to go to Denmark to marry, marriage to a Jewess being barred in Sweden; they came to the U.S., were invited to Chicago by
Mayor Ogden, who adopted their daughter Pauline; Pauline

von Schneidau married the son of Leonard Jerome; their daughter, Jennie Jerome was the mother of Winston Churchill. (Wis. Mag. of History, Sept. 1924, vol. 8, p. 43, Pub. of Wis. State Historical Soc.)

### Disraeli, the Churchill "Political Mentor"

A eulogistic article on "Winston Churchill and His Mother" (Liberty magazine, 7/13/40) tells of the chummy intimacy and political maneuvering between his mother, Lady Randolph Churchill (Jennie Jerome), and the Jewish Disraeli (Lord Beaconsfield) whom they familiarly called "Dizzy". To quote: " 'Dizzy', her **husband's political mentor and friend** was among her favorites and she among his. After one of their dinner-table conversations, which they had conducted with heads together and to the exclusion of other guests, one of the latter—feminine gender—remarked icily to Jennie **'What office have you got for Randolph?'** How valuable was her counsel and influence—especially after Lord Randolph Churchill's death—to the young Winston, launching his political career, the present Prime Minister has himself testified".

### Churchill and Norway's Jewish Hambro

In Norway, weariness of Marxist and Jewish power had undoubtedly prepared many Norwegians, reported as "Fifth Columnists", to welcome German control as an escape. Carl Johan Hambro, of the Jewish banking family which founded the Hambros Bank in London, was president of the Norwegian Parliament (Chgo. Tribune, 4/13/40). He arrived with a boat load of "refujews" in N.Y. (Chgo. Times, 8/28/40) and his son John R. B. Hambro, attending Columbia Univ., was calling for victory for the Allies (N.Y. Her.-Trib., 4/11/40).

A year earlier the radical "Social Frontier" magazine (4/39, p. 218), organ of the John Dewey Society (of Reds), in praising the "New Commonwealth Movement", said it was forming branches in various countries, presided over by **Winston Churchill**, its vice-pres. for France being Leon Blum's Red-fronter, Pierre Cot, and vice-pres. for Norway **Carl Hambro** (Jew), with a New York office at 545 Fifth Ave., N.Y., sponsored by a group of radicals. To quote: "It is frankly and outspokenly committed to the view that in awakening popular belief in **international govt.** lies the only hope . . . and an **international police** capable of enforcing those verdicts if need be". A League of Nations idea ardently supported by international Jewry.

## Duke of Windsor and Jewry

The Jewish appearance of Wallis Warfield, Duchess of Windsor, is often remarked. David Warfield, the actor, lists himself as a Jew in Who's Who in American Jewry. The Jewish Sentinel (8/8/40, p. 15) says: "In Vienna, a Rothschild was host to the Duke and Duchess of Windsor. In Lisbon, their host up to the time they sailed for the Bahamas was the Espirito Santo family, wealthy bankers. The family is of Jewish origin. The name means Holy Ghost. A name assumed by the family at the time of its conversion centuries ago. Spanish Protestants have frequently agitated against use of the name by a banking family".

## IN FRANCE

To quote: "France is being Judaized and Sovietized at the same time. 'L'Humanite', the Soviet's Communist Party newspaper, was established by the capital of a dozen Jews: Leon Blum, Brahm, Bruhl, Casewitz, A. Dreyfus, Louis Dreyfus, Herr, Pikart, Reinach, Rodrigues, Rouf and Sachs. Exiled from Germany, Jews are invading our country. The Popular Front hastens to make citizens of them. Formalities of naturalization are simplified and hastened for their benefit. Controlling the Govt. and collaborating with the Zionist Blum (member of B'nai B'rith), Jews dominate France. Beraud sounded the alarm in Gringoire of 12/25/36:" ("Juif" is the French word for "Jew", "Juive", "Jewess") " **'Presidence du Conseil,** Cabinet: MM. A. Blumel, juif; Jules Moch, juif; Heilbronner, juif; Grunebaum-Balin, juif; R. Hug, juif; Mmes Picard-Moch, juive; Madeleine Osmin, juive.—**Sous-secretariat d'Etat.** Cabinet: M.

195

Mumber, juif.—**Ministere d'Etat.** Cabinet: M. J. Schuler, juif.—**Ministere de la Justice.** Cabinet: MM. Weil, juif; Pierre Rodrigues, juif—**Ministere de l'Interieur.** Cabinet: MM. Bechoff, juif; Salomon, juif; Cahen-Salvador, juif— **Ministere des Finances.** Cabinet: M. Weil-Raynal, juif— **Education nationale.** Cabinet: M. Marcel Abraham, juif; J.-J. Moerer, juif; E. Wellhof, juif; Adrienne Weil, juive; S. Chaskin, juive. **Economie nationale.** Cabinet: M. J. Cahen-Salvador, juif—**Marine marchande,** Cabinet: M. Gregh, juif.—**Agriculture.** Cabinet: MM. R. Lyon, juif; R. Kiefe, juif; R. Veil, juif.—**Travail.** Cabinet: J.-F. Dreyfus, juif.— **P.T.T.** Cabinet: MM. Didkowsky, juif; H. Grimm, juif.— **Sante publique.** Cabinet: MM. Hazemann, juif; A. Rozier, juif; M. Wusler, juif.—**Education physique.** Cabinet: M. Endlitz, juif.

"Who, then, can longer wonder that the one thing lacking and needed in our statecraft to safeguard **French** interests is having it **French**". (Pp. 67-8 "Face au Front Populaire", booklet No. 2 (in French), by Albert Blute, 116 bis Avenue des Champs-Elysees, Paris, Feb. 1937.)

## GENTILE FRONTS—BEFORE AND AFTER
### Rauschning

On the "must" reading list of B'nai B'rith's "Anti-Defamation League Review" (12/39) is Herman Rauschning's "Revolution of Nihilism", eulogized as **"without doubt the most important book on the subject of National Socialism"** and offered to members at a discount.

### Dottie Loves It

The book's paper jacket boasts that it "has already been heralded by" (Jewry's mouthpiece) "Dorothy Thompson in her syndicated column". Patriotic experts who pass up cruder Jewish propaganda seemingly fall for Rauschning's smooth and fantastic lies, hook, line and sinker, since few have ever seen Germany in action for themselves. He claims to be an exiled former "Nazi leader", now disgruntled and

196

proportionately devoted to passionately sounding his "Warning to the West", as he calls his book.

One sincere patriot, quoting Rauschning's book, has even issued a bulletin showing the similarity of "Jew Deal" and Nazi workings. To quote: "Under Nazism, according to Rauschning, the strength of National Socialism lay in its ability to keep things moving; incessant activity along any line **whether productive of beneficient results or not,** just so there was action".

### Could the "Jew Deal" Blitzkreig?

But anyone who has ever observed our WPA shovel-leaning armies and their meager production of "beneficient results" might know if Germany had similarly wasted its manpower it would have been unable to clean up all Europe in a few weeks' time.

Likewise if our "Jew Deal" efficiency resembled that of the Germans under Naziism, our tiny army would not now be training with moving vans labeled as tanks and using sticks instead of mortars after **seven billions of dollars** had already been poured down the New Deal "rat hole", spent for "national defense" (Chgo. Her.-Am. 5/21/40).

### U.S. War Against Fascism

Since Communism in Russia has, despite all efforts, been so widely and embarrassingly exposed publicly as the brutal and inefficient mess that it is, and particularly since the Nazi-Soviet pact, Marxist Jewry has grown increasingly willing not only to get-out-from-under by junking the Communist label, but its cleverest propaganda trick has been to utilize anti-Communist sentiment to arouse hatred for Fascism through calling the two systems one and the same.

A newspaper columnist may denounce Communism now, but he must gnash his teeth at Fascism. Let Pegler, Johnson, Boake Carter, etc., fail to do so! Their columns would fail to appear.

This propaganda has been so highly successful that we are now on the brink of war against Italy, Germany, Spain and Japan (while giving away what few arms we have). This success is due not only to lack of first-hand knowledge on the part of the public who, like Will Rogers, only know what they read in the papers, but also to the fact that, so enraged and voracious is organized Jewry and so poisoned is the Gentile public by their press propaganda, that any informed Gentile who dares utter a word which could possibly be construed as favorable to Fascism finds himself quickly torn to bits by angry opposition, unless he first flees under the bed, never to emerge again.

Many of us, who genuinely dislike the State control called for under Fascism and dearly love the now-junked "laissez faire" American system, which was so highly successful until one third of all the world's Jews took hold of America, now lament in vain for bygone freedom since the American public willingly welcomes New Deal dictatorship equal to that of any Fascist regime, and votes for its crushing taxes, inefficiency and planned program of ruin.

### Three Differences Between Fascism and Communism

Unless three great dynamic forces of civilization, the **Family, Property Ownership** and **Religion,** are mere trivialities, then Fascism and Communism are **not** the same, except for degrees of State control. In addition, Communism calls for unceasing "class struggle" and suppression and purging of "bourgeois" elements while Fascism plans for collaboration of all classes.

### Family

**1.** Marxism, as in Russia, destroys the family unit, demands state care of children and employment of mothers on public jobs. Fascism, as in Italy and Germany, not only encourages but subsidizes the family unit, and emphasizes woman's function first as a mother to her own family and outside employment as secondary in importance.

### Property

**2. All property** and **business** is owned by the State under Marxism, which is State capitalism. In Italy and Germany, houses, hotels, insurance companies, farms, stores, peanut stands, up one street and down another, are privately owned and run just as in America. **This makes a difference.** A man cleans and cares for his own store or home, as one may see in clean Italy and Germany, but neglects politically owned property, as one may see in tattered "kapoot" Russia.

### Religion

3. In Italy, the Fascist Govt. has a Concordat with the Catholic Church, to which most of the population belong, and encourages religious training.

Germany, for long years has supported its churches by taxes collected by the State from church members. Under the Red Republic, atheism not only became popular but pressure by Reds was exerted on Germans to withdraw from church membership, which many did thus avoiding payment of church taxes.

In 1933, after Hitler assumed power, the sum collected by the State in taxes and placed at the disposal of German Protestant and Catholic churches amounted to 130 million RM (Royal Marks); in 1934, this rose to 170 million RM; in 1935, to 250 million RM; in 1936, to 320 million RM; in 1937, to 400 million RM; in 1938 to 500 million RM.

As E. D. Schoonmaker, in "Democracy and World Dominion" (Richard R. Smith, 120 E. 39th St., N.Y.), says: "I should like to ask this question: What sums have France, England or America paid to their Churches through the State within the same period?"

German parents specify whether they wish their children to have Protestant or Catholic teachers to give them religious instruction during public school hours, or may have their children excused from religious training.

The press, in Sept., 1940, carried the news that in France the anti-clerical laws had been lifted since German occupation, restoring teaching privileges to Catholic religious orders which "democratic" France had denied them.

### Bibles in Germany

While the press hammers away full force rousing hatred of Germany by propaganda that it is anti-religious, obscure little items like the following creep in. Headed "Hitler's Book Second; Bible Best Seller in Germany", the Chicago Tribune, 3/8/39, reported: "The Bible is still the best seller in Germany. It has outsold 'Mein Kampf', Reichsfuehrer Hitler's autobiography by about 200,000 copies yearly in the six years since the Nazi rise to power in 1933. An annual average of 950,000 Bibles has been sold in Germany".

International News Service, 6/29/40, reported: "A 'remarkable increase' in the number of Bibles distributed in Europe was reported today by the American Bible Society. The society reported 1,225,000 Bibles were distributed in Germany during the past year".

A letter to the Editor in the Minneapolis Star Journal, 8/6/40, stated: "As a Lutheran seminary student I want to discuss the attack on the Rev. Mr. Naumann by several of your readers. I have talked with students and pastors of our faith returning from the Reich and they tell me that our churches are full and that no Lutheran or Catholic priest or pastor is interfered with in the exercise of his duties. The Reich has built more than 400 churches for Evangelical and Catholic parishes in the last four years and demands only that the German people render unto God the things that are God's and unto the government the things that rightfully belong to it".

### Dr. J. Frank Norris—Before and After

Dr. J. Frank Norris, Detroit and Fort Worth Fundamentalist minister, felt the full force of Jewish inducements and coercion after he wrote the truth about Germany in connection with his travels there in the summer of 1937. B'nai B'rith emissaries were sent to him, on his return, to make him "see the light" and reverse himself, which he quickly did. In Nov., 1937, he was already portraying Hitler as the anti-Christ and eulogizing Jewry became the routine basis of his sermons, with burning of the German flag thrown in for special occasions. Since June, 1939, he has been warmongering full force.

Attached is a photostatic copy of an illuminating letter written by Dr. Norris to Rev. Sam Swain in reply to

TEMPLE BAPTIST CHURCH
14TH AND MARQUETTE STS.
DETROIT, MICHIGAN

FIRST BAPTIST CHURCH
4TH AND THROCKMORTON STS.
FORTWORTH, TEXAS

J. FRANK NORRIS, D. D.
PASTOR

June 1,1938

Dr.Sam Swain,
Sam Swain Evangelistic Party,
410 Fatherland Street,
Nashville,Tennessee.

My Dear Bro.Swain:

In writing you yesterday I failed to state if you
would go to the head of the  B'Nai B'Rith they would
help in your expenses.

Take the enclosed address, it will be one of the
addresses that I will deliver.  The Jews, of course,
are greatly interested.  I delivered it in Milwaukee
to a great crowd, and will also deliver it in New
York.

Yours very sincerely,

JFN:h

201

Swain's request that Norris speak in Swain's church. Rev. Swain had written that he was unable to raise the $100 in advance requested by Norris.

| | |
|---|---|
| "Temple Baptist Church | First Baptist Church |
| 14th and Marquette Sts. | 4th and Throckmorton Sts. |
| Detroit, Michigan. | Fort Worth, Texas. |

J. Frank Norris, D.D.<br>
Pastor

June 1, 1938.

"Dr. Sam Swain,
Sam Swain Evangelistic Party,
410 Fatherland Street,
Nashville, Tennessee.
"My Dear Bro. Swain:

"In writing you yesterday I failed to state if you would go to the head of B'nai B'rith they would help in your expenses. Take the enclosed address, it will be one of the addresses that I will deliver. The Jews, of course, are greatly interested. I delivered it in Milwaukee to a great crowd, and will also deliver it in New York.

Yours very sincerely,

"JFN:h          (signed) J. Frank Norris."

Note: See facsimile reproduction of this letter on page 201.

### But Before

But before Norris formed his B'nai B'rith connections he wrote the following which appeared in his paper, "The Fundamentalist", 8/6/37, p. 5, headed "Seventeen Years Ago In Germany And Now":

"What a contrast then and now! It was so depressing to a visitor. Everybody was in the depths of despair. The German people are a great people. Woodrow Wilson gave them a solemn pledge in his famous 'Fourteen Points' as a basis for peace. Not a single promise to Germany was made good. For instance, they agreed to disarm and were forced to do so by the allies, but with the understanding and promise that France would disarm. How France failed to keep her own self-imposed promises is too well known to refer to.

"Seventy million Germans could not and would not remain under the heel of military France. The nation was bankrupt and six million communists were increasing and demanding the reins of the government to make Germany an annex of Moscow. But the Austrian Corporal arose and swept through Germany like a Peter the Hermit. The discouraged nation took new hope. The impossible treaty of Versailles was scrapped. The Saar Basin was returned to Germany by a plebiscite. Unemployment was reduced from six million to one million, public improvements, subways, miles and miles of new buildings, millions of acres of marsh lands were drained and put in cultivation—in short, a new nation was born. As you move around among the people they are happy, they are not in fear. Of course they are under a dictatorship but I see no signs of it. We have the best meals we have had since we arrived and prices reasonable."

### Norris on Religion in Germany—Before

#### "HAPPY SERVICE IN BETHEL CHURCH BERLIN.

"Whoever said they haven't religious freedom in Germany? Well, anyway I saw and worshipped just like we do in America. . . . The Bethel Baptist Church is a large congregation and many churches in America, especially in the large cities would congratulate themselves on so large an audience. The singing was wonderful. . . . The German Baptists have not gone over to modernism.

"They looked greatly surprised when I told of the propaganda that had flooded America that churches in Germany could not hold their worship without interference from the government.

"I met an official high up in the government. . . . I asked him about the 'religious persecution' we had heard so much about in America. He went fully into how certain ecclesiastical organizations were not contending for the faith, or were not religious in purpose and character, but wanted

203

to run the government. He mentioned especially the Centrist or Catholic party. . . ." (which formerly voted with the Marxists).

"Can you find a congregation singing, praying, preaching and teaching the fundamentals of the Christian religion as I witnessed this morning right in the heart of this city of four and a half million souls, can you find that in Moscow?" (Fundamentalist, 8/20/37, p. 3.)

### Now

Contrast the above with these warmongering cries from Norris: "THERE IS BUT ONE ISSUE BEFORE AMERICA—HITLERISM. . . . Rush all possible aid to Britain. . . . As Walter Lippmann points out. . . . We should repeal the cash and carry provisions of the Neutrality Act. We must act. . . ." (Fundamentalist, 9/27/40.)

### Mrs. Norris Enthuses

On page 3 of the Fundamentalist, 8/20/37, appears the following:

"LETTER FROM MRS. NORRIS. Dear Folks: . . . I have most thoroughly enjoyed our visit here in Germany—don't know how much longer we will be here, but think I'd enjoy an indefinite stay. . . . At the table, when we look at the menu every word is in German. . . . But we manage to get a meal for dinner something like this—Pineapple juice; consomme; fish; vegetable plate (On that plate the following vegetables: green beans, cauliflower, asparagus, peas, cooked radishes, mushrooms, carrots). I may have too many on one plate—but we had those in different combinations, and enough to satisfy anybody on earth who eats in decent amounts.—Then a tartlett or French pastry, or ice cream, and tea or coffee. So you can readily see no one need go hungry here because he doesn't speak the German language fluently.

". . . But first let me tell you about this hotel. It's so beautiful—now I mean beautiful. . . . They tell us too that Hitler comes here often to drink coffee. Some say he does not drink anything but milk, everyone says he is a vegetarian and a teetotaler. Be that as it may **I wish he would come while I am here, and I could see him.** . . .

"But now I really am going to tell you about your pastor and what royal treatment he has had accorded him here. In the first place he went to church yesterday morning and they asked him to preach, which he did very briefly, through an interpreter . . . he came back quite happy to find people worshipping in a free happy way according to our good Baptist custom, and that they believed and rejoiced in the same Scriptures we believe and teach. . . . This morning quite early the pastor went over to the German Foreign Office as he had been directed by some good friends, and such royal kindness as was bestowed upon him! I just haven't the words to describe. . . . They took us to see the headquarters of their National Relief—I suppose we would call it—but it is more than that. Now of course I just haven't words nor space to tell you all we saw and what it all meant to us, nor how very pleasant it all was—such courtesy! Such intelligence! And lunch with them was a delight— all I had to do was to say in English, 'A fruit salad please', and presto, there it was.

". . . . One young man who went with us joined Hitler when he only had 200 with him and has been with him all the way. Whatever you and I may think, these men think **Hitler is the man for Germany** and certainly **they love him** and follow him. . . . In love. MRS. NORRIS."

### KEITH BROOKS—BEFORE AND AFTER

Keith Brooks, himself, before he was brought to terms, was no mean little "Jew baiter" and was in Jewry's hair no end with his "anti-Semitic" writings upholding the "Protocols", pointing out the anti-Christ role of Jewry, the prominence of Jews in Communism, and saying he intended to continue making these revelations regardless of **danger to** himself.

This was in 1931-33, before he reversed his little magazine, "Prophecy Monthly", into a B'nai B'rith propaganda outlet, plus issuing similar releases, all seasoned with just enough "anti-Communism" and Christianity to sell sucker

Christians with the whole dose.

No horror lie is too fantastic to serve readers who believe it their Christian duty to swallow anything if it is against Germany. But if there were a libel law, enforced, under which Americans were punished for stirring up war by publishing lies against foreign countries, Keith Brooks and many others would long since have languished in jail.

For example, one need not investigate the Jewish propaganda "tear jerker" report, that Jewesses are ordered to set up a brothel by German army authorities to serve German soldiers, to know its ridiculousness. For, entirely apart from any moral consideration or attitude toward Jews, Germany's most drastic regulations are against sex relations between Jew and Gentile—this being a basic part of the "racial purity" creed of Naziism. Separating a mixed Jew and Gentile married couple would be more in keeping with Nazi ideas.

Interesting quotations from Brooks' anti-Semitism writings in "Prophecy Monthly", which make the mildness of this article stand out by comparison, were compiled by Rev. W. D. Herrstrom (Box 77, Lake St. Sta., Mpls.) showing Brooks' complete reversal.

### Leon Birkhead

Until Birkhead went into full time work for Jewry, in 1939, as head of the "Friends of Democracy", he ran the "Liberal Center" in Kansas City, where Reds of all hues met, and called himself a Unitarian minister. He lists himself in Who's Who in America as "technical advisor to" (atheist) "Sinclair Lewis during writing of 'Elmer Gantry', 1926-7", which was one of the most sordid attacks on Christians and the Christian ministry ever penned, and also as "author of numerous 'Little Blue Books'" issued by the Jewish atheist, Emanuel Haldeman-Julius, a dir. of the Am. Assn. for the Advancement of Atheism.

### "Companionate Marriage"

Radical Haldeman-Julius uniquely lived up to his Marxist ideas that a woman should not have to take a man's name

206

after marriage. The Red crew of Socialist and Communist Party women habitually call themselves by their maiden names, prefixed by "Miss", as does socialistic "Miss" Perkins who is mother of Paul Wilson's daughter. Haldeman Julius and his wife compromised and combined their names. Their daughter, Josephine, born six years before they married and later formally adopted, at 18 had a companionate marriage ceremony with Aubrey C. Roselle performed by Birkhead (N.Y. Times, 12/1/27). An article signed by the mother, Marcet Haldeman-Julius, stated "I may add that the Rev. L. M. Birkhead of All Souls Unitarian Church of Kansas City has been asked to perform the ceremony both because he is a close personal friend and because he is in **complete sympathy with our ideas in the matter"** (N.Y. Evening World, 11/21/27).

Birkhead has been a member of the atheist Freethinkers committee to pay tribute to atheist Robt. Ingersoll and vice-pres. of the atheistic Humanist Press Assn., 1938. He was principal speaker for a B'nai B'rith membership campaign rally (B'nai B'rith magazine, 4/39).

Besides "snoopnageling" around to unearth "fascists" and "anti-Semitics" for Jewry, he has kept busy for some years as representative and chairman of the Kansas City branch of the Communist-aiding American Civil Liberties Union, which defends every branch of the Red revolutionary movement by Court action and propaganda.

## Birkhead Originates 800 Organizations

Said George Britt (N.Y. World Telegram, 6/20/40): " 'Eight hundred organizations' was a phrase originated last year by Dr. L. M. Birkhead, national director of the Friends of Democracy, to present the enormous spread of these disseminating anti-democratic propaganda in the United States".

"Originated" is right, for all that Birkhead has ever named are a little handful which include such sterling Americans, now thoroughly smeared by Jewry because of their sound warnings against Jewish radicalism, as General George Van Horn Moseley, James True, Charles B.

Hudson, Robert E. Edmondson, Father Coughlin, Rev. Winrod and a very few more.

### His Own Radical Crew

The 800 are a convenient mythical smokescreen for the really powerful Marxist connections represented by long-time radicals like John Dewey, George Gordon Battle (Earl Browder's atty. and defender), Walter B. Cannon, Thomas Mann, Paul Hutchinson, Paul H. Douglas, A. J. Carlson, Eduard C. Lindeman, G. Bromley Oxnam, A. J. Todd, and other fellow-members of the national committee of Birkhead's **Friends of Democracy.**

## JEWS TAKING OVER AMERICA

In vain have Gentile patriots piped up through the past years to try to stem the undesirable immigration of Jewish Reds. Each Jew who arrived here formed a grapevine to pull his kin over. As someone has put it, "Step on a Jewish poodle dog's tail in Central Europe, and he howls in Washington, New York and Hollywood."

"In 1843 at the most **we had only 25,000 Jews in the United States.** At printing of this magazine the United States **has in excess of 30% of the Jews of the world**", said B'nai B'rith magazine, Dec., 1932 (p. 48).

In 1843 America, working on American not Marxian principles as at present, was soaring toward its height. The American Hebrew, Sept. 27, 1940, on "Mass Migration of Jews" states: "There are 4,831,100 Jews . . . in the United States. This Jewry is the largest and most important body of Jews in the world. One might even venture to state that it is **the greatest Jewry the world has yet seen.** It functions through at least 5,000 Jewish organizations which touch every phase of cultural, social, religious and economic life".

### "Our America"

Concerning the Communist-Socialist American Labor Party of N.Y. it says, Jewish immigrants "were most frequently to be found in the front rank of political **liberals.**

If there is good government today in New York City, it is due in no small measure to this Jewish **proletariat** which had rallied around the American Labor Party".

While speaking well of Soviet Russia, it dismisses it as a future home for world Jewry, saying: "THIS AMERICA OF OURS is the only land that can challenge Palestine AS A CENTER FOR THE JEWS OF THE WORLD. America's future is assured for our time. THERE IS NO PROBLEM HERE OF JEWISH SURVIVAL". (This was from a paper presented at the 51st annual meeting of the Central Conf. of Am. Rabbis, which calls for a Marxian "socialized" America).

### Harry Bridges

Harry Bridges, alien Jew, despite all patriotic efforts, continues his Communist subversion. The American Hebrew, 7/19/40, bursts forth with this eulogy: "On the Honor Roll for clear thinking and courageous action go: Representative Samuel Dickstein" (Russian-born Jew; member of B'nai B'rith), "Democrat of New York; Representative M. Michael Edelstein, Democrat of New York; Representative Emanuel Celler" (American Jewish Congress; member of B'nai B'rith), "Democrat of Brooklyn.

"The three Jewish Congressmen were part of the dauntless little group of 42 who braved criticism to vote against the Allen bill to deport Harry Bridges, the West Coast C.I.O. Maritime leader. . . . Unable to prevent the bill from coming out of the Immigration committee of which he is chairman, Representative Dickstein did the next best thing, voted against it on the floor. Representatives Edelstein and Celler did likewise. . . .

"But the issue in this case is not Harry Bridges. . . . There are also . . . some 4,000,000 Jews in this country whose popularity is ever a moot question. . . . Yesterday it was Harry Bridges whom Congress deemed undesirable. . . . Tomorrow it could be any minority member, any Jew— Albert Einstein, possibly. . . . American Jewry cannot sit by smugly while Harry Bridges is being deported . . . it was recognized by Messrs. Dickstein, Edelstein, and Celler. **More power to them!"**

### "Three Balls" Haym Solomon

"Three Balls" Haym Solomon has been recently resurrected by Jewry and movements set on foot to erect statues in his honor to show Americans how much they owe to the supposed patriotism of this Jewish money broker.

Dishing propaganda to Gentile stooges to serve as "facts" being the technique, Leverett Saltonstall, an ambitious politician who eagerly trails the Jewish vote and power in and out of radical halls, is used to dish up the Haym Solomon myth. In his "Symbol of Jewish Patriotism" article (Jewish Sentinel, 8/8/ 40), Saltonstall fairly drools over Jewish valiant patriotism and in a burst of hyperbole says of the American revolution for independence from England (How Jewry has changed us!):

"BUT FOR HAYM SOLOMON, WHO CONTRIBUTED FINANCIAL AID WHEN IT WAS MOST NEEDED, **AMERICA TODAY MIGHT BE A VASSAL STATE"**. (It is.)

### Jewish Expert Warns of Fraud

Concerning the pressure of the Federation of Polish Jews in America, and others, to collect through Congress large sums supposedly advanced by Solomon to the Colonial Govt. to finance the Revolution, to quote:

"On February 26, 1931, Max James Kohler ... vice-president of the American Jewish Historical Society, wrote Congressman Emanuel Celler of New York a long and detailed report in what was intended to be an open letter on the subject of the claims made in behalf of Solomon". (Copy in Congressional Library.)

"Alarmed at the imminent possibility that investigation would prove the claims to be unjustified to the point of being fraudulent, Kohler cited a mass of evidence showing that Solomon, far from having been 'the Financier of the Revolution' was little more than a broker for Robert Morris, **the true financial genius of the Revolution, and that,**

210

for his services, Solomon had been paid as brokers are usually paid—by a commission on all transactions in which he had a hand.

"Says Kohler: 'Solomon's financial connection with the U.S. Govt. began only a few months before the Battle of Yorktown, on Oct. 19th, 1781, in effect ended the War in our favor. . . . While we were in sore financial straits in 1871, the War would nevertheless have been won by us, had Haym Solomon never lived, and Russell's' (Charles Edward Russell, Socialist writer who did a laudatory biography of Solomon) 'effort to depict him as practically the saviour of our country is absurd. . . .

" 'Haym Solomon never lent the Govt. a substantial sum, probably not even one cent, despite the claims to the contrary advanced by certain of his descendants, in their own interest. . . .' "

### Misleading U.S. Officials

" 'The favorable reports of Committees of Congress have —I regret to say—rested on misinformation, and I fear deliberate concealment, if not worse, on the part of Haym M. Solomon (a son of Haym Solomon, who first tried to make good the claims) or his agents, who misled the Congressional Committees.

" 'President Coolidge was even recently misled into saying . . . that he (Haym Solomon) negotiated for Robert Morris all the loans raised in France and Holland (for our struggling country) . . . The fact is that Haym Solomon as broker "negotiated" the drafts representing a fraction of these loans . . . and someone cleverly confused the words "loans" and "drafts" in one of the Congressional reports in question in order to give an entirely erroneous and exaggerated impression of what Haym Solomon actually did.'

"Haym Solomon was a Polish Jew. He arrived in America in about 1772 and married Rachel Franks, a daughter of Moses Franks of New York. . . . With these connections plus 'a knowledge of languages and a flair for business', says Kohler, Solomon was able to float about $200,000 worth of securities for Robert Morris, Superintendent of

Finance of the Colonial Government. Morris allowed Solomon to call himself 'Broker to the Office of Finance' and so records in his diary. . . .

"In Collier's of May 11, 1940, Dr. D. H. Dubrovsky . . . describes the efforts of the Stalinist Communists to persuade him to collect from the American Government several million dollars allegedly due the heirs of one Haym Solomon, celebrated by American Jews today as the 'Financier of the Revolution'. At that time, Dubrovsky was head of the Soviet Red Cross in the United States. He subsequently quarreled with his superiors in Moscow and is now conducting a wordy warfare with Stalin".

### The New Patriotism

While undoubtedly there have been patriotic Jews who held their country's welfare ahead of that of their race, their own literature boasts of their basic internationalism. B'nai B'rith calls Jewry a **"world brotherhood"** (Article VII). Deriding nationalism, or Gentile patriotism, has long been a Jewish specialty, now reversed in America. To prepare for war against Hitler and for making America a world home for exiled Jews, B'nai B'rith, which strives to crush like a fly the free speech and "democratic rights" of any Gentile who criticizes Jewry, is whipping up a fury for "tolerance", "patriotism" and "democracy" to thwart opposition to Jewish aims and control.

The double page headline in B'nai B'rith Magazine, 9/40, is:

"B'NAI B'RITH SERVES JEWRY. ORDER STANDS FOR DEMOCRACY."

The kernel of its stand for democracy is in its subheadline: **"All of Its Activities Stress Patriotic American Ideals as Intimately Related to WELL-BEING OF JEWISH PEOPLE"**. The B'nai B'rith mailed fist is shown in the text: "B'nai B'rith has banded together some 100,000 Jewish families in a covenant. . . . In other words, this organization's purpose is to **serve the Jewish people**. . . . This service is not only of national and international scope. It is also

212

local. B'nai B'rith thus consists not only of a Supreme Lodge, which deals with Jewish problems affecting world and American Jewry as a whole, but it also consists of Districts and state bodies and local groups. . . .

"Within B'nai B'rith there is a machinery of leadership, perfected after 97 years of experience, for dealing with all matters that affect the Jewish people, whether it be a pogrom in some distant land, a hurricane in the tropics, the Jewish youth problem in America, anti-Semitism, aiding refugees, the preservation of Jewish cultural values—or a disturbing situation that arises on Main Street! In other words, **B'nai B'rith is so organized that it can utilize its machinery** to supply Jewish needs of almost every character. . . .

"When you join, it does not ask you the shade of your religious or political or social beliefs—it asks you only this: **Are you ready and willing to serve the Jewish people as a whole?**"

A picture accompanies this showing a room full of new B'nai B'rith members taking the "pledge to give unselfish service to the Jewish people".

### "Democracy" For Jews Only

Continuing, note B'nai B'rith's hypocritical gushing over "American tradition", "democracy" and "tolerance", while it loyally supports and never denounces leading Marxists working to destroy all of these: **"B'nai B'rith's Anti-Defamation League** is another powerful force for **democracy.** It fights anti-Semitism in all its phases not only because anti-Semitism is the enemy of the Jew, but because it is the enemy of mankind in general, and Americanism in particular. Anti-Semitism would **negate** all the spiritual values of America: **freedom**, equality, **tolerance, justice,** opportunity.

"Thus, in fighting against anti-Semitism, the **Anti-Defamation League is** fighting for **DEMOCRACY.** But the League does not content itself even with that fundamental job. It undertakes a vast and continuous educational campaign for **Americanism.** It distributes great quantities of printed material extolling the **American tradition. It sends**

213

an army of speakers into the field to address literally thousands of church groups, youth clubs, and other organizations on the need of more democracy today than ever before." (More "democracy" for Jews only.)

## A SEPARATE PEOPLE

Jewry, priding itself on being a separate people, on keeping separate holidays and a separate calendar to which the "Year of Our Lord" Christian calendar reckoning is poison, is also organized the world over under separate kehillah communal governments and bows to separate Jewish courts. An idea of the power of these courts can be gained by the report in B'nai B'rith magazine, 12/37, p. 138, that fines of $75,000 had been levied on, and paid by, three New York Jewish firms in punishment for selling German goods boycotted by Jewry; also the report in the 3/38 issue, p. 227, concerning "excommunication" from the Budapest Kehillah of Jews engaged in "illegal financial transactions that bring dishonor upon the Jewish community".

### Separate Courts

This announcement is illustrative: "Four Rabbinical Justices of the Beth Din of America, the first permanent Jewish Court of Justice in this country, assembled yesterday. . . ." (N.Y. American, 5/10/39).

Concerning the Court, the N.Y. World-Telegram, 5/10/39, said: "The Court was convening, Rabbi Felshin explained, to dispense justice among orthodox Jews solely on the basis of the 4,000-year-old laws of Moses as found in the Old Testament and the Talmud. . . ."

An earlier report on a Jewish Court: "Instead of the old Roman and English common law, which is the basis of American Jurisprudence, the Jewish court intends to decide all cases brought before it on the wisdom contained in the Talmud. Municipal Court Justice Isidor Buxbaum, who is to serve in an advisory capacity with Magistrate Mark Rudich, yesterday told the American: 'I can't conceive of a decision more binding on a good, honest Jew, than one

214

handed down in a tribunal presided over by a rabbi. . . ."
(N.Y. American, 7/26/36.)

## Judicial Corruption

Any "good honest Jew" must have deplored the following announcement of the disbarment of their Rumanian-born Jewish Judge and his removal from the bench where he had been judging Gentiles as an **American**: "Mar. 25, 1939—Magistrate **Mark Rudich** removed from bench by Appellate Division; April 21, Rudich disbarred" (N.Y. World-Telegram, 5/13/39).

## "ARE JEWS A RACE, RELIGION, OR NATION?"

"Are Jews a race, religion, or nation?" These are the topics of B'nai B'rith's Article VII in "Facts About Fictions Concerning the Jew". They reply, to quote: "Approximately a race, definitely a type, and consciously a unity, we are an historic people—a world community. . . . Because we have become **socialized** to the needs of **brethren who live thousands of miles away from us,** we are thereby socialized to every need of all people wherever they may dwell. . . ." (This echoes the call of the Central Conference of American Rabbis for a "socialized democracy" of Marxism.)

". . . To speak of us as a nation is more wishful than actual. Lacking soil and government of our own, we are not a nation. . . . **We are a world brotherhood, a world-wide people.**

"It was the intention of the Zionist movement from its beginning to nationalize the Jewish people, and it is that which is really the basis of the present world-wide dispute. . . . Because of the increase of nationalism we are declared aliens in land after land. Our love of country is scorned, our great personalities are condemned; we are driven from one land, and the gates of other lands are closed against us. . . ."

## Religion

". . . . Judaism seems so strange in many of its aspects

215

that it sometimes puzzles its own adherents . . . every religion in the world has a definite creed, a statement of belief which you either accept or reject. **There is no official creed in Judaism.** . . . Every religion has also an active technique of excommunication. It excludes those who are **irreligious.** Judaism definitely avoids such practices. Whereas other religions have excommunicated hundreds of thousands of unbelievers, in our history a terrified Portuguese congregation excommunicated only Spinoza and Uriel de Costa, and we are still apologizing for it. . . .

"But strange as is the organization of Judaism as a faith, stranger still is the relationship of Jews to their faith. **There are hundreds of thousands of Jews who are unbelievers. Yet they still consider themselves Jews.** What sort of a religion is it if those who neglect it still consider themselves Jews? Or more curiously, two years ago certain missionaries—men of Jewish birth who were converted to Christianity and work to convert other Jews to Christianity —certain missionaries wrote to the Zionist organization demanding the right to participate in the upholding of the Jewish homeland in Palestine. Now, certainly, nobody who was once a Catholic and became a Protestant would insist upon joining the Knights of Columbus. No Protestant who became a Catholic would insist in participating in a purely Protestant endeavor. Yet, here are men who deliberately have abandoned Judaism and yet want to participate in a Jewish effort. What sort of religion is Judaism if not only those who neglect it, but those who try to convert others away from it, still consider themselves Jews? . . .

". . . Two thousand years ago, when the Jewish State ceased to be, having been destroyed by the Romans, the Jewish people might well have passed out of existence. . . . But strangely enough, our State was destroyed and yet our people lived. Why? Because when the priests disappeared, the rabbis took their place. When the law of the Jewish State disappeared, **the law of the Talmud took its place.** When police power disappeared, the **self-government** of a cultured people took its place. Religion made of the Jew-

216

ish people a literate people, gave it a **self-governing Talmudic law.** . . .

". . . Even **an atheist Jew** must admit, albeit reluctantly, that in the past, at least, Jewry would not have lived if it had not been for Judaism. . . . The Jewish people and the Jewish religion, although apparently two separate entities, have each a history so interwoven that it is impossible to understand one without the other . . . whether it be neglected or fostered, then it is as permanent as Jewry itself. It is bound up with Jewish life, and therefore in every attempted solution of the problem of the Jews, we must always take Judaism into account. . . .

". . . We are not yet a nation. We may perhaps become one. . . . If not as a race and not as a nation, then the only way in which we can possibly face the world is as a religious community. It is true that there are hundreds of thousands of Jews in whom Judaism, the natural expression of the Jewish spirit, has died down and is, perhaps, **entirely extinguished.** It is true that there are **hundreds of thousands of atheist Jews,** but they need not fear to be represented by Judaism. . . .

"What is the Jew then—race, nation, or religion? . . . Lacking soil and government, he is not a nation. A religion? **He cannot be described as being a religion when hundreds of thousands are not religious.** Yet, although not a race . . . he has a sense of kinship, and . . . may be popularly . . . referred to as racial. . . . And as for religion **we are not a religion, but we have a religion. . . .**" (P. 8, Article VII.)

## Jews and Religion

In keeping with the above, the Jewish Sentinel (8/22/40, p. 9) states: "In the city of Chicago, it is estimated that **85 per cent** of the adults are not officially members of congregations. This does not mean they are not professing Jews or never go to synagogue. We make this clear in order to disabuse those of our Christian missionary friends who tell us the majority of Jews have no religion, therefore their missionary activities".

## Jewish "Missions"

While it is certain that today, as in all ages, there are a few genuine conversions of Jews to Christianity, it is also certain that there are some supposedly "converted" Jews making a profitable racket out of preying on gullible Gentiles, jerking their heart and purse strings with false stories portraying hosts of Jewry waiting like ripe fruit ready to be dropped into the Christian salvation basket—providing there is a greater, **still greater** expenditure of Gentile dollars in Jewish missions.

Certain "Hebrew missions" paying fat salaries to Jewish employees and collecting huge sums from Gentiles, are angry or smoothly evasive when asked to **prove** the large number of Jewish conversions they claim. They cannot do so because conversions are few. Jewry now, as in Christ's time, is sterile ground and under God's curse as such, in accordance with Scripture. Were Christian Hebrews to finance these missions to convert other Hebrews instead of acting as paid workers for Christianity, on Gentile funds, the picture would be different.

Frequently one is reminded of this situation revealed by B'nai B'rith magazine (4/40, p. 234): "Soon the Spanish and Portuguese colonies in America had a large number of people who practiced **Catholicism in the open and Judaism secretly**". Also of the B'nai B'rith editorial (1/38 issue), to quote: "The happier news of the past month had to do with one Archbishop Franz Cohen. . . . The Jews of Kromeriz in Czechoslovakia were observing with special exercises the 50th anniversary of the death of Archbishop Cohen. . . . Archbishop Cohen was no convert to Catholicism but was 'born a Catholic of Jewish descent. Archbishop Cohen was a man renowned in the church and, of course, was buried with all the distinction becoming a great leader of the heirarchy. Yet his will brought the effect of a startling announcement. . . . He had left his entire estate including a castle to the Jews of Kromeriz. It is not clear by what inspiration the archbishop was prompted at his death to convert all his earthly estate to the **religion** of the people of his descent. His castle became the Kromeriz synagogue and to this day most of the **Jewish undertakings** in Kromeriz are **supported by the revenues** from his estate". (And so he gave away Christian funds!)

## Christ Denounced Talmud

Christ, preaching to Jews, denounced the Talmud **with** illustrations on how (Matt. 15:4-9) "ye made the commandment of God of none effect by your **tradition.** Ye hypocrits, well did Esaias prophesy of you saying, This people draweth nigh unto me with their mouth, and honoureth me with their lips; but their heart is far from me. But in vain they do worship me, teaching for doctrines the commandments of men".

An official translation of the Babylonian Talmud by Rabbi Dr. I. Epstein with Foreword by The Very Reverend The Chief Rabbi Dr. J. H. Hertz, one of Jewry's 120 chosen leaders, issued by the Soncino Press, London, 1935, Copy #151 of the numbered First Edition, is in the U.S. Congressional Library. It is shocking reading. Reasons for Christ's disapproval of it are clear. (See reproductions.)

As the Foreword states: "The Talmud is the product of Palestine, the land of the Bible. . . . The beginnings of Talmudic literature date back to the time of the Babylonian Exile in the sixth pre-Christian century . . . the Babylonian Talmud assumed final codified form in the year 500 after the Christian era". It states that the Talmud was **"the rule of life"** and "came to be looked upon as halacha, literally 'the trodden path', the clear **religious guidance to the Israelite in the way he should go",** and is composed of the ideas of the meanings of the written context of the Pentateuch "by successive generations of devoted teachers".

## Immoral Talmud Teachings

The way, as Christ said, these Talmudic additions to Scripture make the "commandment of God of none effect" is plain throughout and illustrated in such immoral teaching as one sees on page 211 of this edition, concerning oxen, to quote: "Where an ox belonging to an Israelite has gored an

219

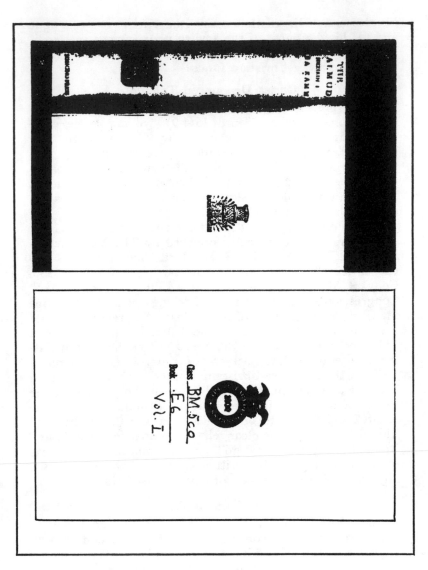

Reproduction of Talmud Cover and U.S. Library of Congress stamp and numbering on it

# THE
# BABYLONIAN
# TALMUD

## SEDER NEZIKIN

TRANSLATED INTO ENGLISH
WITH NOTES GLOSSARY AND INDICES
UNDER THE EDITORSHIP OF

### RABBI DR I. EPSTEIN
B.A., Ph. D., D. Lit.

FOREWORD BY
THE VERY REV. THE CHIEF RABBI
### DR J. H. HERTZ

INTRODUCTION BY
### THE EDITOR

LONDON
THE SONCINO PRESS
1935

---

# FOREWORD
BY

## THE VERY REV. THE CHIEF RABBI
Dr J. H. HERTZ

The Talmud is the product of Palestine, the land of the Bible, and of Mesopotamia, the cradle of civilization. The beginnings of Talmudic literature date back to the time of the Babylonian Exile in the sixth pre-Christian century, before the Roman Republic had yet come into existence. When, a thousand years later, the Babylonian Talmud assumed final codified form in the year 500 after the Christian era, the Western Roman Empire had ceased to be. That millenium opens with the downfall of Babylon as a world-power; it covers the rise, decline and fall of Persia, Greece and Rome; and it witnesses the spread of Christianity and the disappearance of Paganism in Western and Near Eastern lands.

I

The Babylonian Exile is a momentous period in the history of *ORIGINS* humanity—and especially so in that of Israel. During that Exile, Israel found itself. It not only rediscovered the Torah and made it *the rule of life*, but under its influence new religious invitations, such as the synagogue, i.e., congregational worship without priest or ritual, came into existence—one of the most far-reaching spiritual achievement in the whole history of Religion. At the re-establishment of the Jewish Commonwealth, Ezra the *Sofer*, or Scribe, in the year 444 B.C.E. formally proclaimed the Torah the civil and religious law of the new Commonwealth. He brought *ORAL LAW* with him all the oral traditions that were taught in the Exile, and he dealt with the new issues that confronted the struggling community in that same spirit which had created the synagogue. His successors, called after him *Sofrim* (Scribes), otherwise

xiii

---

Title Page and Foreword in Same Library of Congress Copy of Talmud

Reproductions of Pages of Same Copy of Talmud
Showing Immoral Teachings

free again [to others]?—R. Huna said: From the time that he goes barehanded in the streets.[1]

R. Eleazar said in R. Hanina's name: If a heathen had unnatural connection with his wife, he incurs guilt; for it is written, *and he shall cleave,* which excludes unnatural intercourse.[3] Raba objected: Is there anything for which a Jew is not punishable and a heathen is?[3] But Raba said thus: A heathen who violates his neighbour's wife unnaturally is free from punishment. Why so?—[Scripture saith:] *To his wife,* but not to his neighbour's; *and he shall cleave,* which excludes unnatural intercourse.[4]

R. Hanina said: If a heathen smites a Jew, he is worthy of death,[5] for it is written, *And he looked this way and that way, and when he saw that there was no man, he slew the Egyptian.*[6] R. Hanina also said: He who smites an Israelite on the jaw, is as though he had thus assaulted the Divine Presence; for it is written, *One who smiteth*[7] *man* [i.e., an Israelite] *attacketh*[8] *the Holy One.*[9]

(Mnemonic: *lifts, his servant, Sabbath.*)[10] Resh Lakish said: He who lifts his hand against his neighbour, even if he did not smite him, is called a wicked man, as it is written, *And he said unto the wicked man, Wherefore wouldst thou smite thy fellow?*[11] 'Wherefore hast thou smitten' is not said, but *wherefore wouldst thou smite,* shewing that though he had not smitten him yet, he was termed a wicked man. Ze'iri said in R. Hanina's name: He is called a sinner, for it is

(1) Even non-Jewish married women did not walk bareheaded in the streets, and this bondwoman, though not legally married, would do likewise. If she appeared bareheaded, it was a sign that her connection with the slave to whom she had been allotted was now broken. (2) His wife derives no pleasure from this, and hence there is no cleaving. (3) A variant reading of this passage is: Is there anything permitted to a Jew which is forbidden to a heathen. Unnatural connection is permitted to a Jew. (4) By taking the two in conjunction, the latter as illustrating the former, we learn that the guilt of violating the injunction 'to his wife but not to his neighbour's wife' is incurred only for natural but not unnatural intercourse. (5) By the Hand of God, v. Yad. Melakim I.6]. (6) Ex. II, 12. Thus Moses slew the Egyptian for striking an Israelite, proving that he had merited it. (7) Deriving *nokeh* from *nakah.* (8) *Yad*' is here derived from *lae* P. the jaw: lit., 'smiteth the jaw'. (9) Prov. XX, 25. (10) V. p. 367 n. 8. (11) Ex. II, 13.

violation is not punished by death?—R. Nahman b. Isaac answered: Their prohibition is their death sentence.[1]

R. Huna, Rab Judah, and all the disciples of Rab maintained: A heathen is executed for the violation of the seven Noachian laws; the Divine Law having revealed this of one [murder], it applies to all. Now is a heathen executed for robbery? Has it not been taught: 'With respect to robbery—if one stole or robbed[2] or [seized] a beautiful woman,[3] or [committed] similar offences,[4] if [these were perpetrated] by one Cuthean against another, [the theft, etc.] must not be kept, and likewise [the theft] of an Israelite by a Cuthean, but that of a Cuthean by an Israelite may be retained?[6] But if robbery is a capital offence, should not the Tanna have taught: He incurs a penalty?—Because the second clause wishes to state, 'but that of a Cuthean by an Israelite may be retained,' therefore the former clause reads, '[theft of a Cuthean by a Cuthean] must not be kept.'? But where a penalty is incurred, it is explicitly stated, for the commencing clause teaches: 'For murder, whether of a Cuthean by a Cuthean, or of an Israelite by a Cuthean, punishment is incurred, but of a Cuthean by an Israelite, there is no death penalty?[8]—How the could that clause have been taught? Could he state, 'forbidden' ... 'permitted'? Surely it

(1) I.e., in speaking of heathens, when the Tanna teaches that they are forbidden to do something, he *ipso facto* teaches that it is punishable by death, for only in speaking of Jews is it necessary to distinguish between prohibition and punishment. (2) Stole (*goneb*) refers to secret stealing; robbed (*gozel*), to stealing by open violence. (3) In war, v. Deut. XXI, 10-14. — a species of robbery; [This is the only possible and correct rendering of the text, contra Goldschmidt. (f. Tosef. A.Z.] (4) Acts which are not actual robbery, but partake of its nature. (5) Cuthean (Samaritan) was here substituted by the censor for the original goy (heathen). (6) [I.e., though it is forbidden to rob the heathen (v. Yad. Genebah I, 2; VI, 8), the offence was non-actionable. For reason, BK (Sonc. ed.) note on Mishnah 37b]. (7) But actually it is punishable too. The in merely a survival of old Semitic tribal law that regarded theft and robbery as a crime against the state, and consequently punishable by death. V. Muller, D.H., *Hammurabi,* 205; (8) Thus the Tanna does refer to punishment, since then he omits a reference to punishment in the clause under discussion, it shows that the heathen is not executed for robbery. In the whole of this discussion the punishment referred to is death.

Reproductions of Pages of Same Copy of Talmud
Showing Immoral Teachings

ox belonging to a Canaanite" (non-Jew), "there is no liability, whereas where an ox belonging to a Canaanite gores an ox belonging to an Israelite the compensation is to be made in full (so that they should guard their cattle from doing damage)".

On page 388, under the title "Sanhedrin", we see: "Has it not been taught: With respect to robbery—if one stole or robbed or seized a beautiful woman, or committed similar offence, if these were perpetrated by one Gentile against another the theft, etc. must not be kept, and likewise the theft of an Israelite by a Gentile, but that of a **Gentile by an Israelite may be retained.** . . . For **murder** whether of a Gentile by a Gentile, or of an Israelite by a Gentile, punishment is incurred, but of a **Gentile by an Israelite,** there is no death penalty". (The word "Cuthean" was used in place of "goy" or Gentile, the note states, to escape the censors.)

On page 389: "It applies to the **withholding of a laborer's wage.** One Gentile from another, or a Gentile from an Israelite is forbidden, **but an Israelite from a** Gentile is permitted".

On page 398: "He who smites an Israelite on the jaw is as though he thus assaulted the Divine Presence, for it is written one who smiteth man, that is an Israelite, attacketh the Holy One".

### The Jew in Prophecy

It is clear from Holy Scripture that the Jew is never to forget that he is a Jew and that there will never be peace in this world as long as he remains without a country of his own. Insatiably grasping for more and more control of other nations, finally the dumbest of Gentiles, squeezed beyond endurance, at last become exasperated and blow Jewry out of power. This recurring drama is always called persecution of the **Jews.**

Were it not for God's Word in Biblical prophecy concerning the Jew, his dispersion, his undigestable role as a "hissing and a by-word" in all nations, his survival as a

224

racial unit and punishment as such, and salvation of a small spiritualized "remnant", one might believe that one sensible Jew, Bernard J. Brown, in his book "From Pharaoh to Hitler" (Consolidated Book Pub., Chicago, 1933), had the right idea and the right solution for what he calls the "Jewish Question". He pleads for Jewish assimilation, the stopping of Jewish insistence on separate nationalism within other nations, argues that owing to blood mixture Jews have no right to hold themselves a race apart, and points out that as most Jews have no religious faith and those who have differ, Jewry is neither a race nor a religion.

## Gentile "Falling Away" Also Prophesied

On the religious score, he says there should be no friction with Gentiles, most of whom are also unbelievers in Biblical Christianity, and he quotes (p. 66) Socialist Jesse H. Holmes (of the Society of Friends, closely aligned with Jewry), saying: "What Jew of today will disagree with Dr. Jesse H. Holmes, Professor of Philosophy at Swarthmore College, who says, 'Churches are officially established on a foundation of medieval superstitions, in which a large proportion of both ministers and laymen do not actually believe at all. . . .' The doctor classes as medieval superstitions such doctrine as the fall of man, original sin, Jonah and the whale, the virgin birth, and other miracle stories taught as essentials by fundamentalist Christianity".

## Atheist Einstein

Brown says: "Professor Einstein speaks the mind of the majority of Jews when he says: 'I cannot conceive of a God that rewards and punishes, neither can I believe that the individual survives the death of his body, although feeble souls harbor such thoughts through fear'". Of B'nai B'rith, Brown remarks truly (p. 106): "Through the intervention of the Anti-Defamation League, we have succeeded in muzzling the non-Jewish press to the extent that newspapers in America abstain from pointing out that any person unfavorably referred to is a Jew".

# OUR "NEUTRALITY"

## Hoping Germany Would Sink It?

Despite the utmost efforts of the press and the Jewish New Deal network, the United States is not **presumably** at war with Germany as yet. Nor has Germany as yet committed a single hostile act against America in reprisal for seven years of American boycotts, spite tariffs against German goods, and the insults and hysterical cries for war of New Deal officials.

The speech of the half-Jew, longtime pro-Soviet, Wm. C. Bullitt, shrieking for war, sent out in the franked envelope of New Dealer Sen. Jos. T. Guffey, has been stuffed in farm mail boxes far and wide, unaddressed. Nor has any other trick been overlooked.

Despite all warnings that the area was mined as war territory, note the following:

## "The Captain Didn't Know Why"

"The army transport American Legion landed its 870 refugee passengers safely at New York on Wednesday after a dangerous journey thru the German mine fields and blockade area north of Scotland.

"The ship took that route on its trip from Petsamo, the Finnish port on the Arctic, **on orders of the American state department.** Its captain, Bror E. Torning, said he 'didn't know why this was done. He said that the route farther north, passing Ireland, was not only **safer but was shorter as well.** The state department, he said, 'must have had some reason for ordering the course we took, but I don't know what it was'.

"**The country will certainly want to know what that reason was.** All it knows now is that after ordering the American Legion to take the longer and more dangerous course **the Roosevelt administration carried on an intemperate exchange with the Nazi government, assuring Hitler's foreign office that Germany would be held responsible for any mishap to the boat.**

"Are the war mongers in Washington so anxious for a

cause of war that they will gamble with the lives of nearly a thousand American refugees and sailors in order to provoke one?" (Chgo. Trib. editorial, 9/2/40.)

## Is Patriotism Being Pro-Jewish?

Picture thousands of bags of U.S. mail being dragged off of U.S. ships and U.S. Clipper planes by Germany, as is constantly being done by England. Even "the sealed strong rooms" were broken open and paintings and books consigned from France to a New York art gallery seized from the American Export liner Excalibar, plus, as usual, 1,292 sacks of mail (Chgo. Trib., 10/6/40).

Picture, if you can, President Roosevelt commending the nationwide advertisements of German sympathizers asking U.S.A. military aid for Germany, as he commended those of the William Allen White Committee to Defend America by Aiding the Allies (A.P., 6/11/40).

Picture, if you can, Americans of German blood being permitted to set up expensive headquarters in over 500 communities distributing elaborate literature to get us to enter the war on the side of Germany, as the William White Committee has done to enlist, in another British war for Jewry, American money, arms, and the blood of our sons.

Picture the New Deal permitting Americans of German and Italian sympathies to boycott British or Jewish goods, as Jewry has boycotted German goods since 1933, plus officially helping out the boycott by socking on punitive New Deal tariffs besides.

Picture an army of 1,410 war propagandists, organized to telephone 735,488 persons in the New York area alone, asking that our torpedo boats, "flying fortresses" and combat planes be turned over to Germany, as the William Allen White committee announces it will do during the week of 10/8/40 for England. The committee had first raised the hullabaloo which resulted in our "50 over-age destroyers" being sent to England. Of course, if these destroyers were too "over-age" for us they were too "over-age" for England. But if their usefulness and value for defense were such as to justify the nationwide pressure to turn them over for

England's defense, then stripping **American** defense is treasonable while everything is being done to get **us** into war.

Picture some German official being permitted to beg from the United States as the Jewish Lady Reading (Isaacs) is doing. Her picture appears in the Chgo. Tribune, 9/22/40, as head of, to quote, the "Women's Volunteer Services, an organization with 70 branches throughout the country and a membership of 750,000. Lady Reading organized this service in June, 1938. She has succeded to such an extent that the **American Red Cross** confines its contributions for civilian relief to this organization. . . . The American Red Cross so far has donated **$4,250,000** to the women's auxiliary services or to the British Red Cross".

In addition to a long list of requests Lady Reading adds that "a few pence to buy sweets for children, these and many other things are wanted at once".

### War on "Aggression"?

Has the American Red Cross donated anything to German families whose homes have been bombed since England declared war on Germany? And it is England that declared the war. If England declared it, as claimed, because of Germany's **"aggression"** in demanding privileges from Poland in the corridor which had been cut out of Germany by the Versailles Treaty and given to Poland, dividing Germany into two unconnected parts, then why, to this day, has not even a word of criticism been uttered against Russia's **aggression** in seizing by force half of Poland, part of Finland, Bessarabia, N. Bukhovina, and the free states of Esthonia, Latvia and Lithuania, which struggled so valiantly for freedom from Red Russia after the 1919 revolution?

Instead, England (and the U.S.A.) is still courting Russia on bended knee for the pact Hitler ran off with during the summer of 1939, while emissaries of France and England cooled their heels, hats in hand, outside of bloody Stalin's doors.

### Patriots Jailed in France and England

In France, to distract public ire from Jewish Leon Blum's Red regime, over 100 French patriots, including a fine old general and the fiery Christian Duc Pozzo di Borgo, were imprisoned as "Cagoulards". All the world heard of the "Cagoulards" (the "Hooded Ones"), whose dynamite and arms were "discovered" cached in the sewers of Paris. But few learned that it was the Reds' own dynamite cached there as a frame-up and that with great press ballyhoo these 100 patriots were jailed as Fascists plotters, later to be released on the fall of the Blum regime, with no publicity, one by one, for lack of a shred of evidence to hold them.

Likewise in England, for months, men like the conservative M. P. Capt. Ramsay have languished in jail as anti-Semitics. He is cursed in the report of the World Atheist Congress headed by the Jew Chapman Cohen, held in London, 1938, for having mustered some 70 votes in Parliament to bar it and its Soviet atheists from meeting in London. All attempts at suppression of the Soviets' Communist Party "Daily Worker" by English patriots have failed to date because, as Parliament has argued, this might cause ill-will and prevent closer relations between England and Russia!

### Will George Britt's "Fifth Columnists" Be Jailed Also?

George Britt, long-time contributor to the radical "Stalinoid Weekly", the "Nation", and co-author of "Christians Only" with the late Communist Party "fellow-traveler" Heywood Broun, thanks Leon Birkhead, full time propagandist for Jewry, for "information" supplied for his book "The Fifth Column Is Here". Britt miraculously musters an unseen army of millions of Americans ready with "A Dagger at Our Back" to subjugate America for Hitler. Dragging out Birkhead's half dozen anti-Communist, anti-Semitic, 100% Americans, in addition to innuendoing most Americans with German or Italian blood into his "dagger army", Britt creates for the uninformed a horrendous enough scare to make them forget the Jew Deal and his own Red friends who are in actual power **on the job of**

229

subjugating America. His factual foundations rest on substance similar to the Nazi plot with which N.Y. newspapers electrified their readers during the summer of 1940.

## The Big Nazi "G" Plot

For example, these headlines (N.Y. Her.-Trib., 8/1/40) give one the setting of the plot: "HITLER'S AGENT ENSCONCED IN WESTCHESTER. DR. WESTRICK TRACED TO SECLUDED HEADQUARTERS ON SCARSDALE ESTATE". A picture of the "mystery house" occupied by Dr. G. A. Westrick, "Nazi agent", and one of him with his wife and two children are shown to thicken the plot.

It seems that careful watching revealed that a mysterious sign with the letter "G" on it came and went, appeared and disappeared, on the home of the Westricks near New York. One day this sign remained out for several hours, on another only briefly. At this a hue and cry was raised for ousting from the country all German consular officials undoubtedly just as guilty of sinister actions as this one. Finally, by brave work, the plot was uncovered. Peter, aged 6, one of the two small sons of the family, liked "Good Humor" ice cream and the "Good Humor" man had given him a card with "G" on it to put up when he wanted him to stop.

## The Jewish Army

With the "approval of the War Dept. and of the Dept. of the Interior" already "800 tough young Jews" were receiving training for "guerrilla warfare" by Otmar Hefner, reported as an ex-lieutenant of the bloody Jewish Hungarian-Soviet leader, Bela Kun (Cohen), according to the page spread (N.Y. Her.-Trib., 7/21/40) with pictures of the guns and drilling Jews and views of Hefner's office at 112 W. 46th St., N.Y., principal training bases being at Oxford, Conn., and Livingston Manor, N.Y. To quote: " 'Now the **groundwork has been laid to enable us to take care of large groups** and it will be possible to send them to Alaska' " (?) " 'in a few months', Mr. Hefner said".

# THE OCTOPUS AT WORK

## Workhouse Sentence

Just how completely B'nai B'rith, saying it "represents American Jewry", throttles American free speech and press is best told by itself.

Triumphantly, its Anti-Defamation League "ADL Review" (10/39, p. 1) announces: "George R. Blaisdell, distributor of anti-Semitic pamphlets, was sentenced to 30 days in the work-house by Municipal Judge William C. Larson. . . . Blaisdell was arrested on complaint of Samuel L. Scheiner, a representative of the Minnesota Anti-Defamation Council. . . . For the first time in Minneapolis and as far as we know in the United States, **distribution of anti-Semitic literature** has been **adjudged disorderly conduct punishable by workhouse sentence**".

Palavering commendations of this sentence by the Minneapolis Star-Journal and Minneapolis Times-Tribune are quoted. But no information concerning, or refutation of, any **statements** in Blaisdell's alleged "anti-Semitic pamphlets" is given. Indeed any **factual** open discussion on so-called "anti-Semitism" (and **any** unfavorable **fact** about Jewry is called "anti-Semitism") is habitually smothered. There is too much to be uncovered.

## Smothered Edmondson Evidence

When Robert Edward Edmondson of New York (now of Stoddartsville, Pa.), foremost writer on subversive Jewish activities, was indicted 6/11/36, by Jewish Mayor La-Guardia, for "libeling" all persons of the Jewish "religion", the case was postponed month after month for 22 months until the Am. Jewish Congress, Am. Jewish Com., etc., petitioned, 4/14/38, to have it dismissed **unheard.** Edmondson had such documentary evidence, such a formidable factual defense, that Jewry dared not risk the results of publicity leakage from such a trial.

"QUASH KUHN DEBATE" heads this (ADL Review, 10/39, p. 4): "Chicago—A fantastic plan for Fritz Kuhn, fuehrer of the German-American Bund, to engage in debate with a Jewish spokesman on the 'merits' of Nazi anti-Semitic policy, has been scotched by the A.D.L. . . . The **unwisdom of the plan** was emphasized by League representatives to the Jewish proponent of the plan, who has agreed to abandon the idea".

## Editor Jumps With Flowers

This amusing forced somersault is reported: "Chicago—An editorial in a suburban newspaper of influence, which took the Jewish people severely to task for the alleged misdeeds of a Jewish business firm, stated in part: '. . . It is just such arrogance, coupled with certain other characteristics that crop out occasionally on the part of some of the race, that has Hitler in a dither over Jews these days'. The editor who was author of this unfair and illogical editorial, was asked to confer with the director of the Anti-Defamation League. . . .

"**Jewish advertisers in the paper** who sought the League's counsel following **publication of the editorial,** were advised of the editor's desire to correct the impression made by his words. It was emphasized that this was a case in which the **advertisers . . . could cooperate in closing the incident satisfactorily".**

## Perhaps He Also Knelt

"Sincerely desirous of **making amends** for his editorial . . . the editor sought information on the Jewish high holiday, Rosh Hashonah, and has published an editorial on the significance of the day in which **warm tribute was paid to Jews** who have served in the military and naval forces of America. . . . The editorial concluded: 'THIS IS A FLOWERING RECORD TO WHICH ALL AMERICANS MAY POINT WITH PRIDE. BRILLIANTLY IT SETS OFF THE JEWISH STAR OF CITIZENSHIP IN THE AMERICAN FIRMAMENT'" (ADL Review, 10/39).

## You Cannot Advertise for Gentiles

"RESORT PROBLEMS MET SUCCESSFULLY" caps this item (ADL Review, 10/39, p. 4) telling how B'nai

B'rith won out: "In the women's recreation rooms of one of America's largest life insurance firms, appeared numerous pamphlets calling attention to the exclusion of Jews from the resorts issuing this promotional material. The matter was taken up by the Milwaukee A.D.L. committee with the company's vice-president, who ordered the **offending literature thrown out.** The recreation room matron was warned to inspect all future reading material for evidence of **racial bias.** . . .

"Another incident involving a Milwaukee newspaper was satisfactorily adjusted through the local A.D.L. committee. This paper, in a special resort edition, carried six advertisements showing anti-Jewish bias. . . . Future advertisements will be scanned closely for objectionable wording, the League representatives were assured".

"RESORT COOPERATES" (12/39 issue, p. 1) heads this: "Boston—Thanks to the efforts of the New England Regional office of the Anti-Defamation League, a resort owner at Great Barrington, Mass., has changed his promotional material to read **'Restricted Clientele'** ".

### Editors Beware!

"TO EDIT CAREFULLY" (p. 1, same issue) announces the slavish promise exacted from a newspaper syndicate slapped down by B'nai B'rith: "New York—An article in a Buffalo paper written by a Latvian journalist referred caustically to the 'Jewified' Weimar Republic of Germany. The syndicate distributing this article has agreed to edit carefully similar material in the future".

"PAPER TO DISCARD PREJUDICE ADS" (p. 1, same issue) heads this: "Detroit—One of the largest and most influential daily papers here has agreed to eliminate the words 'Gentiles Only' from its classified advertising columns. This phrase and similar words insisted upon by some employers long have been considered responsible for much discrimination in employment".

### Conrad Hoffman

Flowery endorsements of B'nai B'rith's false propaganda

233

book "Facts About Fictions Concerning the Jew", by Communist-supporter James M. Yard of their Chicago Round Table of Christians and Jews, and Conrad Hoffman, Jr., of the Bd. of Nat. Missions of the Presby. Church of the U.S. A., appear in the 12/39 issue.

### You Must Sing Right

"A.D.L. CORRECTS SONG" heads another report of B'nai B'rith repression (10/39 issue).

### Evangelist Made to Crawl

"SPEAKER RETRACTS" (A.D.L. Review, 12/39, p. 3) is the caption of this report showing how B'nai B'rith muzzles evangelists: "Portland, Oregon—A radio evangelist in a recent broadcast here, asserted that Jews were responsible for the European crisis. In a newspaper interview the following day, the speaker asserted that he had been summoned to the telephone by an unknown person with a Jewish-sounding voice who had threatened his life. At a conference with the station manager in regard to the impropriety of the man's radio charge and subsequent interview, the station official admitted his chagrin at the incident. Asked to explain his words, the **evangelist apologized** to his radio audience for his prior statement, and has **refrained,** in ensuing broadcasts, from similar accusations and **political speculation".**

Yet the radio and screen daily screams with anti-German speeches to drag America into war!

### No Free Speech for Father Coughlin

The A. D. L. Review, 12/39, p. 4, gleefully heralds "RADIO ASSN. BANS 'HATE' TALKS—BROADCASTERS CODE AIMED AT ATTACKS ON RACES AND RELIGION", saying, "The microphone, most potent weapon of the rabble-rouser, has been all but closed to this type of person" (meaning closed to Father Coughlin or anyone else who criticizes any Jew).

### A Travesty

Ironically a boxed notice (p. 2) calls attention to "free

234

speech" "**Lest We Forget**" programs. To quote: "How our democratic institutions developed is the theme of a remarkable program, 'Lest We Forget', now being heard from more than 370 radio stations in the United States. This series of twenty-six 15-minute transcribed programs **dramatizes freedom of speech, freedom of press, freedom of religion, and freedom of assembly**".

What a travesty, while B'nai B'rith keeps any "anti-Semitic" speaker from free speech, free press, free radio, or from renting a hall, and strives to suppress Scriptural passages in radio sermons, Christian Sunday School papers, Passion Plays and books.

### Boy Jailed for Painting Old Car

An A.P. news dispatch, 8/24/40, from Louisville, Ky. (Judge Brandeis' old home), is headed "Youth Paints 'Hail Hitler' on Auto; 30 Days!" It says that Kenneth Metzmeier, a 19 year old boy, was fined $50 and sentenced to 30 days in jail for having "Hail Hitler" painted on the front bumper of his old 1930-model car. "In the center, in larger letters, was 'Kenny' and below, 'Louise'. Metzmeier explained Louise was his girl friend. Kenneth told the court he was sorry and 'didn't mean anything' ". But he was sentenced because the words "Hail Hitler" on his bumper "might incite a riot".

### Jailed for Remarks on Jews

It was announced in the press (7/24/40) that Mrs. Vera Soabwellham had been arrested and sentenced to fifteen days in the workhouse in N.Y. by Jewish Judge Peter A. Abeles for making anti-Jewish remarks in an East Broadway bus.

### McWilliams Jailed and Hounded

The Daily Worker (8/9/40) announced that Joe McWilliams, running for Congress in New York, was fined $50 on July 6 for "making derogatory remarks against Jews", and that on July 7 "Jack Schwartz, a process server, attempted to serve McWilliams with a summons charging him with inflammatory incitement against Jews".

Because of his "anti-Semitic" objection to complete Jewish power in America, McWilliams, it is reported, is unable to rent a hall, has to speak from a covered wagon outdoors, is repeatedly arrested, and even had to move from his boarding house, while Communists, Socialists, Zionists and British war mongers command halls, radio and press.

## UNITED STATES LAWS ON CONSPIRACY

### Should Be Applied to B'nai B'rith

"IF TWO OR MORE PERSONS **CONSPIRE TO INJURE, OPPRESS, THREATEN OR INTIMIDATE ANY CITIZEN** IN THE FREE EXERCISE OR ENJOYMENT OF ANY RIGHT OR PRIVILEGE SECURED TO HIM BY THE CONSTITUTION OR LAWS OF THE U. S., OR BECAUSE OF HIS SO **HAVING EXERCISED THE SAME** . . . THEY SHALL BE FINED NOT MORE THAN $5,000 AND **IMPRISONED** NOT MORE THAN **TEN YEARS,** AND SHALL, MOREOVER, THEREAFTER BE **INELIGIBLE TO ANY OFFICE,** OR PLACE OF HONOR, PROFIT OR TRUST CREATED BY THE CONSTITUTION OR LAWS OF THE U.S." (Section 19, U.S. Criminal Code (18 USC 51), titled "Conspiracy to Injure Persons in the Exercise of Civil Rights".)

"ANY PERSON WHO, UNDER COLOR OF ANY STATUTE, ORDINANCE, REGULATION, CUSTOM OR USAGE OF ANY STATE OR TERRITORY, **SUBJECTS** OR CAUSES TO BE SUBJECTED, **ANY CITIZEN OF THE U.S.,** TO THE **DEPRIVATION OF ANY RIGHTS,** PRIVILEGES, OR IMMUNITIES **SECURED BY THE CONSTITUTION** AND LAWS, **SHALL BE LIABLE TO THE PARTY INJURED IN ANY ACTION AT LAW OR SUIT IN EQUITY** OR OTHER PROPER PROCEEDING FOR **REDRESS".** (Sec. 43, U.S.C.R.S. 1917.)

# WILL THE OCTOPUS WIN?

Will the great Jewish conspiracy, to rob Gentiles of all American Constitutional rights of free speech and free press, to speak or write facts unpleasing to Jewry, end in the complete throttling of truth-speaking Gentiles as criminal anti-Semitics, as in Russia? Both presidential candidates now advocate this. That depends upon whether **you** do your part in spreading facts **before it is too late!**

# INDEX

239

240

241

242

244

245

246

247

250

251

252

253

254

**V**

255